From Farm to Firm

From Farm to Firm

Rural-Urban Transition in Developing Countries

Nora Dudwick, Katy Hull, Roy Katayama,
Forhad Shilpi, and Kenneth Simler

THE WORLD BANK
Washington, D.C.

ISBN: 978-0-8213-8623-1
eISBN: 978-0-8213-8640-8
DOI: 10.1596/978-0-8213-8623-1

Cover photo: copyright © Ariadne Van Zandbergen.

Library of Congress Cataloging-in-Publication Data
From farm to firm : rural-urban transition in developing countries / Nora Dudwick ... [et al.].
   p. cm.
   Includes bibliographical references and index.
   ISBN 978-0-8213-8623-1 — ISBN 978-0-8213-8640-8 (electronic)
   1. Rural-urban migration—Developing countries. I. Dudwick, Nora.
HB2160.F76 2011
307.2'4091724—dc22   2011008873

Contents

Boxes

Figures

Tables

Foreword

The World Bank's *World Development Report 2009: Reshaping Economic Geography* (*WDR 2009*) represented a turning point in the Bank's thinking about the links among geography, poverty reduction, and growth. In presenting this new thinking, the book sparked a rich intellectual debate within the development community from which emerged the following paradigm-shifting notion: Spreading investment across a territory does not necessarily promote convergence in welfare across regions; rather, improving the welfare of poor people might be better achieved by allowing capital investment to flow to where it can be the most productive, while enabling people to move to those areas offering economic opportunities. Their mobility could be supported through a combination of human capital investment and connective infrastructure investments.

In the same way that it pushed economists and policy makers alike in a new direction, *WDR 2009* also generated a great deal of curiosity about how this conceptual framework could be applied to different regions, different types of countries, and different situations. The two studies that make up this volume, one featuring Sub-Saharan Africa and the other South Asia, represent an effort to provide texture to the propositions and models set out in *WDR 2009*. Relying on development professionals from various Bank departments—those with experience in geography and urban and rural development policy, along with experts in poverty and inequality analysis and policy—these studies tested analytical methodologies adapted to relatively data-poor economies, as well as those that could benefit from more sophisticated data foundations. The studies benefited from the guidance and advice of a group of experienced economists and policy experts both within and outside the Bank. Possibly more important from the viewpoint of their contribution to development policy, these studies focus attention and resources on the links between geography and poverty in the world's poorest regions—Sub-Saharan Africa and South Asia—adding new value to the knowledge base created by *WDR 2009*.

We are pleased to present this collection to the economists, social scientists, and policy makers concerned with issues of geography and development in poor countries, and we hope it will continue to spark useful and evidence-based debates aimed at reshaping economic geography.

Jaime Saavedra
Acting Director
Poverty Reduction and Equity
Poverty Reduction and Economic
    Management Network
The World Bank

Marisela Montoliu
Adviser and Former Head
Spatial and Local Development
Sustainable Development
    Network
The World Bank

Acknowledgments

The World Bank work program on rural-urban transformation, co-sponsored by the Poverty Reduction and Economic Management (PREM) Network and Sustainable Development (SD) Network vice presidencies, spanned two years, from mid-2008 to mid-2010, and benefited from the contributions of development analysts and practitioners from the World Bank and other international organizations and academic institutions.

The authors would like to thank the Poverty Reduction and Equity Group, led by Ana Revenga, sector director, Jaime Saavedra, sector manager, and Louise Cord, former sector manager, and the Finance, Economics, and Urban Department, led by Zoubida Allaoua, sector director, for their ongoing support of this work program. Special thanks go to Marisela Montoliu, who initiated the cross-sectoral work program as head of the Spatial and Local Development team in the SD Network. Her intellectual leadership and hands-on engagement throughout the research and writing process—including her own contribution of the overview chapter—enhanced the relevance and impact of the work program.

The authors also gratefully acknowledge the substantial contributions of the panel of peer reviewers—Christopher Delgado, Paul Dorosh, Antonio Estache, Maria Emilia Freire, Chorching Goh, Steve Haggblade, Peter Lanjouw, and Stephen Mink—who provided substantive feedback and guidance throughout the process. The guidance of Louise Cord and Jaime Saavedra, and the feedback provided at different stages of the process by Judy Baker, Luc Christiaensen, Gaurav Datt, Marianne Fay, Gershon Feder, Louise Fox, Stephen Karam, Alexander Kremer, Somik Lall, Emmanuel Skoufias, Robert Townsend, and Hassan Zaman, contributed to the progress and quality of the studies. The input of country team staff was also important, and included comments from Sébastien Dessus, Chris Jackson, Dino Merotto, Antonio Nucifora, Uri Raich, and Rachel Sebudde. Shaohua Chen, Kalpana Mehra, Toru Nishiuchi, Prem Sangraula, Daan Struyven, Wei Xiao, and Haomiao Yu supported the data analysis and provided figures and graphs. Brian Blankespoor, Dana Thomson, and Emily Schmidt conducted the geographic information system (GIS) analyses, including production of maps. Paul Cahu contributed to the analysis and the overview chapter.

Finally, the authors would like to acknowledge the organizational and logistical support provided by Alexander Arenas, Ramu Bishwakarma, Lanto Ramanankasina, and Grace Sorensen.

Overview

The transition from predominantly rural to increasingly urban economies is one of the greatest development challenges of these times. Urbanization spurs growth and reduces poverty, but also can engender inequalities. Managing the rural-to-urban transition in a way that ensures shared growth is therefore a major concern of developing country policy makers and the development community.

Rural-urban transformations have been the focus of two consecutive *World Development Reports* (*WDRs*): *WDR 2008, Agriculture for Development* and *WDR 2009, Reshaping Economic Geography* (World Bank 2007, 2008). Our research agenda picks up where the *WDRs* left off by providing more finely tuned insights into the transformation process across rural and urban spaces. This overview distills some of the principal messages of the *WDRs*. It then outlines the main objectives of our work program before summarizing our key findings and their policy implications.

WDR 2008 and *WDR 2009*: Rural and Urban Perspectives on Transformation

The two most recent *WDRs* provided a starting point for our complementary studies of the rural-urban transformation. *WDR 2008,*

Agriculture for Development, studies the structural transformation of the economy from a rural development perspective. *WDR 2009, Reshaping Economic Geography*, addresses the spatial transformations that accompany those structural changes—but it does so primarily from an urbanization perspective.

WDR 2008 notes that developing countries are at very different stages in the transition from predominantly rural to largely urban-based economies. It classifies countries into three different groups: "agriculture-based," "transforming," and "urbanized" (see box 1 later in this overview). These classifications are far from static, although invariably agriculture contributes to a declining share of growth as countries develop. For example, over the course of two to three decades China and India changed from agriculture-based to transforming countries, Indonesia became increasingly urbanized, and Brazil developed into a full-fledged urbanized country (figure 1).

The speed at which countries make the transition from largely agriculture-based to urbanized economies varies greatly. Likewise, the pace of change within countries may vary dramatically. Large countries, in particular, have regional disparities that replicate "the three worlds of

Figure 1   *WDR 2008*'s Classification of Agriculture-Based, Transforming, and Urbanized Countries

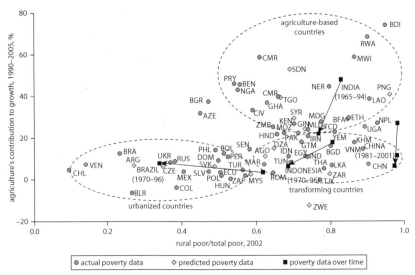

agriculture." Thus India, a "transforming" country, has agriculture-based states such as Uttar Pradesh and Bihar and urbanized states such as Goa.

WDR 2009 further explores geographically uneven development, whether it is local, national, or international. It classifies areas according to whether their principal challenges are related to "density," "distance," or "division" (see box 1). According to these categories, China is best described as a "1-D" country, where the principal challenge is how to increase the density of economic activity. Brazil is characterized as a "2-D" country, where an additional challenge rests in increasing the connectivity between "leading" (mostly urban) and "lagging" (typically rural) regions. India is described as a "3-D" country, where internal divisions represent a further challenge. The 1-D, 2-D, and 3-D distinctions can be applied as well on both narrower and broader geographical scales. For example, a 1-D town is one with insufficient agglomeration, and a 3-D continent is one facing the challenges of inadequate economic density, lagging regions, *and* major economic barriers.

According to *WDR 2009*, urbanization is initially associated with a divergence of living standards between leading and lagging areas. Divergence occurs because the concentration of capital and labor brings with it productivity and cost advantages, resulting in higher wages in urban areas. Concentration also enables the provision of better infrastructure and social services in towns and cities. *WDR 2009* finds that rural-urban welfare disparities begin to converge once countries reach upper-middle-income levels (figure 2). Various phenomena explain this expected convergence: out-migration from rural areas reduces surplus labor; rural productivity benefits from technological advances; and governments become more sophisticated, expanding their fiscal bases and investing in rural infrastructure and services. Essential household consumption is predicted to converge first, followed by access to basic public services and, finally, wages and incomes. Within-city spatial disparities, manifested in slums, are predicted to last longer than rural-urban disparities, persisting until countries reach high-income status.

Both *WDR*s argue that when governments and others are considering how best to manage the rural-urban transition, they must tailor policies to the country's (or area's) stage of transformation. According to *WDR 2008*, in agriculture-based economies policies should focus on boosting productivity in smallholder farming. In transforming economies, policies should also promote growth of the rural nonfarm sector. And in urbanized economies, policies should help to link farmers to modern food markets, agroindustry, and environmental services. *WDR 2009* asserts that in 1-D

Figure 2   Divergence, Then Convergence, in Rural-Urban Gaps

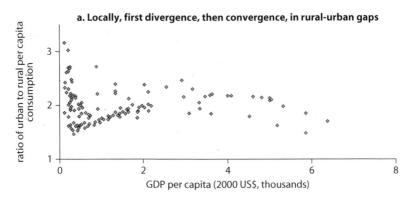

a. Locally, first divergence, then convergence, in rural-urban gaps

b. Nationally, divergence, then convergence, in incomes between leading and lagging areas

—— Sweden, 1920–61	—— United States, 1840–1960
- - - Spain, 1860–1975	······ Habsburg Empire, 1756–1910
—·— Japan, 1955–83	—— — United Kingdom, 1871–1955

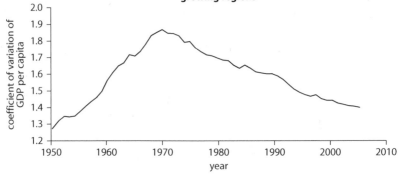

c. Internationally, divergence, then convergence—but only in growing regions

Source: World Bank 2008.

Box 1

Country-Level Policy Recommendations Derived from the *WDR*s

WDR 2008 classifies countries according to the contribution of agriculture to economic growth and the share of the poor in the rural sector. In "agriculture-based" economies, agriculture contributes 20 percent or more to growth, and more than half of the poor live in rural areas. In "transforming" economies, agriculture contributes on average 7 percent to growth, but poverty remains overwhelmingly rural. In "urbanized" economies, agriculture contributes even less to overall growth, and poverty is mostly urban.

WDR 2009 classifies countries according to the relative importance of "density," "distance," and "division." Density refers to the economic output per unit of land area and is the principal challenge in "1-D" countries. Distance is manifested in densely populated lagging regions in "2-D" countries. Divisions—for example, between ethnic groups—are an additional obstacle in "3-D" countries. The seven countries in Sub-Saharan Africa and South Asia featured in our study would fit into the categories shown in the table.

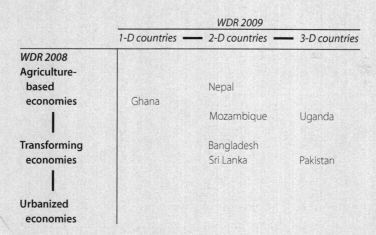

	WDR 2009		
	1-D countries ──	*2-D countries* ──	*3-D countries*
WDR 2008			
Agriculture-based economies	Ghana	Nepal	
		Mozambique	Uganda
Transforming economies		Bangladesh	
		Sri Lanka	Pakistan
Urbanized economies			

Based on these classifications, the *WDR*s might suggest the following policy responses. For Ghana, an agriculture-based economy, *WDR 2008* might recommend public investments to promote agricultural growth and food security. And because the principal challenge on a national level is one of insufficient density, *WDR 2009* might recommend instigating spatially neutral institutions such as improved land policies or country-wide education and health initiatives.

(continued next page)

Box 1   *(continued)*

In Nepal, another agriculture-based country, a relatively large share of the total population is in lagging and poorly connected regions. It thus faces issues of both distance and density. In addition to the policy menu proposed for Ghana, *WDR 2009* might therefore recommend increased investments in connective infrastructure.

Bangladesh, Mozambique, Pakistan, and Uganda are all on the brink of entering the transforming economy category. Thus *WDR 2008* might call for interventions to boost rural nonfarm productivity through investments in human capital and nonagricultural activities in small- and medium-size towns. Free from major cultural divides but with significant barriers to mobility, Bangladesh and Mozambique qualify as 2-D countries that, as *WDR 2009* might suggest, would benefit from connective infrastructure in addition to spatially unbiased institutions. By contrast, the ethnic, cultural, or political divisions present in Pakistan and Uganda might justify territorially targeted programs, in addition to aspatial institutions and connective infrastructure.

For Sri Lanka, the only country in our sample that fits squarely in the transforming economy category, *WDR 2008* might recommend programs to promote nonfarm activities in small and secondary towns. *WDR 2009* might call for sound, spatially blind policies and investments in connective infrastructure.

Because of the different perspectives of these two *WDRs*, some of the broad policy implications emerging from them may seem at odds. For example, for low-density, agriculture-based economies *WDR 2008* might recommend targeted investments in rural areas, whereas *WDR 2009* might suggest that spatially neutral investments be the main priority. But both *WDRs* would concur that a detailed country-level analysis should guide the specifics of policy design and that a narrower lens—for example, a focus on a particular region or city within each country—could unearth more complex challenges.

countries policies should focus on the provision of "spatially blind" institutions, such as sound macroeconomic policies, broadly distributed social services, and good land laws. In 2-D countries, governments should also implement connective infrastructure—such as good roads—so that the benefits of agglomeration economies can be shared as widely as possible. And in 3-D countries, institutions and infrastructure should be supplemented with spatially targeted interventions in order to overcome ethnic and cultural divisions. Box 1 indicates how the policy recommendations of the two *WDRs* might be applied to the countries featured in our studies.

Building on the *WDRs*: Our Work Program

Our work program builds on the findings of the *WDRs* on the rural-urban transformation, focusing specifically on Sub-Saharan Africa and South Asia—two regions that pose particularly urgent issues for policy makers. Although each region is still largely agricultural, each is undergoing rapid rates of urbanization. In fact, cities within the two regions have the highest prevalence of slums in the world: UN-HABITAT (2008) estimates that more than 6 out of 10 city dwellers in Sub-Saharan Africa and 4 out of 10 in South Asia live in slums. These slums are a powerful reminder that even though the rural-urban transformation may be good for national development, it can incur inequitable outcomes for households.

Our country-level focus helps to add nuance to the broad typologies provided in each *WDR*. For example, with agriculture contributing 35 percent to its gross domestic product (GDP), Nepal is classified squarely as an agriculture-based country. But a narrower lens indicates that the country is in fact a patchwork of largely urbanized areas, such as the Kathmandu Valley, and almost entirely rural areas, such as the eastern hills region. Similarly, although Mozambique as a whole is making the transition from an agricultural to an urban economy, the pace of change is by no means even. Its capital, Maputo, in the south, is growing at a very fast pace, but a significant share of the poor population remains in the rural northern regions.

WDR 2008 has a rural focus and *WDR 2009* an urban one. Although by virtue of their subject matter both reports acknowledge the interdependence of rural and urban areas, they sometimes overlook distortions and spillovers that flow from rural to urban spaces, and vice versa. We aim to look across the rural-urban continuum to consider the interaction between rural and urban transformations. For example, what are the push and pull factors shaping migration decisions? And how do institutions such as land laws affect transformation in both rural and urban areas?

Our approaches are interdisciplinary, demonstrating how analytical methods can be tailored to the quantity and quality of data available. In relatively data-poor countries, such as many of those of Sub-Saharan Africa, it makes more sense to analyze patterns and trends in rural-urban disparities using decomposition tools rather than attempt to address causality. In more data-rich countries, such as those of South Asia, regression-based tools can provide indications of causality.

Our studies, as reported in this volume, use three different levels of analysis—global, national, and local—to look at the patterns and trends in the ongoing rural-urban transformation and the reasons for the uneven economic landscapes. The first level of analysis is global, encompassing more than 40 low- and middle-income countries. Taking a global perspective (chapter 2), we examine rural-urban welfare differences, using both monetary and nonmonetary measures. We then use cross-sectional surveys to assess the degree of convergence or divergence in rural and urban living standards as national income and the urban share of the population increase over time. Finally, we look at covariates to help explain why spatial inequalities are increasing in some countries and decreasing in others.

We then move to the national level of analysis (chapter 3), homing in on rural-urban differences in three African countries—Ghana, Mozambique, and Uganda. For the national-level analysis, we use Oaxaca-Blinder decomposition techniques to determine whether rural-urban inequalities stem from differences in endowments, such as levels of education, or from differences in returns to those endowments. Put simply, this technique helps us to understand whether rural-urban welfare disparities in these three African countries stem from *people* or from *places*.

Moving on from the national-level analysis, we address the rural-urban transformation from the perspective of intraurban and intraregional differences. After the discussion of the rural-urban transformation in Sub-Saharan Africa, we consider patterns and trends in welfare within three African cities—Accra, Kampala, and Maputo—investigating the relationship between inequalities in living standards and location within these cities (chapter 4). We then look at the causes of urban inequalities, focusing especially on colonial legacies, land policies, and weak governance.

In part II of this report, we return to the national level of analysis but use examples of countries in South Asia. Chapter 5 introduces the regional perspective on managing the rural-urban transformation, and chapter 6 looks at the patterns in South Asia—specifically Bangladesh, Nepal, Pakistan, and Sri Lanka. This case study approach, employing both regression-based tools and qualitative analysis, enables us to look beyond the question of "people or places" to uncover in chapter 7 the effects of policies and institutions—whether land distribution and property rights, or access to infrastructure and services—on rural-urban transformations in the four countries. We then move to describing land market institutions (chapter 8), geographical links (chapter 9), and labor mobility (chapter 10) in relation to the rural-urban transformation. Chapter 11 presents our summary and conclusions.

Main Findings

Many of the key findings in the studies described here are complementary. First, they confirm that, on average, urban areas enjoy a higher standard of living than rural areas. But beyond this broad (and far from surprising) finding, they discover a high level of variation. For example, chapter 2 finds that the size of the rural-urban gap is highly variable across the 41 developing countries, especially among the poorest countries. And even in countries with the same levels of urbanization or GDP per capita, the rural-urban differences may be enormous or relatively small. Chapter 6 reveals that within-country differences in economic structure and well-being can be even larger than the differences between countries. For example, even in Sri Lanka, the most urbanized country in South Asia, the poorer regions are more than 15 hours away from the nearest medium-size city.

Like the two *WDRs*, our studies confirm the existence of bumpy economic landscapes. But they also suggest that patterns of convergence and divergence may not be neatly tied up with a country's level of development, at least within the observable time horizon for countries in Africa and South Asia. For example, our cross-country analysis finds little evidence to suggest that welfare differences are either consistently expanding or consistently diverging as GDP per capita grows. And both our Africa and Asia studies suggest that more than the level of development, the kinds of policies and institutions that a country has in place as it develops will determine the texture of the economic landscape.

Our report echoes the call by *WDR 2009* for spatially neutral institutions as a *sine qua non* of the effective management of the rural-urban transformation. Land institutions emerge as particularly important. For example, the case study on Sri Lanka shows how restrictions on the sale of rural land increase the cost of migration, thereby impeding rural-urban transitions. Our study of three African cities also reveals how inadequate legal frameworks, poor land management, and corruption have combined to create extremely tight markets for formal land and housing, contributing to the precipitous growth of slums. But our studies also indicate that land is a very difficult area to reform from a political economy perspective. According to the case studies on Pakistan and Sri Lanka, if political economy factors make full-fledged land policy reform impossible, intermediate measures—such as greater access to credit and improved efficiency of land markets—can mitigate the negative impact of land tenure conditions on the rural-urban transformation.

Like *WDR 2009*, our studies also highlight the importance of spatially unbiased access to services, in particular basic education. In the African countries analyzed, human capital disparities play a bigger role than differences in returns to education in accounting for the observed gaps in rural-urban welfare. Similarly, regression results for the South Asia countries confirm that people with higher levels of education can reap considerable positive returns in the labor market. Thus, the studies of both Sub-Saharan Africa and South Asia suggest that nationwide human capital standards could be powerful instruments for narrowing rural-urban disparities.

Similarly, uneven access to services is found to underpin spatial divides, whether they are between rural and urban areas, smaller and larger towns, or different parts of the same city. Our study of three African countries finds that rural-urban migration choices are based not only on income prospects but also on prospective access to schools and health care centers. Meanwhile, our study of three African cities reveals that the uneven living standards across income quintiles are closely correlated with the level of services people can access in their neighborhood. Combined, these findings suggest that policies to broaden access to basic services would both remove pressures on congested metropolises and contribute to more geographically balanced development.

Both *WDRs* suggest that policies should be carefully sequenced to a country or area's level of development. But our studies underscore that the appropriate policy mix will depend on the unit of analysis. For example, at the country level Ghana is indeed a 1-D country that would benefit, first and foremost, from spatially blind institutions (see box 1). But at the city level, Accra faces vast socioeconomic divides that might call for the kind of spatially targeted interventions recommended for 3-D areas. Moreover, our studies suggest that because of observed interactions across policies, a combination of measures can often have a much stronger impact on the rural-urban transformation than a sequence of policies. For example, we find that the benefits of infrastructure investments are larger in areas with better agricultural potential and fewer restrictions in factor markets.

These studies serve as a reminder that, although the rural-urban distinction is helpful from an analytical perspective, a rural-urban continuum may be more useful from a policy perspective, because interventions are likely to have second-round impacts in areas beyond their immediate geographical target. For example, in Pakistan the impact of rural land inequality is felt in the higher pace of migration and lower wages for unskilled workers in towns and cities. In Sri Lanka, although public investment in irrigation has satisfied an immediate goal of boosting agricultural productivity, it has resulted in less employment diversification, slower migration, and lower overall living standards. Meanwhile, our study of three African cities suggests that not all policies to address urban inequalities should target urban areas—for example, introducing better services in rural areas would reduce the push factors that drive people to cities in the first place.

The implications that emerge from our work are only some of the many considerations facing policy makers. Above all, leaders often face restrictive political environments that limit the likelihood that many of the "first best" solutions will be implemented—political economy issues we only touched on in our studies. We have, however, demonstrated the high cost of inaction: a failure to institute reforms is impeding, and will continue to impede, the extent to which everyone can share in the economic benefits of rural-to-urban transformations. We hope that these studies will help to tip the political economy in favor of change.

References

UN-HABITAT (United Nations Human Settlements Programme). 2008. *State of the World's Cities 2008/2009: Harmonious Cities.* Nairobi: UN-HABITAT.

World Bank. 2007. *World Development Report 2008: Agriculture for Development.* Washington, DC: World Bank.

———. 2008. *World Development Report 2009: Reshaping Economic Geography.* Washington, DC: World Bank.

PART I

Global, National, and Local Perspectives on Urbanization and Inclusive Growth: Examples from Africa

CHAPTER 1

Urbanization: Essential for Development

The world is becoming increasingly urbanized.[1] Indeed, half of humanity is now living in urban areas, and more than 70 percent of the populations of Latin America, North America, and Europe are living in cities (see box 1.1 for definitions of the term *urban*). Although 60 percent of the people in Sub-Saharan Africa still live in rural areas, it is the fastest-urbanizing region of the world. In fact, the United Nations predicts that by 2030 Africa will be a predominantly urban continent. Urbanization stems in part from rural-to-urban migration, in part from natural increase, and in part from the reclassification of urban boundaries as cities expand outward and small population centers grow and are designated as urban areas.

Urbanization is therefore happening, and it will continue to happen. This trend is inevitable because urban development is an integral part of economic development. Economic growth is invariably accompanied by a transition from a predominantly agrarian economy to an economy dominated by the production of nonagricultural goods and services. Although some of this transformation can take place in situ as the rural nonfarm economy grows and diversifies, the overriding pattern is one of increasing urbanization. Firms take advantage of agglomeration economies (sharing of infrastructure, better matching of workers to jobs, and knowledge

Box 1.1

Defining *Urban*

There is no uniform global definition of *urban*. The United Nations (2004) argues that "given the variety of situations in the countries of the world, it is not possible or desirable to adopt uniform criteria to distinguish urban areas from rural areas." Statistical definitions of urban areas vary from country to country (or even within countries) and can be based on administrative boundaries, size, level of services, or population density (World Bank 2008).

This report delineates rural and urban areas following the classification used by the Population Division of the UN Secretariat in its regular report *World Urbanization Prospects* (*WUP*)—see United Nations (2005). Thus rural areas and urban areas, and rural and urban populations, are defined according to the criteria used by each country. Details on data sources and methods used for specific countries are available on the *WUP* Web site (http://esa.un.org/unup/).

This classification, although admittedly imperfect, is an attempt to balance competing demands. In choosing it, we give considerable weight to the representativity of the household survey data that are the basis for our empirical analysis. All of these surveys were designed to be nationally representative, as well as representative of rural and urban areas, *according to the classification system used in each country*. In principle, it is possible to reclassify areas using more rigorous and consistent criteria, such as the agglomeration index developed for the 2009 *World Development Report* (World Bank 2008). Such a reclassification would have many benefits, but in the context of this report those benefits would be offset by an enormous cost: the survey data would no longer be statistically representative of rural or urban areas, which in turn casts doubt on inferences made from the observed rural-urban welfare differences.

In addition to consistency issues across countries, simple categorization within a country inevitably involves a loss of information. In reality, there is a rural-to-urban continuum, ranging from sparsely populated isolated settlements to small towns to secondary cities to megacities. Thus, in any given country there is heterogeneity within areas that are classified as rural or urban. Although a few countries stratify their household surveys into three or four levels of the rural-urban continuum (e.g., rural, urban, and metropolitan in Brazil), they are the exceptions.

Figure 1.1   Urbanization and Per Capita GDP across Countries, 2000

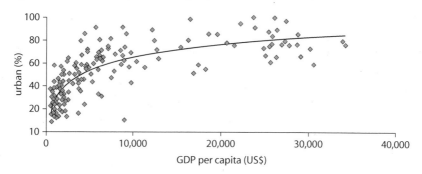

Source: Annez and Buckley 2008.
Note: GDP = gross domestic product.

spillovers), which leads to what Arthur (1990) describes as "positive feedback"—a mutually reinforcing relationship between increases in productivity and the concentration of firms. Similarly, people concentrate to take advantage of higher-paying employment opportunities, better prices because of denser markets, and improved amenities.

The suggestion that urbanization is a requirement for economic development is borne out by the empirical evidence: few countries have realized income levels of US$10,000[2] per capita before reaching about 60 percent urbanization (see figure 1.1). And simple bivariate regressions, though no indication of causality, suggest that urbanization is a very strong indicator of productivity growth over the long run (Annez and Buckley 2008).

Urbanization and Inequality

During the early stages of development, economic growth and urbanization tend to increase spatial inequalities. Agglomeration economies create leading areas, characterized by economic dynamism and rising standards of living. Most often, those who are already better-off—that is, have more education and more assets to fall back on—are better placed to take advantage of these new opportunities. But the flip side of leading areas is lagging areas—areas that have not experienced structural transformation and where standards of living are stagnating or even declining.

Spatial inequalities exist at many levels. At the international level, early industrialization has concentrated production in Western Europe and North America, leaving entire regions of the world behind. At the country level, large portions of countries such as northern Ghana or northern

Uganda are considered lagging areas. Disparities also appear within such regions. For example, low living standards have been observed in rural areas of southern Mozambique, only 100–200 kilometers from the booming capital city of Maputo. Drilling down further, even very prosperous cities have squalid slums.

At the country level, because of the nature of structural transformation, inequalities between leading and lagging areas often correspond to rural-urban divides. *World Development Report 2009: Reshaping Economic Geography* (*WDR 2009*) argues that rural-urban living standards diverge as countries develop and become more urbanized, converging only once they reach a relatively high development threshold. Specifically, it finds that "urban-to-rural gaps in consumption levels rise until countries reach upper-middle-income levels" (World Bank 2008).

But policy makers cannot afford to sit back and wait for their countries to pass a hypothesized development threshold before spatial inequalities begin to converge, especially when that threshold lies far in the future. Spatial inequalities entail less inclusive growth processes—that is, less poverty reduction for a given rate of growth—and are often associated with social tensions and even conflict, particularly when spatial inequalities are aligned with ethnic, linguistic, or religious divides (Kanbur and Venables 2005). Therefore, a key question emerges: *How can developing countries manage the transition from a predominantly rural economy to a more urbanized economy in a way that produces acceptable growth and equity outcomes in the short and medium term?*

Part I of this report aims to help the development community gain insights into this question of how to manage the urbanization process in a way that preserves growth and promotes equity. It complements recent and forthcoming publications on spatial inequalities at the global and regional levels (the regional level, using examples from South Asia, is covered in part II of this report). In contrast to the long-term view provided by *WDR 2009*, part I presents a more medium-term picture of patterns and trends in spatial inequalities. In painting that picture, part I focuses on Sub-Saharan Africa.

Why Africa?

The focus on Africa in part I is intended in part to address questions of African exceptionalism. The notion that Africa, contrary to other regions, has experienced "urbanization without growth" (Fay and Opal 2000) is probably overstated, holding true only for small African countries at low levels of urbanization or failed states that are experiencing "push" as opposed to "pull" rural-to-urban migration (Annez and Buckley 2008). Even though the "urbanization without growth" paradigm is misleading, the region has experienced urbanization with lower levels of *shared* growth. Ravallion, Chen, and Sangraula (2007) point out that urbanization in Sub-Saharan Africa has been associated with less poverty reduction than in other regions. And, alongside Latin America, Sub-Saharan Africa is experiencing the highest levels of urban inequality in the world.[3] Thus higher average levels of well-being in urban areas may mask high levels of deprivation among poor urban residents. According to UN-Habitat (2008) estimations, a higher proportion of city dwellers in Sub-Saharan Africa live in slums than anywhere else in the world (figure 1.2). Although the slum classification says nothing about the depth of deprivation, examination of conditions across regions by UN-Habitat's Global Urban Observatory suggests that slum dwellers in Sub-Saharan Africa experience a higher level of *multiple* shelter deprivations compared with slum dwellers in other regions (UN-Habitat 2008).

Meanwhile, African policy makers appear to be particularly ambivalent about the process of rural-urban transformation: a UN survey of population policies indicates that 83 percent of African governments are implementing policies to reduce rural-to-urban migration, and 78 percent are intervening to reduce migration to large cities in particular. These percentages are notably higher than the world averages (United Nations 2008a). Because the urban population of Africa will almost double over the next two decades, growing from about 290 million in 2007 to 540 million in 2025 (United Nations 2008b), the question "Is Africa's urbanization different, and if so, why?" is of growing urgency from a policy perspective.

Why focus here on three particular countries in Sub-Saharan Africa— Ghana, Mozambique, and Uganda? These countries are not intended to be representative of the entire region, but they do bear certain common characteristics that enable us to draw some indicative conclusions about processes of structural and spatial transformation. First, they are all at an early stage of economic development and structural transformation, albeit to slightly different degrees. Second, all three countries have experienced urbanization over the course of the last three decades. And third, each has experienced robust growth in its gross domestic product (GDP) over the past 15–20 years, which enables us to observe the trends in spatial inequality associated with economic development.[4]

After looking at rural-urban disparities in Ghana, Mozambique, and Uganda, we narrow the lens of analysis further to examine intraurban

Figure 1.2   Proportion of Urban Populations Living in Slums by Region, 2005

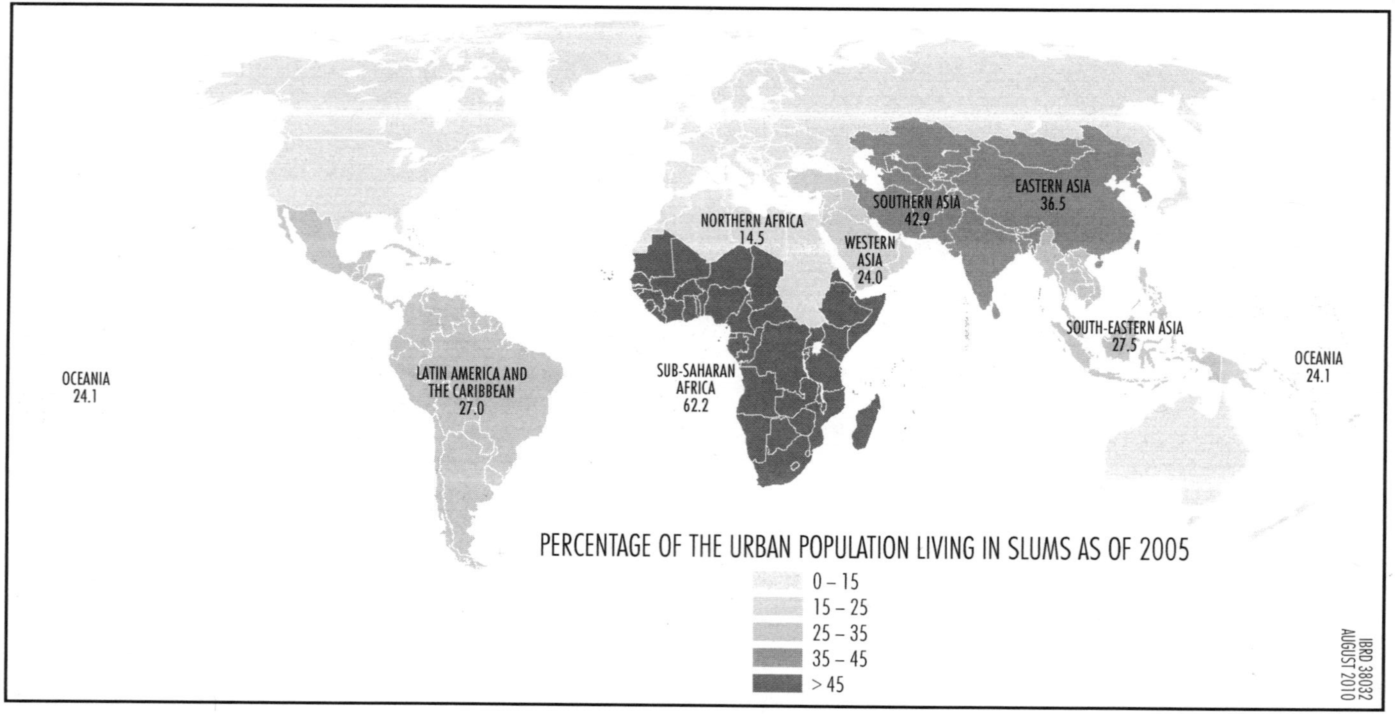

IBRD 38032
AUGUST 2010

OCEANIA
24.1

SOUTH-EASTERN ASIA
27.5

EASTERN ASIA
36.5

SOUTHERN ASIA
42.9

WESTERN
ASIA
24.0

NORTHERN AFRICA
14.5

SUB-SAHARAN
AFRICA
62.2

LATIN AMERICA AND
THE CARIBBEAN
27.0

OCEANIA
24.1

PERCENTAGE OF THE URBAN POPULATION LIVING IN SLUMS AS OF 2005

0 – 15
15 – 25
25 – 35
35 – 45
> 45

Data source: UN-Habitat 2008.

inequalities in the capitals of these countries: Accra, Maputo, and Kampala. Three observations informed a decision to focus on these capital cities. First, across Sub-Saharan Africa, large cities (of between 1 and 5 million) have been growing at a faster rate than medium-size and small cities and thus account for a rising share of Africa's urban population. Growth in the primary city, it seems, will represent the dominant trend for the foreseeable future. Second, spatial inequalities in big cities tend to be larger than in smaller cities (Kilroy 2007). And third, the greater quantity of data available for capital cities as opposed to secondary cities in each of these countries allow a more thorough investigation of patterns and trends across income and nonincome welfare measures.

Organization of Part I

The chapters that follow investigate urbanization and rural-urban welfare inequalities on three geographic scales: global, national, and local.

At the global level, we examine in chapter 2 cross-country evidence of rural-urban welfare inequalities in 41 low- and middle-income countries. Specifically, we look at differences in rural and urban welfare based on both monetary and nonmonetary measures. We then use household survey data to uncover patterns of divergence or convergence over time. Finally, we investigate whether these patterns are associated with other covariates, such as per capita GDP. The findings indicate that investigators should be cautious in predicting welfare convergence or divergence based on a country's level of development alone. Although urban welfare is consistently higher than rural welfare, the magnitude of the gap is extremely variable, even in countries with similar levels of urbanization or per capita GDP. Over time, few clear patterns of convergence or divergence emerge. Rather than reinforcing the broad prediction in *WDR 2009* of convergence-then-divergence as countries develop, the findings indicate that deeper analysis of the institutional and policy environment is required to understand the dynamics of rural-urban transitions at the country level.

Chapter 3 therefore takes the analysis to the national scale as we try to uncover the sources of rural-urban consumption inequalities. Focusing on Ghana, Mozambique, and Uganda, we investigate why urban welfare is higher than rural welfare in these three countries. We use decomposition techniques to determine whether these inequalities stem from differences in endowments (such as levels of education) or differences in returns to those endowments. In other words, would the rural poor, by virtue of their household characteristics, remain poor if they lived in urban areas? Or would a move to the city entail higher returns, all other things being equal? Differences in endowments emerge as the principal explanation of rural-urban inequalities, particularly in Uganda and Mozambique. These results indicate that barriers to mobility are not the principal explanation of welfare inequalities between rural and urban areas and suggest that measures to boost rural education would have a significant impact on spatial inequalities.

To gain a yet more finely tuned picture, we consider in chapter 4 disparities at the local level in Accra, Maputo, and Kampala, relying on data on demographic and physical changes in these three capital cities. We then look at income and nonincome welfare in the capitals versus the countries as a whole before examining the extent of intraurban inequalities. In the final section, we investigate the principal causes of spatial inequalities in these cities, highlighting colonial legacies, dysfunctional land markets, and weak governance.

Concluding chapter 11 of this report pulls together the findings of each of the levels of analysis to reflect on policy implications and outlines an agenda for future research. The findings reinforce the call in WDR 2009 for spatially blind institutions to promote equality of opportunities in rural and urban areas. But the findings also question the extent to which such institutions can be effective without concurrent investments in connective infrastructure and carefully targeted interventions, even in relatively low-income environments. Avenues for future research include more spatially sensitive poverty analysis and further investigation into the impact of land tenure on rural-urban transitions. Urbanization may be part and parcel of development, but concerted policy making—based on sound analytics—is required to ensure that it incorporates shared growth and opportunities for all.

Notes

1. Part I of this report was produced by a team led by Kenneth Simler and Nora Dudwick of the Poverty Reduction and Equity Group (PRMPR) under the Poverty Reduction and Economic Management (PREM) vice presidency. Team members were Paul Cahu, Katy Hull, Roy Katayama, and Kalpana Mehra. The chapters were prepared under the supervision of Louise Cord and Jaime Saavedra. This work is part of a joint work program between PRMPR and FEUSE (Finance, Economics and Urban Department, Spatial and Economics Unit). The FEUSE team was led by Forhad Shilpi and supervised by Marisela Montoliu.

2. All dollar amounts are U.S. dollars unless otherwise indicated.

3. According to UN-Habitat (2008), the two regions exhibit "exceptionally high levels of urban inequality": a subset of 26 cities in Africa and 19 in Latin America have average Gini coefficients of 0.54 and 0.55, respectively.

4. An additional reason for choosing these countries is the availability of repeated cross sections of good-quality household survey data.

References

Annez, P. C., and R. M. Buckley. 2008. "Urbanization and Growth: Setting the Context." In *Urbanization and Growth*, ed. M. Spence, P. C. Annez, and R. M. Buckley. Commission on Growth and Development. Washington, DC: World Bank.

Arthur, B. W. 1990. "Positive Feedbacks in the Economy." *Scientific American* 262: 92–99.

Fay, M., and C. Opal. 2000. "Urbanization without Growth: A Not So Uncommon Phenomenon." Policy Research Working Paper 2412, World Bank, Washington, DC.

Kanbur, R., and A. Venables. 2005. "Rising Spatial Disparities and Development." Policy Brief No. 3, United Nations University, World Institute for Development Economics Research, Helsinki.

Kilroy, A. 2007. "Intra-Urban Spatial Inequality: Cities as 'Urban Regions.'" *World Development Report 2009* Background Paper, World Bank, Washington, DC.

Ravallion, M., S. Chen, and P. Sangraula. 2007. "New Evidence on the Urbanization of Global Poverty." Policy Research Working Paper 4199, World Bank, Washington, DC.

UN-Habitat. 2008. *State of the World's Cities 2008/9: Harmonious Cities.* Nairobi: United Nations Human Settlements Programme.

United Nations. 2004. *World Urbanization Prospects: The 2003 Revision.* Department of Economic and Social Affairs, Population Division. New York: United Nations.

———. 2005. *World Urbanization Prospects: The 2004 Revision.* Department of Economic and Social Affairs, Population Division. New York: United Nations.

———. 2008a. *Urban Indigenous Peoples and Migration Factsheet.* http://www.un.org/esa/socdev/unpfii/documents/factsheet_migration_final.pdf.

———. 2008b. *World Urbanization Prospects: The 2007 Revision.* Department of Economic and Social Affairs, Population Division. New York: United Nations.

World Bank. 2008. *World Development Report 2009: Reshaping Economic Geography.* Washington, DC: World Bank.

CHAPTER 2

Global Level: Recent Patterns and Trends in Rural and Urban Welfare Inequality

In almost every country in the world, average living standards in urban areas are superior to those in rural areas. This pattern is observed whether welfare is measured by average income, consumption, poverty indexes, infant mortality, health, access to services, or numerous other variables. Likewise, the superiority of average urban living standards is the norm regardless of national income levels and tends to be maintained during the development process, even as countries move from predominantly rural agrarian economies to more urbanized economies with larger industrial and service sectors.

However, the *size* of rural-urban welfare gaps varies a great deal across countries, and some argue that the evolution of these gaps follows a predictable pattern as a country grows and develops. According to the *World Development Report 2009: Reshaping Economic Geography (WDR 2009)* (World Bank 2008), the rural-urban gap in consumption increases until countries reach upper-middle-income levels, or $4,000–$12,000 in gross national income per capita. After that point, the rural-urban gap is expected to diminish as the urban share of the population grows, the domestic product and factor markets become more efficient, and the delivery of public services becomes more equal over space. As described

in *WDR 2009*, in industrial economies, rural-urban welfare differences
are small, but not completely eliminated.

The development trajectories of today's industrialized countries con-
form well to the paradigm of rural-urban divergence-then-convergence in
living standards. The current low-income countries may follow the same
path, and yet the available data also pose some critical questions, as illustrated in figure 2.1 taken from *WDR 2009*. The figure shows the ratios of
urban-rural per capita consumption as revealed by 120 cross-sectional
household surveys conducted in 75 countries. On the right-hand side of
the distribution, the urban-rural consumption ratio drops from about
2.2:1 to about 1.6:1. The left-hand side of the distribution in figure 2.1 is
almost L-shaped. The bottom part of the L reveals greater urban-rural
inequality accompanying higher levels of gross domestic product (GDP)
(in the cross section), as described in *WDR 2009*. However, along the vertical part of the L are the poorest countries, all with per capita GDP of less
than $1,000 (not adjusted for purchasing power parity), in which average
urban consumption is anywhere from 150 percent to over 300 percent of
rural consumption. What accounts for this large range of urban-rural
inequalities among countries at roughly similar stages of development?

In this chapter, we seek to complement *WDR 2009*, and other recent
studies summarized in box 2.1, by examining more closely rural-urban

**Figure 2.1   Cross-Sectional Data from *WDR 2009* on Urban-Rural Consumption
Differences**

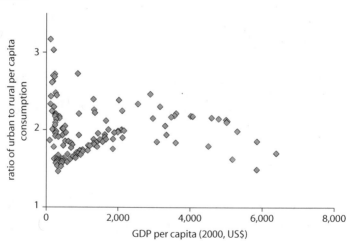

Source: World Bank 2008.

Box 2.1

Are Rural-Urban Welfare Differences Shrinking or Growing?

The evidence on the evolution of rural-urban welfare inequalities over time is mixed. Considerable literature exists on both the theoretical and empirical aspects of the convergence or divergence of rural and urban living standards as countries develop. Taking a long-term view, *WDR 2009* asserts that an economic divide will emerge between rural and urban areas as the processes of urbanization and development proceed (World Bank 2008). This view is consistent with the notion of an industrializing core undergoing a virtuous circle of development, with positive feedback between productivity and the concentration of firms, while a rural periphery suffers from slower growth or even stagnation. According to *WDR 2009*, once countries reach the upper-middle-income level, rural-urban disparities tend to narrow. Essential household consumption is hypothesized to converge first, followed by access to basic public services and, finally, wages and incomes.

The World Institute for Development Economics Research of the United Nations University (UNU/WIDER) research project found divergence of rural-urban living standards not only in low-income countries but also in middle-income countries such as the Czech Republic, Hungary, Mexico, Poland, and the Russian Federation. For low-income countries, divergence was stronger for income measures than nonincome measures. Limited convergence was found among nonincome measures, with many cases of neither convergence nor divergence over time.

By contrast, there is evidence that rural-urban differences in poverty rates are narrowing, but only in some regions. Ravallion, Chen, and Sangraula (2007) find that since the early 1990s, rural poverty rates have, in the aggregate, been falling faster than urban poverty rates. They attribute this finding to poor people "urbanizing even more rapidly than the population as a whole." In other words, the narrowing of rural and urban poverty rates is largely the product of a compositional effect, with rural-urban population shifts accounting for much of the more rapid poverty reduction in rural areas. The authors note pronounced regional differences in the differences in rural and urban poverty rates. For example, in China and in the Europe and Central Asia region, the rural-urban poverty rates diverged over the period 1993–2002, whereas in Sub-Saharan Africa and South Asia, there is no clear trend in the differences between rural and urban poverty rates.

welfare inequalities among the low- and middle-income countries that make up the L-shaped scatter on the left side of figure 2.1. These countries represent the bulk of the World Bank's clients. In addition to comparing mean consumption, we analyze more distribution-sensitive welfare indicators such as the poverty headcount and poverty gap. We also address two nonmonetary welfare indicators, undernutrition and school enrollment.

In addition to examining the cross-sectional evidence, we use repeated surveys in these countries to better understand the dynamics of changes in rural-urban welfare gaps and whether they are increasing or decreasing over time as these countries become richer and more urbanized. If the dynamics look anything like the cross-sectional information in figure 2.1, one would expect divergence of rural-urban living standards in the countries with a low rural-urban gap and convergence in the countries with a large gap. An alternative hypothesis would be that in all cases the rural-urban divergence accompanies growth, which would imply extremely large rural-urban inequalities in the future for those low-income countries that already have urban-rural ratios of 2:1 or greater. Finally, in this chapter we use cross-country regressions to explore possible country characteristics or typologies associated with rural-urban welfare divergence or convergence.

Sources of Data

The data used in the cross-country analysis presented in this chapter were drawn from two main sources. For the monetary-based welfare measures, we use an updated version of the data set constructed by Ravallion, Chen, and Sangraula (2007) for their study of the rural-urban distribution of poverty. The data set is compiled from dozens of household living standards surveys that use broadly similar methods for defining a monetary measure of individual welfare based on consumption or income,[1] including both cash transactions and imputed values for items produced and consumed by the household. The welfare measure and the national poverty lines are converted to internationally comparable terms by applying purchasing power parity (PPP) exchange rates to the local currency values.

The purpose of PPP exchange rates is to adjust for spatial differences *across countries* in the purchasing power of a nominal unit of currency; they make no adjustment for spatial differences in purchasing power *within* countries. Such differences can be large, especially between rural and urban areas and in low-income countries with poorly integrated markets. For example, Ravallion, Chen, and Sangraula (2007) report that urban poverty lines are frequently 40–50 percent higher than rural poverty lines, with the difference reaching as high as 79 percent. If the higher cost of basic needs in urban areas is ignored, then urban poverty is underestimated and rural-urban differences in poverty are overstated in countries where urban poverty is lower than rural poverty, which is the vast majority. In their data set, Ravallion and his colleagues correct this deficiency by setting the rural extreme poverty line in each country at $1.25 per day (in PPP terms), and then using the ratio of urban to rural poverty lines observed in each country to set an urban extreme poverty line (also in PPP terms) for each country that reflects its prevailing rural-urban differences in the cost of basic needs. A similar procedure is used for the $2.00 per day poverty line. The data set distinguishes rural and urban areas using the definitions given in *World Urbanization Prospects* (*WUP*), a regular publication of the Population Division of the United Nations Secretariat (United Nations 2005). *WUP* largely follows definitions used by national statistical offices.

The analysis in this section employs a subset of these data that has been updated to use the 2005 PPP exchange rates (Ravallion, Chen, and Sangraula [2007] used the 1993 PPP exchange rates). The data in this subset cover 41 countries, with two surveys for each country. The subset of countries was chosen on the basis of four criteria: (1) interval between the oldest and most recent available Living Standards Measurement Study (LSMS) surveys (longer intervals preferred), (2) range of national income levels, (3) geographic distribution, and (4) availability of Demographic and Health Surveys (DHS) data for nonmonetary welfare measures. The 41 countries in the data set are listed in appendix A, along with the year of the surveys and the GDP per capita (in 2005 international PPP dollars) corresponding to the survey year.

The second data source is the Demographic and Health Surveys collected by ICF Macro. The DHS, which collects extensive information on nutrition, education, and access to services, has an extremely high degree of comparability across countries and survey years. Our analysis focuses on the nutritional status of children and school enrollment rates. DHS data are available for 27 of the 41 countries with LSMS data (the 27 countries in the DHS sample and years of the surveys are listed in appendix A).

A significant limitation of both data sets is the time span covered. The surveys in the data sets were conducted between 1990 and 2006. The intervals between the two surveys in any given country range from

4 to 16 years, which is short when compared with the rural-urban and structural transformations that typically take decades to achieve. Noise in the form of interannual fluctuations, such as from a particularly good or bad agricultural year, is likely to be high relative to the signal of long-term trends of divergence or convergence. But they are the best data available. Also noteworthy, because the surveys are repeated cross sections, little can be said about the changes in rural-urban welfare gaps caused by compositional changes, such as the artificial "convergence" that would occur if a group of poor people moved from a poor rural area to a less poor urban area. However, this factor is addressed in chapter 3 for the three Sub-Saharan African countries featured in that chapter.

Methods

The comparisons in this chapter are intended to be exploratory and descriptive; they are not designed to establish causal inferences. The approach is straightforward. First, we compare the initial levels of welfare measures in rural and urban areas within each country. This comparison is carried out only for the first year of survey data, and so provides a baseline against which one can assess the convergence or divergence of welfare levels.

In the second set of analyses, we examine whether welfare—as captured by the selected measures—is improving more rapidly in urban areas or rural areas. Because the time period between the two surveys is relatively short, the results are unlikely to support statistically robust statements about convergence or divergence of the kind posited in *WDR 2009*. Instead, we use an approach similar to that adopted by Sahn and Stifel (2003) in their analysis of nonmonetary welfare measures in Sub-Saharan Africa. Changes in welfare between the two surveys are calculated separately for rural and urban areas in each country for each welfare measure. This calculation is made first using the absolute changes in levels between the two periods (e.g., mean consumption in 2004 minus rural mean consumption in 1996 in a given country). A similar comparison is then made using the Kakwani improvement index, which is based on the idea that for finite measures of welfare an incremental improvement is more difficult to achieve when the initial level is closer to the maximum (see box 2.2). Finally, we investigate patterns across countries in the convergence or divergence of welfare measures, looking specifically at national income levels and regional groupings as potential correlates.

Box 2.2

Comparing Welfare Differences and Changes

Multiple methods are used for comparing rural and urban performance on the various welfare measures. A commonly used approach is to express the difference as a ratio, such as the ratio of mean urban consumption to mean rural consumption (e.g., World Bank 2008). The ratio is extremely intuitive, with values closer to 1 indicating greater equality between groups on the welfare measure. This approach may be appropriate for comparing means, such as mean consumption, but it can be misleading for the five other welfare measures we consider, which are based on proportions of the population above or below a certain threshold. For example, consider a country whose poverty headcount of 60 percent in rural areas and 30 percent in urban areas later fell to 6 percent and 3 percent, respectively. In *relative* terms, the difference is unchanged, because the probability of being in poverty is twice as high in rural areas in each period. However, in *absolute* terms, the rural-urban gap has been narrowed tremendously—a fact that is missed by the ratio measure. Therefore, for the poverty, nutritional status, and school enrollment measures, we use the absolute differences between rural and urban areas.

However, absolute differences can be misleading in assessing development progress over time, either within a country or between countries. As Sen (1981) and others have argued, the relationship between achievement and the values of many common welfare indicators is nonlinear. In particular, as the standard of living reaches higher levels, incremental improvement becomes more difficult. It is arguably easier to reduce poverty by three percentage points if the initial level is 60 percent than if the initial level is 6 percent. Kakwani's *achievement index* compares levels of welfare measures to their minimum and maximum possible levels (Kakwani 1993). For an increasing welfare measure x (i.e., higher levels imply greater welfare) recorded at time t, the Kakwani achievement index takes the form

$$f(x_t, M_0, M) = \frac{\ln(M - M_0) - \ln(M - x_t)}{\ln(M - M_0)},$$

where M_0 and M are the lower and upper bounds of the welfare measure, respectively. Because poverty and stunting are measures of negative outcomes—that is, lower values represent higher welfare—for those variables we define x_t as equal to $100 - w_t$, where w_t is the conventional poverty index or undernutrition

(continued next page)

Box 2.2   *(continued)*

prevalence. If the welfare measures in periods 1 and 2 are defined as x_1 and x_2, it is possible to define an *improvement index* that is equal to the difference in the achievement indexes for the two periods:

$$Q(x_1,x_2,M_0,M) = f(x_2,M_0,M) - f(x_1,M_0,M)$$
$$= \frac{\ln (M-x_1) - \ln (M-x_2)}{\ln (M-M_0)}.$$

The improvement index satisfies several important axioms of welfare comparisons; for details, see Kakwani (1993).

In our study, we use six different welfare measures, four monetary and two nonmonetary.[2] The comparisons are made using aggregate rural and urban statistics for each survey. The monetary measures, based on consumption per capita, are mean consumption (in 2005 international PPP dollars), the poverty headcount index using both the $1.25 per day and $2.00 per day thresholds, and the poverty gap index (FGT1) for $2.00 per day. By employing two poverty lines and two poverty indexes, we are able to detect changes in the distribution of welfare that often are not apparent from comparison of mean consumption alone.

The two nonmonetary welfare measures used are school enrollment and child undernutrition. The education measure is the proportion of children between the ages of 6 and 15 (inclusive) who were attending school, at any level, at the time of the survey. For child undernutrition, we use the incidence of stunting (measured by height more than two standard deviations below the median for the child's age and sex) among children under 3 years of age. Stunting is generally the result of a combination of insufficient nutrient intake and repeated illness and can therefore be interpreted as a measure of chronic deprivation.

Results

The results that follow aim to answer two principal sets of questions, one static and the other dynamic. The first set of questions relates to welfare *levels*: Is welfare consistently higher in urban areas than in rural areas? Are these disparities higher or lower in middle-income countries than in low-income countries? The second set of questions relates to *changes* in welfare: Are rural-urban differences shrinking or growing over time? Do trends vary according to countries' levels of development?

Rural-Urban Inequalities: The Static Picture

In almost all countries (40 of 41), mean consumption is higher in urban areas than in rural areas. Panel (a) of figure 2.2 plots the ratio of urban to rural mean consumption per capita against log national GDP per capita.[3] All countries except Armenia have a ratio greater than 1.0. The ratio is extremely variable among the low-income countries, ranging from 1.2 in Tanzania and Madagascar to over 3.5 in Burkina Faso. For most of the lower-middle- and upper-middle-income countries, mean consumption in urban areas is two to three times larger than that in rural areas. Although a few low-income, high urban-rural ratio countries appear in the upper left-hand corner of panel (a), overall the plot shows a strong positive cross-sectional correlation between the urban-rural consumption ratio and GDP per capita, indicating larger welfare gaps in middle-income countries than in low-income countries.[4]

In almost all cases, the poverty headcount rate is higher in rural areas, although the extent of the disparity varies across countries. Panel (b) of figure 2.2 presents the differences in rural and urban poverty using the extreme poverty line of $1.25/day (in 2005 PPP dollars). The rural-urban differences are highly variable among the low-income countries, ranging from just a few percentage points to over 40 percentage points in Burkina Faso and India. These differences are smaller in the middle-income countries, because for middle-income countries the percentage of the population below the extreme poverty line is very low in both rural and urban areas. By contrast, when the $2.00 per day poverty line is used (panel (c), the average difference in poverty rates appears to be about the same for both low- and middle-income countries.

Consistent with the mean consumption and poverty headcount results, the poverty gap, which captures both the proportion of the population below the poverty line and the average depth of their poverty, is higher in rural areas in almost all of the 41 countries in the sample. Panel (d) of figure 2.2 shows the rural-urban differences in the poverty gap index for the initial period using the $2.00 per day poverty line. The rural-urban differences in the poverty gap range from 0 to 30 percentage points. Overall, the rural-urban differences in the poverty gap are smaller in the middle-income countries, dropping to 12 percentage points or less for countries in the sample with annual GDP per capita greater than

Figure 2.2 Rural-Urban Welfare Differences in Initial Survey Year, Selected Countries

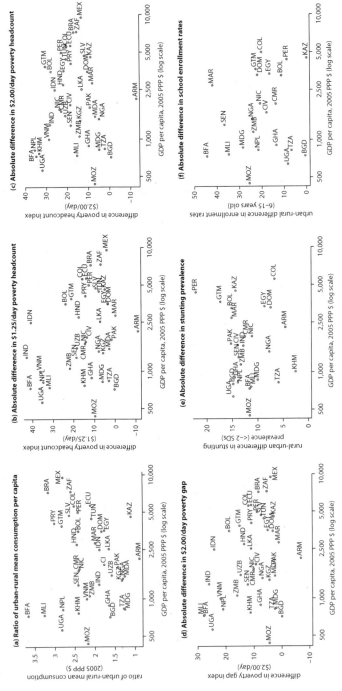

Source: Authors' calculations using LSMS and DHS data (see appendix A).
Note: SD = standard deviation. See appendix A for country abbreviations.

$5,000 (PPP). Taken together, panels (c) and (d) indicate that, among the poor, the depth of poverty tends to be greater among the rural poor, which is somewhat surprising in view of the higher inequality that generally characterizes urban areas.

The undernutrition (stunting) rates in the initial survey year are higher in rural areas in all 27 countries in the DHS sample. As shown in panel (e) of figure 2.2, in the initial survey years the stunting rates are 1–22 percentage points higher in rural areas than in urban areas, with most countries exhibiting differences of 10–15 percentage points. The rural-urban differences in stunting rates do not diminish in the middle-income countries, and in fact, the largest differences are in some of the richest countries in the sample in strong contrast with the mean consumption and poverty differences on view in panels (a)–(d). Several explanations are possible for this finding. One is that basic nonfood living expenses are much higher in the more urbanized middle-income countries, leaving a smaller share of the budgets of poor households to meet food needs. Another possibility is that the more urbanized middle-income countries have greater problems with congestion and inadequacy of public health and sanitation in poor areas, contributing to urban undernutrition through the morbidity pathway.

The rural-urban differences in school enrollment rates, especially among low-income countries, vary a great deal. Panel (f) of figure 2.2 shows the difference in the percentage of children aged 6–15 who are enrolled in school.[5] For example, in Bangladesh and Kazakhstan the rural and urban enrollment rates in this age group are almost equal, whereas in Burkina Faso the difference in enrollment rates is 44 percentage points (63 percent in urban areas versus 19 percent in rural areas). The rural-urban enrollment gaps are generally smaller among the lower-middle-income countries in the sample, although even in the lower-middle-income countries the difference in enrollment rates is generally between 10 and 20 percentage points.

To summarize, three observations emerge from the data on initial levels of welfare in rural and urban areas. First, in both low- and middle-income countries urban areas are almost always better off than rural areas. This not surprising observation is consistent with the conventional wisdom about the average rural-urban welfare differences described at the outset of this chapter. Second, the size of the rural-urban gaps is highly variable, especially among the poorest countries. This variability was observed previously for mean consumption, but it also holds for poverty measures, nutritional status, and school enrollment. Third, the size of rural-urban differences in mean consumption, the $2.00 per day poverty headcount, and undernutrition do not appear to vary systematically with GDP per capita. The cross-sectional evidence presented thus far provides little, if any, support for the hypothesis of diverging rural-urban welfare levels during the early stages of development. In the sections that follow, we address the question of spatial convergence more adequately by using two surveys for each country.

Rural-Urban Inequalities: The Dynamic Picture

Turning to the data on changes in welfare, the uniformity of the finding that initial welfare levels are almost always higher in urban areas than in rural areas allows us to conclude that, with only a few exceptions, a more rapid improvement (or less dramatic decline) in welfare in rural areas would represent convergence. Because GDP per capita grew over the interval between surveys in 38 of the 41 countries in the sample,[6] we also can conclude that whatever patterns that emerge can be associated with growing and developing economies, with minimal noise from countries that are economically struggling or in crisis during the period under consideration.

Table 2.1 summarizes the results for the absolute changes in the six welfare measures. Similar to the approach of Sahn and Stifel (2003), the entries in the table refer to the question, did rural welfare improve more than urban welfare?—that is, is there rural-urban welfare convergence? A "yes" entry indicates that the absolute improvement in the welfare measure was larger in the rural sector than in the urban sector, or that the welfare measure improved in the rural sector and declined in the urban sector. A "(yes)" entry indicates that the welfare measure declined in both rural and urban areas, but that the deterioration was less in rural areas. Conversely, a "no" entry indicates that the welfare measure improved more in the urban area than in the rural area, or improved in the urban area and declined in the rural area. A "(no)" entry indicates that the welfare measure declined in both areas, but that the decline was less in urban areas. Therefore, entries of "yes" and "(yes)" may be interpreted as indicators of rural-urban convergence in living standards, and entries of "no" and "(no)" are indicators of welfare divergence.[7] The bottom rows of the table summarize instances of convergence and divergence via simple counts.

The data on changes in welfare levels do not yield clear patterns of either convergence or divergence. Among the 41 countries in the sample, mean consumption and $2.00 per day poverty diverge in about twice as many countries as they converge. By contrast, extreme poverty

Table 2.1 Changes over Time in Absolute Levels of Welfare Measures, Selected Countries

Region	Country	Mean consumption	Did rural welfare improve more than urban welfare?				
			Headcount ($1.25/day)	Headcount ($2.00/day)	Poverty gap ($2.00/day)	Stunting	School enrollment
AFR	Burkina Faso	Yes	Yes	Yes	Yes	(No)	No
	Cameroon	No	No	No	No	(Yes)	No
	Côte d'Ivoire	No	Yes	Yes	Yes	Yes	Yes
	Ghana	No	No	No	No	(Yes)	(No)
	Madagascar	No	No	No	No	Yes	Yes
	Mali	Yes	Yes	No	Yes	(Yes)	Yes
	Mozambique	No	Yes	No	Yes	No	Yes
	Nigeria	No	No	No	No	No	Yes
	Senegal	No	Yes	No	Yes	Yes	Yes
	South Africa	(Yes)	(No)	(No)	(No)	—	—
	Tanzania	(No)	(No)	(No)	(No)	No	No
	Uganda	No	No	No	No	Yes	Yes
	Zambia	Yes	Yes	Yes	Yes	(Yes)	(Yes)
EAP	Cambodia	No	No	Yes	No	No	—
	Indonesia	No	Yes	No	Yes	—	—
	Vietnam	No	Yes	No	Yes	—	—

(continued next page)

Table 2.1 (continued)

Region	Country	Did rural welfare improve more than urban welfare?					
		Mean consumption	Headcount ($1.25/day)	Headcount ($2.00/day)	Poverty gap ($2.00/day)	Stunting	School enrollment
ECA	Armenia	No	No	No	No	Yes	—
	Kazakhstan	No	Yes	(No)	(No)	Yes	No
	Kyrgyz Republic	(Yes)	No	(No)	No	—	—
	Moldova	(No)	No	(No)	No	—	—
	Uzbekistan	(Yes)	(Yes)	(No)	(Yes)	—	—
LAC	Bolivia	(No)	(No)	(No)	(No)	No	(No)
	Brazil	Yes	Yes	Yes	Yes	—	—
	Colombia	No	(Yes)	(Yes)	(Yes)	No	Yes
	Dominican Republic	Yes	(Yes)	Yes	(Yes)	Yes	Yes
	Ecuador	No	(Yes)	(No)	(Yes)	—	—
	El Salvador	No	No	No	No	—	—
	Guatemala	Yes	Yes	Yes	(Yes)	Yes	Yes
	Honduras	No	Yes	Yes	Yes	—	—
	Mexico	Yes	Yes	Yes	Yes	—	—
	Nicaragua	(Yes)	Yes	Yes	Yes	No	No
	Paraguay	Yes	(Yes)	(Yes)	Yes	No	—
	Peru	No	No	No	No	No	Yes

MNA	Egypt, Arab Rep.	No	Yes	Yes	Yes	Yes	Yes
	Morocco	(Yes)	No	(No)	(No)	Yes	Yes
	Tunisia	No	Yes	Yes	Yes	—	—
SAR	Bangladesh	No	No	No	No	Yes	Yes
	India	No	No	No	Yes	(Yes)	—
	Nepal	No	Yes	No	No	No	Yes
	Pakistan	(No)	(No)	(No)	(No)	—	—
	Sri Lanka	Yes	Yes	Yes	No	—	—
Number in which rural welfare increased more		14	24	15	21	16	16
	Yes	9	19	13	17	11	15
	(Yes)	5	5	2	4	5	1
Number in which urban welfare increased more		27	17	26	20	10	7
	No	23	13	16	14	9	5
	(No)	4	4	10	6	1	2

Source: Authors' calculations using LSMS and DHS data (see appendix A).

Note: "Yes" indicates that welfare improved more in rural areas, or improved in rural and decreased in urban areas; "(yes)" indicates that welfare decreased in both, but urban decreased more; "no" indicates that welfare improved more in urban areas, or improved in urban and decreased in rural; "(no)" indicates that welfare decreased in both, but rural decreased more; — = not available; AFR = Africa; EAP = East Asia and the Pacific; ECA = Europe and Central Asia; LAC = Latin America and the Caribbean; MNA = Middle East and North Africa; SAR = South Asia.

($1.25 per day) rates and the $2.00 per day poverty gap converge in slightly more countries than they diverge. That convergence is more common for $1.25 per day poverty is to be expected, because as countries get richer the extreme poverty rate eventually approaches zero. As a result, many countries experience convergence of rural-urban poverty rates even while their mean consumption levels and $2.00 per day poverty rates are diverging.

The Latin America and Caribbean (LAC) countries have a much higher prevalence of rural-urban welfare convergence on consumption-based measures than other regions. Convergence occurs in poorer countries such as Honduras and Nicaragua as well as richer countries such as Mexico. This finding may be related to the higher levels of urbanization in the LAC region. Because DHS surveys are available for only 6 of the 12 LAC countries in the sample, it is more difficult to assess the region's performance on the nonmonetary welfare measures. For those LAC countries for which data on the nonmonetary measures are available, there is an equal number of instances of convergence and divergence.

Convergence is slightly more common for absolute changes in nonmonetary welfare measures. The last two columns of table 2.1 reveal that rural-urban stunting rates converged in 16 of 26 countries, and school enrollment rates converged in 16 of 23. Multiple (and nonmutually exclusive) explanations are possible for the higher frequency of convergence for these measures. One explanation might be that children's nutritional status and school enrollment are input measures that lead to changes in output measures—that is, reduced spatial inequality in the formative years may lead to relatively better productivity and labor market outcomes in later years, which in turn would reduce spatial inequality in consumption and poverty in those years. Another possible explanation is related to migration and the changing composition of rural and urban populations over time. If better-nourished and better-educated people are more likely to migrate to urban areas, greater convergence on the nonmonetary welfare input indicators may not translate into greater convergence in monetary indicators in later periods.

When the Kakwani improvement index is applied, the majority of the countries exhibit divergence on the consumption-based welfare measures. Table 2.2 reveals that between one-half and two-thirds of the countries in the sample have increasing spatial inequalities in mean consumption and poverty. In general, the Kakwani index tends to show less convergence than the absolute measures presented in table 2.1, because for a given level of absolute change it gives greater weight to

Table 2.2 Changes over Time in Welfare Measures (Kakwani Improvement Index), Selected Countries

Region	Country	Mean consumption	Did rural welfare improve more than urban welfare? Headcount ($1.25/day)	Headcount ($2.00/day)	Poverty gap ($2.00/day)	Stunting	School enrollment
AFR	Burkina Faso	Yes	Yes	Yes	Yes	(No)	No
	Cameroon	No	No	No	No	(Yes)	No
	Côte d'Ivoire	No	Yes	Yes	Yes	Yes	Yes
	Ghana	No	No	No	No	(Yes)	(Yes)
	Madagascar	No	No	No	No	Yes	Yes
	Mali	Yes	No	No	No	(Yes)	Yes
	Mozambique	No	Yes	No	Yes	No	No
	Nigeria	No	No	No	No	No	Yes
	Senegal	No	No	No	No	No	Yes
	South Africa	(Yes)	(No)	(No)	(No)	—	—
	Tanzania	(No)	(No)	(No)	(No)	No	No
	Uganda	No	No	No	No	Yes	No
	Zambia	Yes	Yes	Yes	Yes	(Yes)	(Yes)
EAP	Cambodia	No	No	No	No	No	—
	Indonesia	No	No	No	No	—	—
	Vietnam	No	No	No	No	—	—

(continued next page)

Table 2.2 (continued)

Region	Country	Mean consumption	Headcount ($1.25/day)	Headcount ($2.00/day)	Poverty gap ($2.00/day)	Stunting	School enrollment
				Did rural welfare improve more than urban welfare?			
ECA	Armenia	No	No	No	No	Yes	—
	Kazakhstan	No	Yes	(No)	(No)	Yes	No
	Kyrgyz Republic	(Yes)	No	(No)	No	—	—
	Moldova	(No)	No	(No)	No	—	—
	Uzbekistan	(Yes)	(Yes)	(Yes)	(Yes)	—	—
LAC	Bolivia	(No)	(No)	(No)	(No)	No	(Yes)
	Brazil	Yes	Yes	Yes	Yes	—	—
	Colombia	No	(Yes)	(Yes)	(Yes)	No	No
	Dominican Republic	Yes	(Yes)	Yes	(Yes)	Yes	Yes
	Ecuador	No	(Yes)	(Yes)	(Yes)	—	—
	El Salvador	No	No	No	No	—	—
	Guatemala	Yes	Yes	Yes	Yes	No	Yes
	Honduras	No	Yes	No	Yes	—	—
	Mexico	Yes	Yes	Yes	Yes	—	—
	Nicaragua	(Yes)	Yes	Yes	Yes	—	—
	Paraguay	Yes	(Yes)	(Yes)	Yes	No	No
	Peru	No	No	No	No	No	No

MNA						
Egypt, Arab Rep.	No	Yes	Yes	Yes	Yes	Yes
Morocco	(Yes)	No	(No)	(Yes)	(No)	No
Tunisia	No	Yes	No	No	Yes	—
SAR						
Bangladesh	No	No	No	No	No	Yes
India	No	No	No	No	No	(Yes)
Nepal	No	No	No	No	No	No
Pakistan	(No)	(No)	(No)	(No)	(No)	—
Sri Lanka	Yes	Yes	Yes	Yes	Yes	—
Number in which rural welfare increased more	*14*	*18*	*15*	*17*	*14*	*13*
Yes	9	13	10	13	9	10
(Yes)	5	5	5	4	5	3
Number in which urban welfare increased more	*27*	*23*	*26*	*24*	*12*	*10*
No	23	19	19	18	11	10
(No)	4	4	7	6	1	0

Source: Authors' calculations using LSMS and DHS data (see appendix A).
Note: See table 2.1 for meaning of yes/(yes)/no/(no) responses and region abbreviations. — = not available.

improvements in the group or sector that has a higher initial welfare level. That said, the instances of divergence in mean consumption and the $2.00 per day headcount are the same whether the absolute differences or the Kakwani index is used. The consistency of the direction of change happens to be particularly strong when the Kakwani index is used on these data. Fully 70 percent of the countries record a uniform divergence ("no") or convergence ("yes") across all four consumption and poverty indicators. Again, the LAC region shows a much stronger tendency to rural-urban welfare convergence of mean consumption and poverty than any of the other regions.

The Kakwani index reveals slightly more instances of convergence than divergence for the nutrition and education welfare measures. In the last two columns of table 2.2, convergence on stunting and school enroll-ment rates is observed in slightly more than half of the countries. It is striking that in many countries the direction of the convergence or diver-gence of the nonmonetary measures is the opposite of what is observed for the consumption-based measures. For example, despite the wide-spread rural-urban convergence of consumption and consumption poverty in the LAC region, there is slightly more divergence on under-nutrition and school enrollment. The opposite pattern is observed in Sub-Saharan Africa and South Asia.

In summary, the data on changes in absolute or relative welfare pro-vide few clear patterns of convergence or divergence. The consumption-based measures diverge over time in about two-thirds of the countries, and the undernutrition and education measures converge in slightly more than half. For any given country, rural-urban convergence or diver-gence on the consumption-based welfare measures is a poor predictor of whether convergence or divergence is observed on the nonmonetary measures. A close look at tables 2.1 and 2.2 also reveals very few clear trends for the common characteristics across countries where conver-gence (or divergence) has occurred in recent years.

The Elusive Quest for Patterns

In this section, we use simple econometric models to detect patterns between rural-urban convergence or divergence on these welfare meas-ures and other covariates, in particular, national income per capita. For these regressions, we chose two different sets of dependent variables, cor-responding to the measures of convergence and divergence in the preced-ing section. In one set of regressions, the dependent variable is the rural-urban difference in the absolute level of the welfare measure. In the second set of regressions, it is the rural-urban difference in the Kakwani achievement index for that welfare measure. We use five different specifications on the right-hand side of the regression equation:

1. A basic pooled data model that regresses the welfare levels on log GDP per capita, log GDP per capita squared, and a set of six control variables related to the level of sectoral and spatial transformation (population density, rate of urban population growth, urban population share, agriculture value added per worker, agriculture share of GDP, and GDP growth rate)[8]
2. Model 1 with a time trend variable added to control for the different years in which the surveys were conducted
3. Model 1 with time trend and region-fixed effects
4. Model 1 with time trend and country-fixed effects
5. Model 1 with time trend, region-fixed effects, and country-fixed effects.

Cross-country regressions on pooled data, such as models 1 and 2, effectively trace the relationship between national income and rural-urban welfare differences using data from diverse countries at different stages of development. Although the set of six variables measuring sectoral and spatial transformation control for the differing stages of development to some degree, meaningful inference from such regressions is problematic and, some would argue, impossible. They are included here largely as a basis of comparison with the fixed effects models, and any interpretations of the results from the pooled cross-country data should be made with caution.

The regression results are summarized in table 2.3, which shows the significance levels for the joint tests of significance of the coefficients on log GDP per capita (linear and quadratic). When estimated on pooled data (models 1 and 2), the regressions show a statistically strong relationship between national income and rural-urban differences in the consumption-based welfare measures, especially when measured by the Kakwani achievement index. The coefficients from the pooled models indicate a U-shaped relationship, with rural-urban inequalities among this group of 41 low- and middle-income countries decreasing and then increasing with the rising levels of GDP per capita. This pattern corresponds roughly with the L-shaped (or "tilted L") pattern in the scatter plots described earlier in this chapter. When region-fixed effects are

Table 2.3 Significance of Relationship between Convergence and Log GDP Per Capita

Dependent variable	Pooled (model 1)	Pooled + time trend (model 2)	Time trend + region-fixed effects (model 3)	Time trend + country-fixed effects (model 4)	Time trend + region- and country-fixed effects (model 5)
Absolute differences					
Log mean consumption	**	**	**	n.s.	n.s.
Poverty headcount ($1.25/day)	n.s.	n.s.	n.s.	n.s.	n.s.
Poverty headcount ($2.00/day)	***	***	*	n.s.	n.s.
Poverty gap ($1.25/day)	n.s.	n.s.	n.s.	n.s.	n.s.
Poverty gap ($2.00/day)	n.s.	*	n.s.	n.s.	n.s.
Stunting	n.s.	n.s.	n.s.	n.s.	n.s.
School enrollment	**	**	*	n.s.	n.s.
Kakwani achievement index					
Log mean consumption	***	***	***	n.s.	n.s.
Poverty headcount ($1.25/day)	***	***	***	n.s.	n.s.
Poverty headcount ($2.00/day)	***	***	***	n.s.	n.s.
Poverty gap ($1.25/day)	**	**	**	n.s.	n.s.
Poverty gap ($2.00/day)	***	***	***	n.s.	n.s.
Stunting	n.s.	n.s.	n.s.	n.s.	n.s.
School enrollment	*	*	n.s.	n.s.	n.s.

Source: Authors' calculations using LSMS and DHS data (see appendix A).
Note: All dependent variables are rural-urban differences.
*$p < .10$.
**$p < .05$.
***$p < .01$.
n.s. = not significant.

introduced (model 3), the significance and the shape of the relationship between rural-urban inequalities and GDP per capita are essentially the same as with the pooled models.

When country-fixed effects are included (models 4 and 5), the coefficients on log GDP per capita are not significant for any of the welfare measures. This result is most likely attributable to data limitations, because for country-fixed effects the regression depends entirely on within-country variations in the variables. When limited to only two observations per country and a relatively short time interval between those observations (from 4 to 16 years), this variation is insufficient to fit a good model with log GDP per capita against any of the rural-urban differences in welfare. Whether more data over a longer time period would uncover a systematic relationship remains an open question.

Conclusion

This chapter has used recent survey data to examine the nature and magnitude of welfare inequalities between rural and urban areas in 41 low- and middle-income countries. The welfare measures are both monetary and nonmonetary aspects of well-being, including mean consumption, several poverty measures, child undernutrition, and school enrollment rates.

According to the first set of analyses described in this chapter, for nearly every country over the time period considered, the standard of living was higher in urban areas across almost all six of the variables used in our study. However, the magnitude of rural-urban inequalities was extremely variable across welfare measures and across countries. Even in countries with the same levels of urbanization or GDP per capita, the rural-urban differences may be enormous or relatively small. For example, rural-urban differences are large in Burkina Faso but small in Tanzania. And Bolivia, which is higher up the national income scale, has a much larger rural-urban gap than the Dominican Republic. The welfare gap is not consistently wider in low-income countries than in middle-income countries. In fact, when measured by consumption and stunting, the average rural-urban welfare difference is roughly the same, irrespective of a country's level of development.

We then compare the improvements in welfare in each country during the interval between two surveys to determine whether the rural-urban welfare gap expanded or contracted. The total number of divergences in rural-urban welfare is slightly greater than the number of convergences.

There is a higher rate of divergence, or increasing rural-urban inequality, for consumption-based welfare measures, whereas the nonmonetary measures show a slightly higher rate of convergence over time.

In the final section, we look for evidence of a relationship between changes in the rural-urban welfare gap and changes in national income. The cross-country results from our sample of low- and middle-income countries indicate a U-shaped relationship, with rural-urban inequalities tending to be largest in the poorest countries in the sample, such as Nepal and Uganda, and also in the richest countries, such as Brazil and South Africa. However, after controlling for country-fixed effects we detect no statistically significant relationship for any of the variables, although the short time span covered by the survey data is likely a major reason for this result.

Our findings, along with those of previous studies described in box 2.1, reveal a wide array of welfare convergence or divergence patterns accompanying growth and urbanization. At least at the low- and middle-income levels, there seems to be little evidence that spatial inequalities automatically diminish as countries develop. These results imply that country-level policies and institutions, rather than particular thresholds of per capita GDP or urbanization, are driving the processes of rural-urban divergence and convergence. This observation in turn suggests the hazards of painting with brushstrokes that are too broad, and the importance of in-depth analysis of each country's "stylized facts" before proceeding to policy prescriptions. In the next chapter, we turn to a more in-depth analysis, examining the sources of inequality in three rapidly growing African countries.

Notes

1. In 10 of the 41 countries used for this report, welfare is measured by income rather than consumption expenditure. All of these countries are in Latin America. It is not clear a priori whether using income in some countries and consumption in others introduces a bias in the comparison of rural-urban welfare gaps, or the direction of the bias if there is one. For the analysis of changes over time, there is unlikely to be any bias, because none of the countries changed the welfare measure from income to consumption, or vice versa, from one survey to the next.

2. Ten welfare measures (five monetary and five nonmonetary) were analyzed for this study, but only six are reported here because of length considerations. The patterns for the other four are similar to the six presented here. Full details are available from the authors upon request.

3. We produced similar versions of these plots showing the urban population share and the agriculture sector share of GDP on the horizontal axis, because these shares are also indicative of a country's stage of development. The alternative plots look almost identical to the plots in figure 2.2 because of the high intercorrelation of the three variables.

4. Note that although the patterns in figure 2.2, panel (a), are similar to those in figure 2.1, the positive correlation in figure 2.2, panel (a), continues up to $10,000, whereas in figure 2.1 the correlation turns negative at about $3,000. This result likely stems from the different base years used (2000 versus 2005) and the PPP adjustment that is incorporated in figure 2.2 but not figure 2.1.

5. In this case, we do not differentiate by the level of schooling, nor do these figures convey any information about the quality of schooling.

6. The three exceptions are Colombia, Côte d'Ivoire, and Paraguay.

7. This interpretation is reversed for the small minority of cells (8 of 209) in which initial welfare was higher in rural areas. These include the following countries and welfare measures: Armenia (mean consumption and all three poverty measures), Bangladesh ($2.00 per day poverty headcount and poverty gap), Kazakhstan (school enrollment), and Morocco ($1.25 per day poverty headcount).

8. Additional regressions without these control variables yielded results that are essentially the same as those reported here.

References

Kakwani, N. 1993. "Performance in Living Standards: An International Comparison." *Journal of Development Economics* 41 (2): 307–36.

Ravallion, M., S. Chen, and P. Sangraula. 2007. "New Evidence on the Urbanization of Global Poverty." Policy Research Working Paper 4199, World Bank, Washington, DC.

Sahn, D., and D. Stifel. 2003. "Urban-Rural Inequality in Living Standards in Africa." *Journal of African Economies* 12 (4): 564–97.

Sen, A. K. 1981. "Public Action and the Quality of Life in Developing Countries." *Oxford Bulletin of Economics and Statistics* 43 (November): 287–319.

United Nations. 2005. *World Urbanization Prospects: The 2004 Revision.* Department of Economic and Social Affairs, Population Division. New York: United Nations.

World Bank. 2008. *World Development Report 2009: Reshaping Economic Geography.* Washington, DC: World Bank.

CHAPTER 3

National Level: Three Country-Level Perspectives on Rural-Urban Transitions

Looking at levels and changes in both income and nonincome measures of welfare, we sought in chapter 2 to determine patterns and trends in rural-urban inequalities across a sample of 41 low- and middle-income countries. It was not possible, however, to identify a consistent trend of either convergence or divergence across such a broad set of countries.

This chapter, then, explores in greater depth the rural-urban inequalities in three countries in Sub-Saharan Africa—Ghana, Mozambique, and Uganda—with the aim of gaining more finely textured insights into country-specific patterns and trends and the mechanics driving the rural-urban divide. We begin by describing for these three countries the present structural and spatial transformations and the accompanying welfare trends. Despite their roughly similar levels of development, these countries present an interesting mix of similarities and differences in urbanization rates, spatial inequalities, and other characteristics. Next, we evaluate the role of differences in household characteristics and the returns to those characteristics in explaining rural-urban inequalities. We find that in Mozambique and Uganda, rural-urban inequalities largely stem from low levels of human capital and other assets, whereas in Ghana, inequalities are attributable to characteristics and returns in almost equal proportions.

Structural and Spatial Transformations in Ghana, Mozambique, and Uganda

The low-income countries of Ghana, Mozambique, and Uganda have made significant progress in growth and poverty reduction since the 1990s. The growth rates for both gross domestic product (GDP) and GDP per capita during the 1990s and 2000s exceeded the average rates for Sub-Saharan Africa (table 3.1). In fact, Ghana, Mozambique, and Uganda are among only eight Sub-Saharan African countries that have attained or outperformed regional averages during these two periods.[1]

In each of these countries, economic growth has also been accompanied by significant structural and spatial transformations. However, a large share (and in Mozambique and Uganda, a clear majority) of the labor force is still in agriculture, and the agricultural share of GDP remains significant. From 1990 to 2005, the average share of labor employed in agriculture and its contribution to GDP were 60 percent (labor) and 40 percent (GDP) in Ghana, 80 percent (labor) and 30 percent (GDP) in Mozambique, and 80 percent (labor) and 40 percent (GDP) in Uganda (figure 3.1). Agricultural output increased over the same period, primarily because of expansion of the areas under cultivation, contributing to overall economic growth. From 1990 to 2005, agriculture accounted for an estimated 36 percent of economic growth in Ghana, 22 percent in Mozambique, and 25 percent in Uganda (figure 3.2).

Even though under the *World Development Report 2008: Agriculture for Development* (*WDR 2008*) (World Bank 2007) typology the three countries can still be classified as "agriculture-based economies," major structural changes have taken place over the last two decades. The relative share of agricultural output in GDP has decreased, and the industrial and service sectors of the economy are growing much more rapidly (figure 3.3). These structural transformations suggest that these countries are moving toward becoming "transforming" countries under the *WDR 2008* typology.

Table 3.1   Growth Rates: Ghana, Mozambique, and Uganda, 1990s and 2000s

	Per capita GDP growth rate		GDP growth rate	
	1990–2000	2000–08	1990–2000	2000–08
Sub-Saharan Africa	−0.2	3.0	2.6	5.6
Ghana	1.5	3.2	4.3	5.6
Mozambique	2.9	5.6	6.1	8.0
Uganda	3.8	4.0	7.1	7.5

Source: Authors' calculations based on World Development Indicators, World Bank (October 2009).

Figure 3.1 Shares of GDP and Labor from Agriculture, Selected Countries

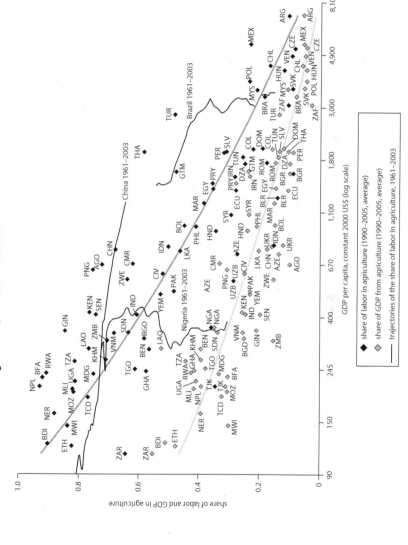

Source: World Bank 2007, fig. 1.2.

Note: To interpret country abbreviations, see World Bank (2007, p. xviii).

Figure 3.2   *WDR 2008*'s Classification of Agriculture-Based, Transforming, and Urbanized Countries

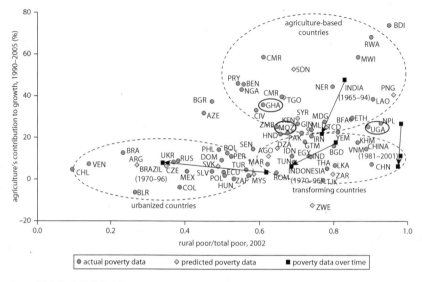

Source: World Bank 2007, fig. 1.3.
Note: To interpret country abbreviations, see World Bank (2007, p. xviii).

Spatial transformations have accompanied structural transformations. One outcome has been the increasing regional divides that largely track agricultural versus industrial (rural versus urban) distinctions. Coincidentally, in all three countries the regional division has broadly manifested itself in a north-south divide. In Ghana, the mostly rural northern regions have lagged behind the more dynamic southern regions. In Mozambique, industrial growth has mainly occurred around Maputo in the south, whereas the northern and central areas of the country have remained agricultural centers. In Uganda, firms have emerged mostly in the areas bordering Kampala, and the northern regions have been left behind, in part because of conflict and instability. Another spatial outcome has been the rural-urban divides that are the focus of the rest of this chapter.

The extent of urbanization varies in Ghana, Mozambique, and Uganda. According to each country's definitions, half of Ghana's population, just over a third of Mozambique's population, and about 13 percent of Uganda's population are now urban.[2] Starting from a relatively high level of urbanization of about 23 percent in 1960, the urban share of the

Figure 3.3   Sectoral Shares of GDP, Value Added: Ghana, Mozambique, and Uganda, 1980–2007

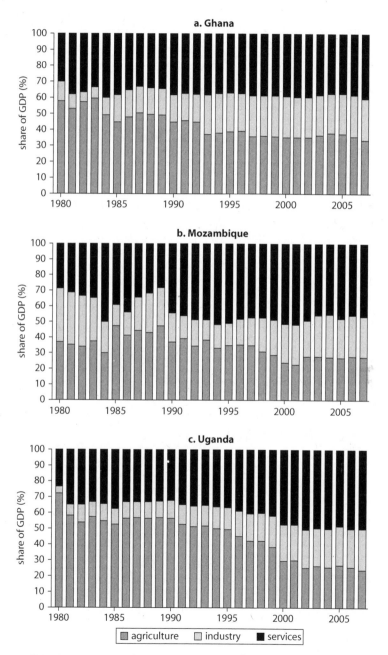

Source: World Development Indicators, World Bank (July 6, 2009).

population in Ghana grew rapidly until the 1970s, when it slowed, and
then resumed rapid growth in the mid-1980s.[3] Mozambique has been
rapidly urbanizing since the early 1970s. In Uganda, although overall
population growth is extremely high, the level of urbanization has only
gradually increased since the 1960s.[4] As seen in figure 3.4, for the last

**Figure 3.4   Population and Urbanization: Ghana, Mozambique, and Uganda,
1960–2007**

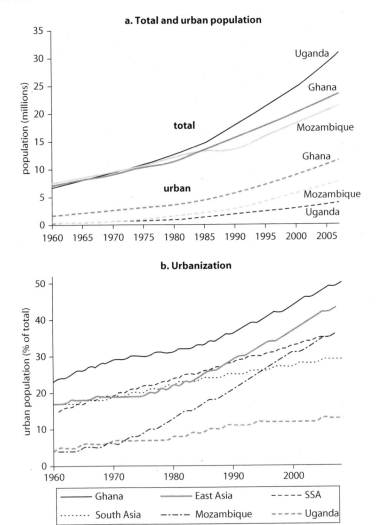

Source: World Development Indicators, World Bank (July 2009).
SSA = Sub-Saharan Africa.

20–30 years Ghana and Mozambique have been urbanizing at a rate close to that of East Asia, and much more rapidly than Sub-Saharan Africa or South Asia.

The size distribution of the 10 largest cities reflects the level of urbanization across the three countries. In line with the urbanization pattern across countries, the estimated total population of the largest 10 cities in 2009 is 6.0 million in Ghana, 4.0 million in Mozambique, and 2.5 million in Uganda (table 3.2).

Rural and Urban Poverty Trends

Changes in the rural and urban poverty profiles have accompanied structural and spatial transformations. According to national poverty lines as opposed to the standard international ones used in chapter 2, poverty rates have fallen in both rural and urban areas in each country (table 3.3). In fact, all three of the Foster-Greer-Thorbecke (FGT) poverty measures (poverty headcount, poverty gap, and poverty gap squared) decreased from the 1990s to the early to mid-2000s (from 1991–92 to 2005–06 in Ghana, from 1996–97 to 2002–03 in Mozambique, and from 1992–93 to 2005–06 in Uganda).[5] Because the large majority of the population is rural, much of the overall national poverty reduction has been driven by the gains in the rural sector, and so the rural-urban poverty divide is converging.[6]

Thus, although the majority of the poor are still in rural areas, poverty is urbanizing in Mozambique. The fall in the proportion of the poor in rural areas of Mozambique is somewhat overstated in the official statistics shown in table 3.3 because of an administrative reclassification of areas from rural to urban between 1996–97 and 2002–03. Nevertheless, the narrowing of rural-urban differences in poverty combined with a genuine increase in the urban population share points to the same qualitative result of an increase in share of the poor in urban areas. In Uganda, the rural share of the poor is essentially unchanged at 93–94 percent between the two survey periods, whereas the proportion of the poor in rural areas of Ghana increased slightly, from 82.3 to 85.7 percent between 1991–92 and 2005–06, indicating a ruralization of the poor (table 3.3).

Not surprisingly, because these countries can still be classified as agriculture-based economies, poverty reduction in rural areas contributed the most to aggregate poverty reduction. Sectoral decompositions of poverty reduction, as in Ravallion and Huppi (1991), indicate that the rural sector accounted for 70 percent of the aggregate headcount poverty reduction in Ghana, 85 percent in Mozambique, and 90 percent in Uganda. The total intrasectoral effects (i.e., poverty reduction within rural

Table 3.2 Ten Largest Cities: Ghana, Mozambique, and Uganda, Selected Census Years

	Ghana				Mozambique				Uganda		
	Census		Estimate		Census		Estimate		Census		Estimate
City	1984	2000	2009	City	1997	2007	2009	City	1991	2002	2009
Accra	867,459	1,659,136	2,365,018	Maputo	989,386	1,099,102	1,120,245	Kampala	774,241	1,208,544	1,560,080
Kumasi	496,628	1,171,311	1,852,449	Matola	440,927	675,422	729,469	Gulu	38,297	113,144	208,268
Tamale	135,952	293,879	447,349	Nampula	314,965	477,900	515,320	Lira	27,568	89,871	174,630
Takoradi	85,280	175,438	308,266	Beira	412,588	436,240	441,957	Jinja	65,169	86,520	101,604
Ashiaman	50,918	150,312	271,850	Chimoio	177,608	238,976	253,259	Mbale	53,987	70,437	84,215
Tema	100,052	141,479	175,717	Nacala	164,309	207,894	217,479	Mbarara	41,031	69,208	93,969
Cape Coast	57,224	118,105	175,710	Quelimane	153,187	192,876	200,788	Masaka	49,585	61,300	70,273
Obuasi	60,617	115,564	166,950	Tete	104,832	152,909	164,201	Entebbe	42,763	57,518	70,052
Sekondi	70,214	114,157	171,032	Lichinga	89,043	142,253	155,277	Kasese	18,750	53,446	91,906
Koforidua	58,731	87,315	109,489	Pemba	88,149	141,316	153,900	Njeru	36,731	52,514	75,380
Total	1,983,075	4,026,696	6,043,830	Total	2,934,994	3,764,888	3,951,895	Total	1,148,122	1,862,502	2,530,377

Sources: Census data and estimates from World Gazetteer, http://www.world-gazetteer.com/.

Table 3.3 Poverty, Inequality, and Population Distribution: Ghana, Mozambique, and Uganda, Selected Years

	Ghana		Mozambique		Uganda	
	1991–92	2005–06	1996–97	2002–03	1992–93	2005–06
Poverty headcount (SE)						
Rural	0.636 (0.010)	0.393 (0.009)	0.705 (0.008)	0.549 (0.010)	0.603 (0.008)	0.342 (0.008)
Urban	0.278 (0.015)	0.108 (0.007)	0.609 (0.014)	0.521 (0.014)	0.288 (0.015)	0.137 (0.012)
Total	0.517 (0.009)	0.286 (0.007)	0.686 (0.007)	0.540 (0.008)	0.564 (0.007)	0.311 (0.007)
Poverty gap (SE)						
Rural	0.240 (0.005)	0.135 (0.004)	0.291 (0.005)	0.205 (0.005)	0.226 (0.004)	0.097 (0.003)
Urban	0.074 (0.005)	0.031 (0.003)	0.257 (0.008)	0.190 (0.007)	0.087 (0.005)	0.035 (0.003)
Total	0.185 (0.004)	0.096 (0.003)	0.284 (0.004)	0.200 (0.004)	0.209 (0.004)	0.087 (0.002)
Poverty gap squared (SE)						
Rural	0.117 (0.004)	0.066 (0.002)	0.153 (0.003)	0.104 (0.004)	0.112 (0.003)	0.039 (0.001)
Urban	0.029 (0.003)	0.013 (0.002)	0.138 (0.006)	0.091 (0.004)	0.037 (0.003)	0.014 (0.002)
Total	0.088 (0.003)	0.046 (0.002)	0.150 (0.003)	0.100 (0.003)	0.103 (0.002)	0.035 (0.001)
Rural share of poverty (% of total)						
Poverty headcount	82.3	85.7	81.8	69.0	93.7	93.0
Poverty gap	86.8	87.9	81.6	69.6	94.7	94.3
Poverty gap squared	89.2	89.3	81.2	70.6	95.3	94.3
Gini						
Rural	0.342	0.408	0.358	0.365	0.328	0.363
Urban	0.347	0.374	0.456	0.463	0.396	0.432
Total	0.373	0.425	0.385	0.404	0.365	0.408
Rural population (%)	66.9	62.4	79.6	67.9	87.6	84.6
Urban population (%)	33.1	37.6	20.4	32.1	12.4	15.4

Source: Authors' calculations based on survey data.
Note: Because of differences in definition, the rural and urban population shares differ from those shown in figure 3.4. SE = standard error.

and urban sectors) accounted for 95 percent or more of the drop in aggregate headcount poverty in each of these countries. Similar patterns are also observed for the poverty gap and poverty gap squared measures (see table 3.4).

Population shifts from rural to urban areas account for only a relatively small share of the poverty reduction. According to the sectoral decompositions, the population shift effects account for 6.9 percent of poverty reduction in Ghana, 7.8 percent in Mozambique, and 3.7 percent in Uganda. Although population shares have been shifting from rural areas with high poverty rates to urban areas with lower rates, the negative values of the population shift effects suggest that rural-urban population movements have been beneficial for overall poverty reduction (table 3.4).

And yet despite progress in poverty reduction, inequality has been on the rise in all three countries. The Gini index has increased within both the rural and urban sectors and for the entire population for the periods evaluated (table 3.3). As explored in much greater detail in chapter 4, urban inequality tends to be greater than rural inequality, as is true for both Mozambique and Uganda. However, in Ghana rural inequality, as measured by the Gini index, was higher than urban inequality in 2005–06. This finding may stem in part from the growing inequalities between the northern and southern regions of the country.

Table 3.4   Sectoral Decomposition of Poverty: Ghana, Mozambique, and Uganda, Selected Years

| | Ghana | | Mozambique | | Uganda | |
| | 1991/92–2005/06 | | 1996/97–2002/03 | | 1992/93–2005/06 | |
	Abs. diff.	%	Abs. diff.	%	Abs. diff.	%
Poverty headcount	−23.1	100.0	−14.6	100.0	−25.3	100.0
Intrasectoral effect	−21.9	94.6	−14.2	97.7	−24.7	97.6
Population shift effect	−1.6	6.9	−1.1	7.8	−0.9	3.7
Interaction effect	0.3	−1.4	0.8	−5.5	0.3	−1.3
Poverty gap	−8.9	100.0	−8.4	100.0	−12.2	100.0
Intrasectoral effect	−8.4	94.8	−8.3	98.0	−12.0	98.5
Population shift effect	−0.7	8.3	−0.4	4.8	−0.4	3.4
Interaction effect	0.3	−3.1	0.2	−2.8	0.2	−1.9
Poverty gap squared	−4.2	100.0	−5.1	100.0	−6.8	100.0
Intrasectoral effect	−3.9	94.4	−4.9	97.0	−6.7	98.9
Population shift effect	−0.4	9.4	−0.2	3.5	−0.2	3.3
Interaction effect	0.2	−3.7	0.0	−0.5	0.1	−2.1

Source: Authors' calculations based on survey data.
Note: Abs. diff. = Absolute difference.

Although consumption measures of poverty have improved for all three countries, trends for nonmonetary indicators of welfare—school attendance, stunting, and access to water—are mixed (figure 3.5). For example, school attendance rates for children aged 6–15 years have increased, and rural-urban disparities are decreasing in both Mozambique and Uganda. This development may be due in part to the Universal Primary Education initiatives in each country. By contrast, school attendance rates in Ghana have fallen, and rural-urban inequalities have remained fairly constant over the 10-year period between surveys.

Similarly, progress in improving the health of children under 3, as measured by the prevalence of stunting, has varied across the three countries. In Uganda, the rural-urban gap has narrowed, with improvements in rural areas. In Ghana, the rural-urban gap also has narrowed, but unfortunately mainly because of increases in urban areas. In Mozambique, we see a slight divergence between the rural and urban stunting prevalence, with a small increase in rural areas and a small decrease in urban areas.

As for indicators of access to improved water sources (such as piped water, tube wells or boreholes, and protected dug wells), in Ghana and Uganda a substantial expansion of access in rural areas has underpinned a narrowing of rural-urban inequalities. But in Mozambique, the rural-urban convergence has been brought about by a decline in access in urban areas. The decline in urban access between 1995 and 2000 may stem in part from a change, following Mozambique's 1997 census, in the definition of *urban* to include small towns. However, the further decline between 2000 and 2006 is indicative of a failure of urban infrastructure to expand at a pace commensurate with population growth. In all three countries, large rural-urban inequalities in access to improved water sources remain, with a 21 percentage point difference in Ghana, a 45 percentage point difference in Mozambique, and a 30 percentage point difference in Uganda.

In summary, not unlike our cross-country observations in chapter 2, the picture for the three countries examined here is mixed. Even though each country experienced significant economic growth and various degrees of structural and spatial transformation, no consistent picture of rural-urban divergence or convergence emerges. Consumption poverty has fallen in both rural and urban areas of Ghana, Mozambique, and Uganda, but progress on reducing rural-urban inequalities in nonmonetary measures of poverty—school attendance, stunting, and access to improved water sources—varies across countries. Uganda, which has seen a much slower pace of urbanization than either Ghana or Mozambique, has shown progress across all three of the nonmonetary measures, with gains in rural areas exceeding those in urban areas. However, not all indicators in Ghana and Mozambique have improved. In Ghana, school attendance rates dropped in both rural and urban areas, and stunting prevalence worsened, in particular in urban areas. In Mozambique, stunting in

Figure 3.5   Nonmonetary Welfare, Rural versus Urban: Ghana, Mozambique, and Uganda

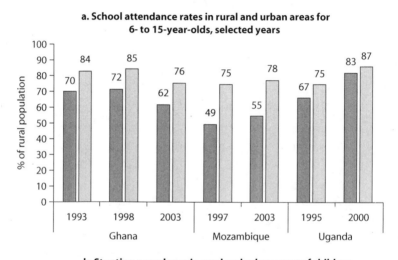

a. School attendance rates in rural and urban areas for 6- to 15-year-olds, selected years

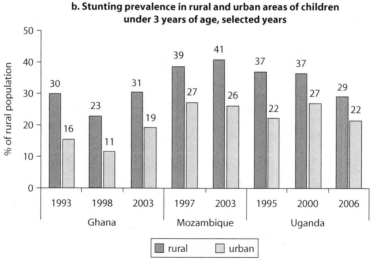

b. Stunting prevalence in rural and urban areas of children under 3 years of age, selected years

(continued next page)

Figure 3.5   *(continued)*

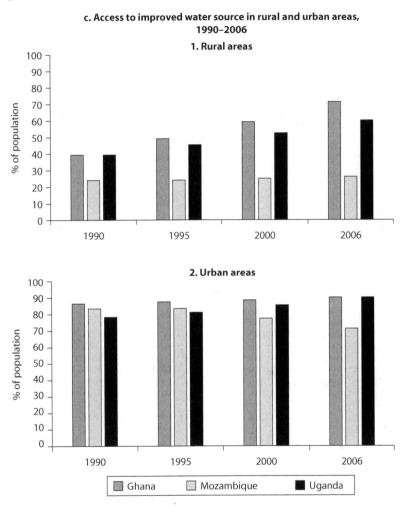

c. Access to improved water source in rural and urban areas,
1990–2006

1. Rural areas

2. Urban areas

☐ Ghana   ☐ Mozambique   ■ Uganda

Sources: Demographic and Health Surveys; World Development Index, World Bank (July 2009).

rural areas increased slightly, and access to improved water sources in urban areas decreased.

Despite substantial progress in poverty reduction and the signs of early structural transformation, the agriculture sectors of these countries are still large, and the manufacturing and service sectors are still in an early stage of development. Any convergence or divergence of different living standards indicators over the last 15 years is small relative to the rural-urban gaps in these indicators.

Sources of Rural-Urban Inequalities

What drives rural-urban inequalities? One way to approach that question is to consider two polar explanations for why some areas of a country are poorer or richer than others. At one end of the spectrum is the "concentration effect"—that is, persistently poor areas emerge from the spatial concentration of people with low levels of productive assets, including human, physical, financial, and social capital. According to this view, poor people in poor areas would most likely be poor even if they lived in richer areas. At the other end of the spectrum is the "geography effect," which attributes persistent geographic differences in living standards to differences in spatial characteristics such as endowments of local public goods and services (e.g., transport, electricity, and water). In other words, differences in living standards are caused by spatially determined differential returns to assets, so that two households with identical observable assets would have different standards of living because the returns to those assets would be higher in the better-endowed area.

This line of analysis has been conducted for several countries in other regions, but to our knowledge not in Sub-Saharan Africa. In a study of Bangladesh, Ravallion and Wodon (1999) found that the geography effect dominated rural-urban welfare differences, with pronounced differences in returns to household characteristics such as education. A subsequent study of Bangladesh by Shilpi (2008) examined not only rural-urban differences, but also differences between a region that is integrated with urban growth poles and a more isolated region that is cut off from the growth centers by major rivers. This study found large geographic differences in returns between integrated and isolated regions. The differential returns were particularly pronounced among higher-income households, which are related to differential public capital and market access. Among poorer households, the geography effect is important in explaining inequalities between integrated and isolated regions, but not inequalities between rural and urban areas *within* each of these regions. The policy implication is that investments in the human capital of poor people can help mitigate rural-urban disparities within regions, but that investments in connective infrastructure are more important for reducing inequalities between integrated and isolated regions. The investments in connective infrastructure facilitate the flow of goods and migrants between regions, which also stimulates the development of growth poles in urban areas of the more isolated region.

A recent regional study by Skoufias and Lopez-Acevedo (2008) looks at these issues in eight countries in Latin America. They find that the concentration effect is the dominant source of inequalities between rural and urban areas within regions, indicating a need for targeted policies to improve the human capital of poor households. However, like Shilpi (2008), their study reveals that large differences in returns (i.e., a dominant geography effect) are responsible for most of the inequalities *between* regions. Thus, policies to remove impediments to labor mobility—such as connective infrastructure and improving the efficiency of credit, land, and labor markets—are appropriate.

Methodology

To better understand the sources of rural-urban welfare inequalities in the three Sub-Saharan countries of interest here, we examine whether welfare differences are attributable primarily to concentration effects or geography effects. We decompose differences in average household welfare (measured in log welfare ratios, which is the log of household consumption per adult equivalent as a proportion of local poverty lines) into components attributable to household endowments and the returns to those endowments using Oaxaca-Blinder decompositions (details on the data and methodology appear in appendix B).[7] For this analysis, we limit ourselves to inequalities in consumption per adult equivalent for several reasons. First, it is a more comprehensive measure of welfare than the other measures examined in the previous section such as school enrollment, stunting, or access to water. Second, unlike stunting or school enrollment, consumption permits a complete ordering of all households in the data set. Third, consumption is a continuous measure, allowing finer distinctions in the welfare levels of households.

According to the classic Lewis and Harris-Todaro models, rural-to-urban migration flows are a function of wage or expected income differentials between rural and urban areas. Similarly, rural-urban differences in the marginal welfare benefits (returns) to certain household endowments may be considered an indicator of the incentives that might exist for rural inhabitants to migrate to urban areas. Expectations of marginal welfare gains associated with moving from rural to urban areas may be partially represented by the differences in coefficients for relevant household endowments in our regressions.[8] Such differences indicate that the geography effect dominates. By contrast, the absence of differences in

coefficients suggests that the concentration effect is the primary explanation for rural-urban welfare inequalities.

Results

Our findings indicate that in Mozambique and Uganda rural-urban
inequalities in average household welfare are primarily attributable to the
concentration effect—or differences in household endowments. In
Ghana, the sources of rural-urban inequalities are divided almost equally
between the concentration and geography effects, or endowments and
returns to those endowments.[9] In Mozambique, endowments accounted
for over 100 percent of the average rural-urban welfare difference in both
1996–97 and 2002–03.[10] In Uganda, endowments accounted for 77 and
73 percent of the rural-urban difference in average welfare in 1992–93 and
2005–06, respectively. In Ghana, returns accounted for 67 percent of the
difference in 1991–92 but dropped to 47 percent in 2005–06, so that
differences in endowments and returns accounted for roughly equal shares
(see table B.5 in appendix B).

By decomposing rural-urban welfare differences, we can identify factors that play a relatively large role in accounting for these welfare
inequalities. Using the Oaxaca-Blinder decompositions, the endowments
and returns components can each be further disaggregated by categories
of variables (see figure 3.6 for the results). The vertical axis of the figure
represents the rural-urban difference in mean (log) welfare ratios, and
each component of the bars represents a contribution to the overall rural-
urban difference. Therefore, the sum of the positive and negative subcom-
ponents of both the endowment and return (coefficients) components
will equal the overall rural-urban difference in mean welfare. Education
and the sector of employment of household heads are typically the two
endowment factors that contribute substantially to rural-urban welfare
inequalities.

Interpretation of the sector of employment variable is ambiguous
because it is to some extent tied to location (e.g., the agriculture sector
is predominantly rural) and because it is a characteristic that is more
amenable to change than other characteristics. The sector of employment variable could appear to capture a particular set of skills, a combination of innate ability and accumulated experience. Alternatively, it
may be viewed as a realization of human capital and a characteristic
that the individual can change in response to the different opportunities available. By including sector of employment as a regressor we are

Figure 3.6   Oaxaca-Blinder Decomposition of Urban-Rural Welfare Differences: Ghana, Mozambique, and Uganda, Selected Years

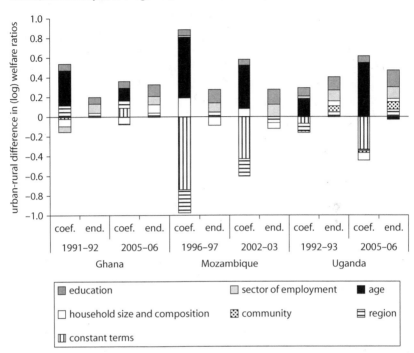

Source: Authors' calculations.
Note: coef. = coefficient; end. = endowment.

interpreting sector of employment as a skill, reflecting the individual's skills and experience.

In all three countries, despite higher returns to education in urban areas, human capital inequalities play a bigger role in accounting for overall rural-urban welfare inequalities. As shown in figure 3.6, the contribution of educational attainment differences in the endowments component is consistently larger than the contribution of education in the coefficients component for each of the three countries and across years. This indicates that the differences in the level of educational attainment of household heads account for more of the mean rural-urban welfare inequalities than do the differences in returns to education.

The scarcity of nonfarm employment in rural areas rather than rural-urban differentials in returns for the same sector explains a large share of rural-urban welfare inequalities. Although differences in returns exist between rural and urban areas, these differences are often negligible in explaining rural-urban welfare inequalities. For example, in figure 3.6 the sector of employment component of the returns effect is very small in most cases. By contrast, differences in sectors of employment make up a relatively large share of the endowment effect for all three countries. The returns differential is marginalized by the fact that employment in agriculture dominates in rural areas. For example, 88 percent of rural household heads in Mozambique were employed in agriculture in 2002–03.

In principle, the higher returns in urban areas to education and in the secondary and tertiary sectors in these countries should draw labor from rural areas to urban areas until returns are equalized. However, rural-urban differentials in returns persist, although these differentials are small relative to the differences in endowments in Mozambique and Uganda. Because migration decisions are based on expected net benefits, not just wage differentials, the low expected probability of finding a good job in the city in view of lower rural education levels and high urban unemployment levels may be reducing the incentives for rural-to-urban migration. Other factors such as migration costs, insufficient land rights in both rural and urban areas, and social segmentation may also be barriers to migration.

Across all three countries, differences in returns to age contribute to much of the rural-urban welfare difference. The positive differentials in figure 3.6 indicate that the returns to age are more favorable in urban areas. Because there are no substantial differences in the mean age between rural and urban areas, the contribution of age to the endowments component is negligible. In urban areas, it is plausible that wage earners earn more as they gain seniority and accumulate skills with age, and that those in the informal sector accumulate assets and social capital with age. However, in rural areas the output of farmers may fall with age as the ability to work hard or improve farming techniques diminishes with age.

Not surprisingly, farmers tend to be better off in rural areas than in urban areas, where little land is devoted to agriculture. Although some high-value agriculture is carried out in or near cities, more often agriculture is a sector of last resort in urban areas, and often represents underemployment. In Mozambique and Uganda, a negative difference for the constant term indicates that household heads with no formal education engaged in agriculture in rural areas of the reference region were better off than their urban counterparts (i.e., uneducated household heads engaged in agriculture in urban areas). In Ghana, uneducated household heads in agriculture in the rural forest zone were slightly worse off in 1991–92 than their urban counterparts in the forest zone, but this trend had reversed by 2005–06.

Negative coefficient differentials for the regional variables indicate that, on average, the marginal benefit of rural households being in non-reference regions (relative to the reference region) tend to be greater than the marginal benefits of urban households being in nonreference regions (relative to the reference region) controlling for other factors. For example, in Mozambique the fact that the breadbasket of the country is the central and northern regions may explain why rural households in those regions tend to be better off than rural households in the southern region, controlling for other factors. For urban areas, because Maputo, the capital city and largest agglomeration, is located in the southern region, it makes sense that, on average, urban households in the central and northern regions tend to be not as well-off as urban households in the southern region.

Decomposition of Welfare Differences over Time

Increases in rural welfare over time stem primarily from the increasing returns in all three countries. The endowments used as regressors tend to change slowly over time—and slower than rising consumption in countries growing as rapidly as these three. Therefore, the share of the difference attributable to the coefficients (returns) will increase almost by construction. More interesting is seeing for which endowments the increase in returns is most significant. In rural areas, the mean welfare ratio (consumption per adult equivalent as a proportion of the poverty line) increased in Ghana from 1.27 to 1.98 between 1991–92 and 2005–06, in Mozambique from 1.08 to 1.29 between 1996–97 and 2002–03, and in Uganda from 1.15 to 1.84 between 1992–93 and 2005–06 (see table B.4 in appendix B). When these differences are decomposed, the returns component accounts for over 90 percent of increases in all three countries. In Ghana and Uganda, greater returns to age of the household head account for much of the rural welfare increases, whereas in Mozambique increases in returns in the central region play a large role (see table B.5). As for improvements in average household endowments, progress in educational attainment occurs mostly in urban areas, although Uganda shows improvements in both rural and urban areas. Also, because of the high population growth rate in Uganda, the average number of adult equivalents per household increased from 3.6 to 4.0 in rural Uganda and from 3.1 to 3.6 in urban Uganda (see table B.4).

Similarly, increases in returns over time account for the majority of the increases in urban welfare. In urban areas, mean welfare ratios increased in Ghana from 2.22 to 3.46 between 1991–92 and 2005–06, in Mozambique from 1.39 to 1.77 between 1996–97 and 2002–03, and in Uganda from 2.07 to 3.79 between 1992–93 and 2005–06. When these differences were decomposed, the returns component accounted for .70 percent of the increase in Ghana, 79 percent of the increase in Mozambique, and all of the increase in Uganda. Similar to findings for rural areas, greater returns to age of the head of household accounted for much of the urban welfare increases in Ghana and Uganda, whereas increases in returns in the northern and central regions played a large role in Mozambique (see table B.6 in appendix B).

Decomposition of Distributional Changes in Rural-Urban Inequalities

Because the relative importance of returns and endowments in explaining rural-urban inequalities may vary considerably for different income groups, we explore the extent of these variations across the distribution by applying the quantile decomposition. This process involves constructing counterfactual welfare distributions and comparing them with the empirical rural and urban welfare distributions (see Machado and Mata 2005 for an example). The counterfactual distribution represents what a welfare distribution might look like if the rural population had obtained urban returns to their (rural) characteristics. If we then compare the counterfactual and rural distributions, the difference between the two distributions can be attributed to differences in returns because characteristics should be the same. Similarly, the difference between the counterfactual and urban distributions can be attributed to differences in characteristics. The cumulative distributions of welfare (in terms of household consumption per adult equivalent) in figure 3.7 indicate different patterns for Ghana, Mozambique, and Uganda.

In Ghana, for 1991–92 the counterfactual distribution runs very close to the actual urban distribution, which demonstrates that differences in the returns to household characteristics account for most of the rural-urban inequalities in welfare for that year. However, for 2005–06 the counterfactual distribution lies about midway between the actual rural and urban distributions, indicating that differences in household characteristics and returns to those characteristics account for about equal shares of the welfare inequalities for that year. The quantile regression approach allows the decomposition between endowments and returns to

Figure 3.7   Cumulative Distributions of Welfare (Household Consumption per Adult Equivalent): Ghana, Mozambique, and Uganda, Selected Years

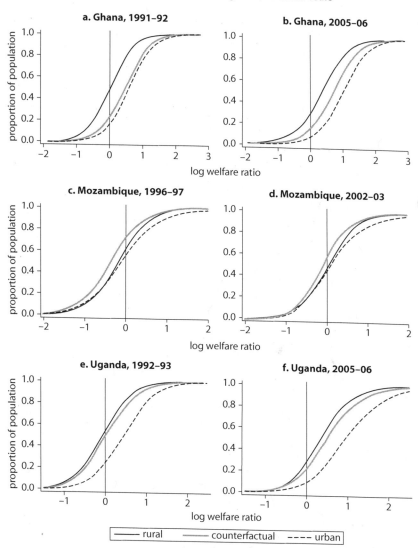

Source: Authors' calculations from household survey data.

Note: These are distributions of households rather than individuals, and therefore the poverty headcount cannot be discerned directly from these cumulative distributions. Because poorer households tend to be larger, headcount poverty rates will typically exceed the share of poor households.

vary across the income spectrum, and so it is striking that the proportions are so similar at all income levels in Ghana. This finding contrasts with those elsewhere, such as for Bangladesh where endowments account for a much larger share of the rural-urban welfare difference among the lowest income groups (Shilpi 2008). This result suggests that if the government seeks to reduce rural-urban inequalities, the same types of policies could be directed at all rural groups as opposed to focusing on human capital development for lower-income groups and interventions to increase mobility for higher-income groups.

In Mozambique, there is very little difference in the actual rural and urban welfare distributions among the poor (the portions of the curves to the left of the vertical line) for both 1996–97 and 2002–03. The rural and urban distributions below the poverty line almost overlap for both 1996–97 and 2002–03, but they widen for the upper parts of the distribution. The lack of any dramatic changes in the lower half of the distribution is attributable in large part to the relatively short period between the surveys, only six years.

Rural household heads in Mozambique are predominantly uneducated farmers, and the estimated returns for uneducated farmers are much lower in urban areas. Thus, simply obtaining urban returns without any change in employment sector or other endowments does not appear to benefit rural households. For this reason, the counterfactual distributions in both years lie to the left of the rural distributions and suggest that the rural households would be worse off if they received urban returns for their low endowment levels. This perhaps overly literal interpretation of the results highlights a limitation of this static decomposition: it does not account for the switching of employment sectors that usually occurs with rural-to-urban migration.

In Uganda, differences in endowments account for most of the rural-urban inequalities throughout the distributions for both 1992–93 and 2005–06. A comparison of the counterfactual distributions and the urban distributions in figure 3.7 reveals that differences in endowments account for most of the observed rural-urban inequalities. The role of differences in endowments appears to be slightly larger at the lower end of the distribution. The role of endowments in accounting for the large majority of welfare inequalities persists from 1992–93 to 2005–06. In Uganda, although the standard of living has improved for both the rural and urban segments of the country, the degree of inequality between the rural and urban distributions is large and increases from 1992–93 to 2005–06, as illustrated by the wider gap between the rural and urban distributions in 2005–06. Also, inequality within rural and urban areas increases over this period.

Implications for Policy

In this chapter, we have sought to gain deeper insights into rural-urban transitions in three African countries that have experienced robust levels of growth over the last two decades. For each country, economic growth and poverty reduction have been accompanied by significant, albeit varying, levels of urbanization. And, as in almost every country of the world, urban areas are outperforming rural areas according to various measures of welfare.

However, beyond these broad similarities each country has a different story to tell about changes in rural and urban welfare. When measured by national poverty lines, consumption poverty has fallen in both rural and urban areas, and at a faster rate in rural areas in Mozambique and Uganda, indicating a degree of convergence. But nonincome measures paint a much more complicated picture: convergence, where it has occurred, has resulted from strong improvements in rural areas (which appears to be the case for school attendance in Mozambique and Uganda) as well as deterioration in urban areas (which appears to be the case for stunting in Ghana or water supply in Mozambique). Thus, both the 41-country overview provided in chapter 2 and the more in-depth study here indicate that consistent trends are not to be expected, either across countries at similar stages of development or even within countries, across different welfare measures.

The Oaxaca-Blinder decompositions and quantile regression extensions are useful for quantifying the relative contributions of the concentration and geography effects to rural-urban inequalities in consumption. However, they are limited in that they are static decompositions that provide an accounting for inequalities, but are not based on a causal model of welfare outcomes and their determinants. The results should also be interpreted with caution because of the high potential for omitted-variable bias in the regressions. This effect biases the coefficient estimates and in turn the relative proportions of characteristics and returns to characteristics. This analysis is probably best viewed as a preliminary step that is suggestive of broad areas for policy and a source of guidance for more in-depth inquiry into specific policy areas such as factor markets or institutions.

Of the three countries, the decomposition results in Uganda are the most straightforward: individual and household characteristics account for a large proportion of rural-urban inequality. This finding parallels the results obtained for Latin America by Skoufias and Lopez-Acevedo (2008) and for low-income households in Bangladesh by Shilpi (2008). Returns to characteristics are not very different across rural and urban areas, but human capital stocks are—most notably in education. Education levels are low in Uganda and particularly so in rural areas. This situation suggests putting a high priority on human capital development, which is consistent with the government policy of universal primary education that was launched in 1997 and expanded to postprimary education and training in 2007. These policies take time to bear fruit, and school quality remains an issue.

Although better rural education is likely to reduce rural-urban inequalities, it is not a panacea for Uganda's growth and development. The population is young and growing faster than 3 percent a year, and job creation will have to keep pace to sustain the current rate of poverty reduction. Complementary public and private investments to accelerate job creation, and returns to employment, are needed as well. Uganda's population is largely rural, and a recent computable general equilibrium (CGE) analysis by Dorosh and Thurlow (2009) points to the important role that greater agricultural productivity plays in generating broad-based welfare improvements in rural areas. Other work by Lall, Schroeder, and Schmidt (2009) indicates that, among urban areas, concentrating infrastructure investments in the Kampala corridor is likely to have the greatest impact on growth and employment.

The decomposition analysis is the least informative for Mozambique, where consumption inequality between rural and urban areas is remarkably low, especially among low-income groups. The decomposition results indicating concentration effects in extremis should not be taken at face value, because the small denominator leads to volatile results. Although the decompositions are not entirely trustworthy, based on results in other countries one would expect concentration effects to indeed dominate in a poor country such as Mozambique, which also has very low levels of education and other human capital. The data on nonmonetary rural-urban welfare gaps presented earlier in this chapter reveal that, despite similar consumption levels, rural areas of Mozambique trail urban areas significantly in school enrollments, child nutrition, and access to safe water. All these findings indicate that high priority should be given to human capital investments in rural areas of Mozambique.

Perhaps as important as the policies suggested by these findings are those not suggested. In particular, the evidence that returns to education are roughly equal in rural and urban areas suggests that labor market seg-mentation or barriers to migration are not significant factors in explaining the spatial divide. These results indicate that regulatory interventions in labor markets are not likely to ease rural-urban divides; indeed, such interventions could create more problems than they solve. The principal challenges appear to be twofold: (1) how to ensure that the rural labor force has sufficient endowments of human capital to take advantage of income-generating opportunities, and (2) how to create an enabling envi-ronment for job creation in both the rural and urban sectors.

Ghana is the only one of the three countries that shows much differ-ence between the two survey years in the decomposition of rural-urban consumption inequalities. Differences in decompositions between sur-veys could arise from normal variability, such as a particularly good or bad crop year, or could reflect an evolution in the sources of rural-urban inequality. Many explanations are possible for the shift from a strong geography effect (returns) in 1991–92 to the almost equal balance between concentration and geography in 2005–06. For example, it would be consistent with a reduction in the inequality of returns, say from improved labor mobility. Unfortunately, that does not appear to be the case. Closer examination of the underlying data shows that during this period both endowments and returns increased in absolute terms in both rural and urban areas.[11] Endowments and returns increased faster in urban areas, which is consistent with the increasing gap in mean con-sumption observed. Of the two components, the rural-urban gap in endowments increased much faster than the gap in returns, which accounts for the leftward shift of the counterfactual line in 2005–06. Because migration is significant in Ghana, it is important to understand how migration is related to this divergence in endowments. Could it be that rural educational services are lagging behind urban ones, or could it be that the rural youth moving to urban areas are disproportionately well-educated?

Certain research areas lie beyond the scope of this chapter but are worthy of in-depth exploration. As noted earlier, spatial inequalities are not limited to rural-urban distinctions; they also have a north-south gra-dient in all three countries. We have not systematically investigated the nature and sources of regional welfare inequality in these countries, but that will be important for informing possible directions for policy. And rural land tenure systems, which have not been discussed here, almost certainly affect incentives to migrate from rural to urban areas. The cus-tomary land tenure systems that prevail in many Sub-Saharan African countries are similar in many ways to the system in Sri Lanka, which has had a major impact on the pace of rural-urban transformation in that country, as described in chapter 8.

Notes

1. The other five countries are Botswana, Equatorial Guinea, Ethiopia, Sudan, and Tanzania.

2. In Ghana, the 1960, 1970, 1984, and 2000 censuses defined *urban* as localities with at least 5,000 inhabitants. In Mozambique, the 1980 census treated 12 cities as urban (Maputo, the nine provincial capitals, Nacala-Porto, and Chokwe), and the 1997 census expanded urban areas to include 23 cities and 68 towns. In Uganda, the 1980 and 1991 censuses defined *urban* as cities, municipalities, towns, town boards, and all trading centers with more than 1,000 inhabitants. The 2002 census changed the definition to gazette cities, municipalities, and towns with more than 2,000 inhabitants (United Nations 2008). Despite the low "urban" population threshold in Uganda, many observers note that Uganda is more urban than indicated by statistics based on administrative classifications. For example, the agglomeration index in the *WDR 2009* classifies 28 percent of Uganda's population as urban (World Bank 2008).

3. Ghana's urban population share of 50 percent would make it an "intermediate" rather than "incipient" urbanizer in the *WDR 2009* classification, but it also shares important characteristics with other incipient urbanizing countries, such as a sparsely populated lagging region in the north and the relatively large contribution of agriculture to GDP growth (figure 3.2).

4. These estimates may differ from household survey estimates.

5. Periods spanning multiple calendar years (for example, 1991–92 or 2005–06) are used for reporting these and other survey results because the household surveys took place over 12- to 14-month periods that were not confined to a single calendar year.

6. Note that the analysis in chapter 2 uses slightly different national poverty lines for cross-country comparisons and can provide slightly different results. Also, the analysis in this chapter is based on adult equivalents unless stated otherwise.

7. The application of Oaxaca-Blinder decompositions and quantile regression extensions is similar to the work by Machado and Mata (2005) on the counterfactual decomposition of changes in wage distributions; more recent works using the quantile regression decomposition include those by Nguyen et al. (2007), Skoufias and Lopez-Acevedo (2008), and Shilpi (2008).

8. When welfare is measured as consumption per adult equivalent in multiples of the local poverty line, spatial differences in preferences and prices are considered in the welfare measure. Although regional price differences may be taken into account in the welfare ratio measures, the static decompositions do not account for factors such as switching employment sectors, changes in the probability of finding employment, the costs associated with migration, support from social networks, or the presence of various push factors.

9. The regression results that underpin the decompositions for Ghana, Mozambique, and Uganda appear in appendix B (tables B.1, B.2, and B.3, respectively). Table B.4 summarizes characteristics of rural and urban households in each of the three countries.

10. In Mozambique, the rural-urban difference in average welfare is very small. When decomposing such very small differences, the results should be interpreted with some caution. To estimate the share of the welfare difference accounted for by either endowments or coefficients, one divides these components by the difference in average welfare. When the denominator is very small, as it is for Mozambique, it is quite easy to obtain percentages larger than 100 for one of the effects (concentration or geography) and offsetting negative percentages for the other effect.

11. This result from the 1991 and 2005 Ghana Living Standards Surveys (GLSS) is not consistent with the Demographic and Health Surveys (DHS) data on school attendance in figure 3.5. The reason for the discrepancy is not clear, but it could be attributed to the different reference populations: school-age children in the DHS and heads of household in the decomposition analysis.

References

Dorosh, P., and J. Thurlow. 2009. "Agglomeration, Migration, and Regional Growth: A CGE Analysis for Uganda." IFPRI Discussion Paper 848, International Food Policy Research Institute, Washington, DC.

Lall, S. V., E. Schroeder, and E. Schmidt. 2009. "Identifying Spatial Efficiency-Equity Tradeoffs in Territorial Development Policies: Evidence from Uganda." Policy Research Working Paper 4966, World Bank, Washington, DC.

Machado, J. A. F., and J. Mata. 2005. "Counterfactual Decomposition of Changes in Wage Distributions Using Quantile Regression." *Journal of Applied Econometrics* 20: 445–65.

Nguyen, B. T., J. W. Albrecht, S. B. Vroman, and M. D. Westbrook. 2007. "A Quantile Regression Decomposition of Urban-Rural Inequality in Vietnam." *Journal of Development Economics* 83: 466–90.

Ravallion, M., and M. Huppi. 1991. "Measuring Changes in Poverty: A Methodological Case Study of Indonesia during an Adjustment Period." *World Bank Economic Review* 5 (1): 57–82.

Ravallion, M., and Q. Wodon. 1999. "Poor Areas or Poor People?" *Journal of Regional Sciences* 39 (4): 689–711.

Shilpi, F. 2008. "Migration, Sorting and Regional Inequality: Evidence from Bangladesh." Policy Research Working Paper 4616, World Bank, Washington, DC.

Skoufias E., and G. Lopez-Acevedo. 2008. "Sources of Welfare Disparities within and between Regions in Latin America and Caribbean Countries. Volume 1: Synthesis." Draft, World Bank, Washington, DC, December 1.

United Nations. 2008. *Urban Indigenous Peoples and Migration Factsheet.* http://www.un.org/esa/socdev/unpfii/documents/factsheet_migration_final .pdf.

World Bank. 2007. *World Development Report 2008: Agriculture for Development.* Washington, DC: World Bank.

———. 2008. *World Development Report 2009: Reshaping Economic Geography.* Washington, DC: World Bank.

CHAPTER 4

Local Level: Intraurban Welfare Disparities and Implications for Development

According to the *World Development Report 2009 (WDR 2009)*, divisions between leading and lagging areas play out not only on a national scale but also within cities (World Bank 2008c). This chapter elaborates on this proposition using data on the capital cities of Accra, Kampala, and Maputo, each of which forms the largest urban agglomeration in its country.

In the first section of this chapter, we consider the demographic and physical changes these cities have undergone over past decades. In the second section, we consider income and nonincome measures of welfare in the capitals versus the countries as a whole. Although the primary cities do offer higher average levels of welfare and services than rural areas, we also find significant within-city disparities, as predicted by the *WDR 2009*. These disparities are the topic of the third section, where we look at income inequalities and inequality in access to services and health outcomes across income quintiles. In the fourth section, we discuss how welfare disparities are linked to location: the "bumpy" economic landscape of the city is manifested in the juxtaposition of well-serviced modern residences with slums. In the fifth section, we analyze why these slums exist, looking at the impact of colonial legacies, land policies, and weak governance on intraurban inequalities. A conclusion follows.

Growing Cities

Each of the cities featured here has undergone profound demographic and physical changes over the last half-century. Figure 4.1 captures the precipitous rate of population growth since the 1960s. At the time of Ghana's independence, Accra's population numbered about 260,000. The current population of the Accra agglomeration, by UN estimates, is 2.4 million, although the metropolitan government claims that the city accommodates up to 3 million people on any given day.[1] In Uganda, Kampala's population was an estimated 100,000 in the early 1960s (Nilsson 2006). With a current population of about 1.6 million, it is by far the largest city in Uganda (the next largest urban center has less than a tenth of Kampala's population). Mozambique is rapidly urbanizing. In 2005, it was the fourth *least* urbanized country in southern Africa, but by 2025, it is projected to be the fourth *most* urbanized country. Maputo had a population of about 100,000 in the early 1960s and under 400,000 at the time of independence in 1975 (Grest 2006). The United Nations estimates the current population of the Maputo agglomeration to be about 1.8 million.[2]

As populations grow, cities must inevitably increase in size or density. Although all three of these cities have experienced an expansion of the urban periphery, Accra appears to have undergone the greatest spatial transformation over the last two decades, particularly to the west of the city center. This transformation may be in part a reaction to ambiguous land laws (discussed in more detail later in this chapter) that may encourage buyers to select land in an area that is unaffected by outstanding disputes (World Bank 2008a).

Figure 4.1   Population Growth: Accra, Kampala, and Maputo, 1970–2009

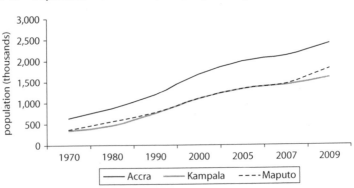

Source: United Nations 2010.

Lower Poverty, Better Services

Population booms in these cities are attributable in part to a reconfiguration of city boundaries, in part to natural increase, and in part to high rates of in-migration from rural areas. Rural migrants are drawn to cities with the expectation of higher standards of living, and *average* measures of income and nonincome welfare tend to bear out this expectation. For example, poverty indicators are better in the capital city than in the country as a whole (see table 4.1). Over the period 1991–2006, Accra was the site of impressive levels of poverty reduction. At 10.6 percent, the poverty headcount in 2005–06 was less than half of what it was in 1991. But contrary to the trend in the rest of the country, where poverty has been steadily declining, in Accra it has been rising since the late 1990s. Indeed, the poverty headcount and poverty gap were higher in 2005–06 than in 1998–99. Nevertheless, the absolute poverty levels remain much lower in the capital than in the rest of the country. Likewise, in Kampala the poverty headcount and poverty gap declined dramatically over the course of the 1990s. Although rural areas also saw high rates of poverty

Table 4.1   Poverty in Capitals versus Nationwide: Ghana, Uganda, and Mozambique

	Poverty headcount (%)[a]	Gini coefficient[a]
Accra-GAMA[b] (Ghana)		
1991–92	23.1 (51.7)	0.364 (0.373)
1998–99	4.4 (39.5)[c]	0.323[d] (0.425),[e]
		0.269[f] (0.388)[g]
2005–06	10.6 (28.5)	0.406 (0.425)
Kampala (Uganda)		
1992–93	20.8 (56.4)	0.394 (0.365)
2002–03	7.8 (38.8)	0.481 (0.428)
2005–06	5.5 (31.1)	0.392 (0.408)
Maputo (Mozambique)		
1996–97	47.8 (69.4)	0.444 (0.396)
2002–03	53.6 (54.1)	0.524 (0.415)

Note: The first values in each column are for the capitals, and the nationwide values appear in parentheses.
a. Authors' calculations based on Living Standard Measurement Surveys except where otherwise noted.
b. GAMA is the Greater Accra Metropolitan Area, which includes the Accra Metropolitan Area, Tema Municipal Area, and the urban areas in the Ga East and Ga West districts.
c. Because survey data are not available, data were taken from Ghana Statistical Service 2007, table 2.
d. Adjasi and Osei 2007, table X.
e. Tuffour and Apallo 2005, table 2.
f. Maxwell et al. 2000.
g. Aryeetey and McKay 2007.

reduction, in 2005–06 absolute poverty was far lower in the capital (with a headcount of 5.5) than in rural areas (34.2) or the country as a whole (31.1).

In terms of monetary welfare, Maputo, where urban poverty worsened between 1996–97 and 2002–03, is an exception to the largely positive story shown in table 4.1. In 1996–97, the poverty headcount of over 47 percent in the capital was significantly lower than that of 71.2 percent in rural areas. Poverty was also less severe, with a poverty gap of 16.5 in Maputo versus a gap of 29.9 in rural areas (Arndt, James, and Simler 2006). But by 2002–03, poverty in the capital had grown in both prevalence and severity, while poverty in rural areas and the country as a whole had decreased significantly. As a result, Maputo had a level of poverty that was strikingly similar to that in the country as a whole in 2002–03.

Like the poverty indicators, measures of nonincome welfare—such as access to services—tend to be much more favorable in urban areas than in rural areas. Because urban populations are dense, the per capita costs of many forms of infrastructure are lower, and competition among alternative service providers can be a force for innovation and efficiency (Kessides 2006). As figure 4.2 indicates, infrastructure services are much better in the capital cities, and generally improved there during the periods between the Demographic and Health Surveys used in this chapter.

In all three countries, access to electricity, piped water, and toilet facilities is much higher in the capital city than in the country as a whole. In Uganda, for example, access to electricity is almost eight times higher in Kampala than across the whole country, and access to piped water is almost six times higher. In Maputo, access to all services is higher than across Mozambique, but lower than access in Kampala and Accra. In Accra, the vast majority of residents have access to electricity and water, whereas less than half of Ghana's population as a whole benefits from similar access. Access to flush toilet facilities is scarcer even in capital cities. But here, too, people in the capitals have higher levels of access than in the countries as a whole.

Welfare Inequalities

These capital cities provide higher levels of income and nonincome welfare *on average*, but they also exhibit high levels of inequality. This finding is by no means atypical. In the developing world, income inequalities in cities are generally high: a subset of 26 cities in Africa and 19 in Latin America have average Gini coefficients of 0.54 and 0.55, respectively

Figure 4.2   Access to Services in Capitals versus Nationwide: Ghana, Uganda, and Mozambique, Selected Years

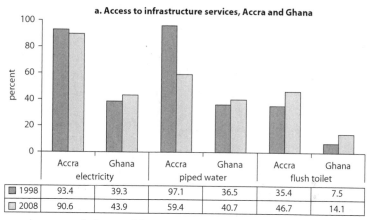

a. Access to infrastructure services, Accra and Ghana

	Accra electricity	Ghana	Accra piped water	Ghana	Accra flush toilet	Ghana
■ 1998	93.4	39.3	97.1	36.5	35.4	7.5
☐ 2008	90.6	43.9	59.4	40.7	46.7	14.1

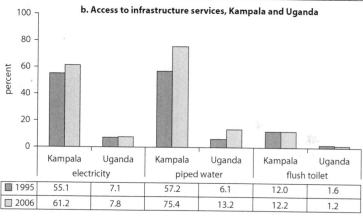

b. Access to infrastructure services, Kampala and Uganda

	Kampala electricity	Uganda	Kampala piped water	Uganda	Kampala flush toilet	Uganda
■ 1995	55.1	7.1	57.2	6.1	12.0	1.6
☐ 2006	61.2	7.8	75.4	13.2	12.2	1.2

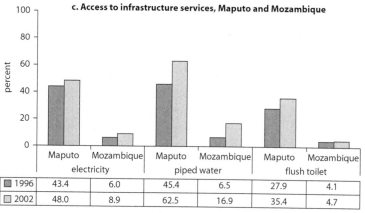

c. Access to infrastructure services, Maputo and Mozambique

	Maputo electricity	Mozambique	Maputo piped water	Mozambique	Maputo flush toilet	Mozambique
■ 1996	43.4	6.0	45.4	6.5	27.9	4.1
☐ 2002	48.0	8.9	62.5	16.9	35.4	4.7

Sources: Demographic and Health Surveys for Ghana and Uganda; Living Standards Survey for Mozambique.

(UN-Habitat 2008). Even in some parts of the developed world—in particular, the United States—some cities exhibit stark income inequalities. Although income inequality, as measured by the Gini coefficient, is relatively low in Accra (0.364 in 1991–92, and 0.269 in 1998–99), it is significantly higher—and increasing—in both Kampala and Maputo (table 4.1). In Uganda, inequality increased in both rural and urban areas between 1992–93 and 2002–03. The story is grimmer still for Mozambique, the poorest of the three countries. There, between 1996–97 and 2002–03 inequality increased sharply in Maputo, from 0.444 to 0.524, whereas it increased only slightly, from 0.396 to 0.415, in the country as a whole.

Likewise, the higher level of average access to services in urban areas obscures significant within-city disparities. When access to basic infrastructure services is broken down by wealth quintile, each city exhibits major disparities (figure 4.3 and tables 4.2 and 4.3). Once more, these findings are typical of cities in general, and particularly those in developing countries. For example, surveying access to services in the cities of Sub-Saharan Africa, Kessides (2006) finds large, statistically significant gaps between the access of the urban poor versus the urban nonpoor. These gaps are often greater than those between the urban poor and rural residents.

In Accra, 68.5 percent of the poorest have access to piped water, but just over half of the poorest in Kampala and only two out of five among the poorest in Maputo have access to piped water. In Kampala, although access for the poorest is still much higher than the national average (56 percent versus 13 percent), congested urban living conditions make alternatives to piped water, such as wells, less feasible than they would be in many rural settings. UN-Habitat estimates that only 17 percent of the residents of Kampala's informal settlements have access to clean and safe piped water; the rest obtain water from "unhygienic and highly contaminated sources."[3]

Differences in sanitation facilities across quintiles are sharper still. In Maputo and Kampala, private flush toilet facilities are extremely rare for all but the richest quintile. Access to shared toilets tends to decrease over the wealthier quintiles as access to private toilets increases. In Accra, the figures suggest that the vast majority of people in all quintiles have access to either private or shared facilities. But in Kampala, and especially Maputo, access is far from complete. Eighty-four percent of the poorest quintile and over 70 percent of the second quintile of residents of Maputo are living without access to either flush or shared toilets.

Figure 4.3   Access to Infrastructure Services by Wealth Quintile: Accra, Kampala, and Maputo

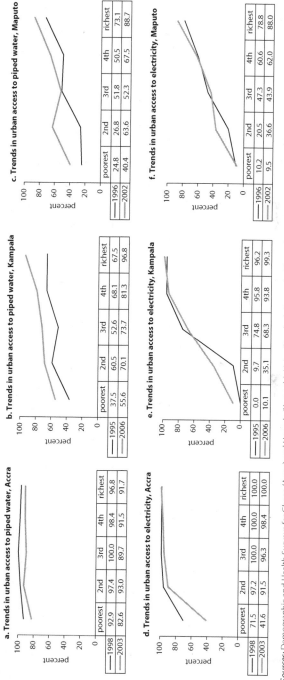

a. Trends in urban access to piped water, Accra

	poorest	2nd	3rd	4th	richest
1998	92.9	97.4	100.0	98.4	96.8
2003	82.6	93.0	89.7	91.5	91.7

b. Trends in urban access to piped water, Kampala

	poorest	2nd	3rd	4th	richest
1995	37.5	60.5	52.6	68.1	67.5
2006	55.6	70.1	73.7	81.3	96.8

c. Trends in urban access to piped water, Maputo

	poorest	2nd	3rd	4th	richest
1996	24.8	26.8	51.8	50.5	73.1
2002	40.4	63.6	52.3	67.5	88.7

d. Trends in urban access to electricity, Accra

	poorest	2nd	3rd	4th	richest
1998	71.5	97.2	100.0	100.0	100.0
2003	41.6	91.5	96.3	98.4	100.0

e. Trends in urban access to electricity, Kampala

	poorest	2nd	3rd	4th	richest
1995	0.0	9.7	74.8	95.8	96.2
2006	10.1	35.1	68.3	93.8	99.3

f. Trends in urban access to electricity, Maputo

	poorest	2nd	3rd	4th	richest
1996	10.2	20.5	47.3	60.6	78.8
2002	9.5	36.6	43.9	62.0	88.0

Sources: Demographic and Health Surveys for Ghana (Accra) and Uganda (Kampala); Living Standards Survey for Mozambique (Maputo).

Note: The wealth index places individuals on a continuous scale of relative wealth. It is a composite measure of household living standards, calculated from data on ownership of assets. Assets include type of water access and sanitation facility, and so although one would expect to see a correlation between income or consumption quintile and asset ownership, these measures are not completely independent.

Table 4.2   Access to a Flush Toilet: Accra, Kampala, and Maputo, Selected Years

City (country)	Quintile of wealth index				
	Poorest	2nd	3rd	4th	Richest
Accra (Ghana, 2008)	18.7	24.5	34.9	63.1	92.6
	(0.0)	(0.5)	(2.9)	(12.0)	(55.0)
Kampala (Uganda, 2006)	0.7	2.4	2.4	1.4	54.1
	(0.0)	(0.0)	(0.0)	(0.02)	(5.82)
Maputo (Mozambique, 2003)	0.0	0.0	1.8	12.0	75.6
	(0.0)	(0.0)	(0.0)	(0.0)	(14.47)

Source: Demographic and Health Surveys.

Table 4.3   Access to a Shared Toilet: Accra, Kampala, and Maputo, Selected Years

City (country)	Quintile of wealth index				
	Poorest	2nd	3rd	4th	Richest
Accra (Ghana, 2008)	96.6	93.4	80.9	65.2	19.5
	(75.4)	(89.4)	(91.4)	(89.8)	(60.7)
Kampala (Uganda, 2006)	88.8	83.8	79.1	70.0	20.3
	(64.71)	(42.54)	(31.1)	(34.44)	(47.0)
Maputo (Mozambique, 2003)	15.7	29.4	11.3	7.0	3.2
	(11.85)	(20.83)	(17.27)	(13.23)	

Source: Demographic and Health Surveys.

Other sanitation services such as waste collection, drains, and sewers are also lacking. For example, Accra has the capacity to collect only 1,200 of the 1,500–1,800 tons of solid waste generated daily (UN-Habitat 2009), and Maputo's Municipal Council collects just 30 percent of the waste generated in the city (World Bank 2006). Large swathes of population live beyond the reach of public water supplies and drainage facilities: Kampala's main sewer line covers less than 3 percent of the city (Nuwagaba 2004), and an estimated 85 percent of Maputo's residents live in areas where there is no rainwater drainage system (Maputo City Council 2005).

What do the data reveal about trends over time? As the figures suggest, although urban infrastructure access generally improved during the period between the two most recent Demographic and Health Surveys, it did not become more equal. For example, access to electricity only marginally improved for the poorest quintiles in Kampala and declined for the poorest in Maputo, with access remaining extremely unequal between top and bottom quintiles in those cities. Accra, which had relatively good electricity service for all quintiles in 1998, saw a drop for the poorest by 2003, which represented an increase in inequality. The one exception to the trend was drinking water in Maputo, where improved access for the poorest meant some narrowing of inequalities between the rich and poor.

Unequal access to water and sanitation affects health. Figure 4.4 considers one indicator of ill health—stunting. Again, there is a clear urban advantage; on average, children in the capital cities are significantly less likely to be stunted than children nationwide. However, less stunting is found among the wealthiest quintiles nationwide than in the lowest (Maputo), bottom two (Accra), or even bottom three (Kampala) quintiles in the capital cities. There is also a considerable spread among wealth quintiles. In Accra, for example, the likelihood of stunting ranges from almost 20 percent among the second and third quintiles to no stunting at all for the top quintile. Ranges are similar in Kampala (almost a quarter of the poorest three quintiles compared with under 5 percent of the top quintile) and Maputo (about 30 percent among the poorest compared with under 10 percent of the wealthiest), although the existence of stunting among the top urban quintiles suggests that, at least in Mozambique and Uganda, even the wealthiest are vulnerable to diseases and other health threats that affect their children's well-being.

Figure 4.4   Stunting: Nationwide versus Capital City

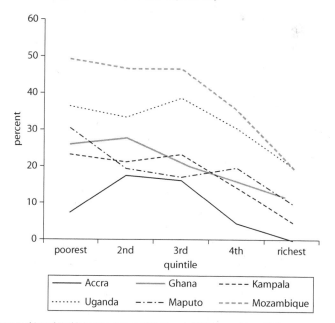

Source: Demographic and Health Surveys (Ghana 2008, Uganda 2006, Mozambique 2003).

Welfare Differences: Linked to Location

Poverty and poor access to services are not evenly distributed throughout these three cities. The differences in consumption and access to services just described reflect spatially based inequalities. Although no small area poverty maps have been created for the three cities in this report, what evidence we do have suggests a strong correlation between poverty and location, with most but certainly not all of the urban poor living in areas defined as slums (see box 4.1).

Maxwell et al. (2000) find high welfare disparities in a survey of 16 areas across Greater Accra. Table 4.4 reports the welfare measures for the one middle-income neighborhood in the survey—Dansoman—and for two slum areas—Tema Newtown and Nima. The results demonstrate a strong correlation between location and measures of well-being. The quality of housing and the immediate environment are much better in Dansoman than in Tema Newtown and Nima. Per capita household expenditures in Dansoman are more than three times higher than in Tema Newtown and 2.5 times higher than in Nima, and a much lower proportion of expenditure is devoted to food. Finally, a child born in Dansoman is eight times more likely to survive than a child born in Tema Newtown and 10 times more likely to survive than one born in Nima.

A 2005 Consultative Citizens' Report Card Survey for Maputo highlights how the inequalities in access to services are closely linked to disparities between the seven municipal districts surveyed (Maputo City Council 2005). In district one—a high-income district—98 percent of people have modern toilet facilities, whereas in district seven—a low-income neighborhood—40 percent of people have no toilet facility whatsoever, and 56 percent use traditional facilities. In district one, 96 percent of people have piped potable water, whereas in district seven, 95 percent of people collect water from wells. Waste collection coverage is 73 percent in district one and nonexistent in district seven.

Similar geographically fine-tuned data do not exist for Kampala. But the combined evidence suggests that most of the city's poor live on former agricultural and vacant lands in the urban periphery, made up of unplanned, inadequately serviced, low-density, poor-quality housing (Giddings 2009). Nuwagaba (2004) describes most of Kampala's poor as concentrated in marginal areas of the city and finds that "slums are an indicator of poverty." Nyakaana, Sengendo, and Lwasa (2005) describe a walk through a typical Kampala slum: houses are constructed in road reserves, children play in front of leaking latrines, and

Box 4.1

Poverty and Slums

Slums are defined as settlements in which more than half of the households lack at least one of the following: improved water, improved sanitation, durable housing, adequate living space, and security of tenure (UN-Habitat 2002). Urban poor households are found not only in slums, and not all those living in slums are poor. However, the strong correlation between being poor and living in a slum leads to the spatial concentration of poverty in many developing country cities.

Relative to other regions, the urban poor in Africa are subjected to particularly severe forms of deprivation. According to UN-Habitat estimations, nearly two-thirds (62 percent) of city dwellers in Sub-Saharan Africa live in a slum—the highest proportion of any region in the world. Moreover, an examination of conditions across regions suggests that slum dwellers in Sub-Saharan Africa experience a higher level of multiple shelter deprivations than slum dwellers in other regions (UN-Habitat 2008).

Slum settlements are closely associated with insecurity because most tenants lack written contracts or any legal mechanism to protect their tenure rights. Unplanned and unsuitable land use heightens vulnerability. Inhabitants of slums are also particularly vulnerable to poverty traps. They tend to experience greater geographic distance from or inadequate and expensive transportation to more productive jobs. Residents in a low-income settlement outside Dar es Salaam, for example, were found to be spending between 10 and 30 percent of their income on transport. Spatial concentrations of crime and violence add to the stigmatization of slums, creating additional hurdles in access to jobs or credit (Kilroy 2007).

Slums are often tacitly accepted by local governments, which find themselves unable to provide basic services for large segments of their city's de facto residents. Not only do slum dwellers receive fewer public services, but they also have to pay more for those they purchase in the private market. Those in the high-income neighborhoods of Accra, for example, have access to a constant water supply at the official rate, whereas those in middle-income neighborhoods must supplement publicly supplied water with water from private vendors at about four times the official rate, and those in slums must rely entirely on these private suppliers. The cost of water from vendors can amount to 10 percent of the monthly income of a low-income household, which in turn limits the amount of water the household uses for drinking, cooking, and hygiene. The result is higher rates of disease, greater loss in workdays, and even higher outlays of expenditure for medical attention (World Bank 2002).

Table 4.4   Welfare Measures in Subareas of Greater Accra

Area	Housing, assets, and environment index[a]	Total per capita household expenditure (1,000 cedis)	Proportion of expenditure spent on food	Proportion of live-born children who died
Dansoman	1.75	1,757	39.0	1.6
Nima	−0.46	699	56.8	16.3
Tema Newtown	−1.42	547	61.9	13.0

Source: Maxwell et al. 2000.
a. An index of quality of housing, assets, and environmental quality was created based on four assets: refrigerator, electric stove, tape deck, and television set. Factor analysis was then used to derive one factor that would summarize variables related to the quality of housing (construction material for roof, walls, and floor), the "possession" index, the source of drinking water, and the availability of sanitary facilities and garbage disposal. The principal components factor extraction method was used. Loadings smaller than 0.5 were excluded from the initial model. The final model had five variables (floor, walls, water source, possession index, and sanitary facilities), all with factor loadings greater than 0.53, and it explained 46 percent of the variance.

the overflow contaminates drinking water sources, making residents particularly vulnerable to cholera.

Understanding Spatial Inequalities

This section examines the causes of the spatially based welfare disparities just documented here. The high inequalities in many cities in both the developed and the developing world suggest that inequality is in part a function of urban growth. But it is by no means inevitable: some Asian cities such as Beijing and Jakarta have managed to grow in size and economic strength while maintaining relatively low levels of inequality. In Malaysia, urban income inequalities have even decreased steadily since the late 1970s as urban populations have grown (UN-Habitat 2008).

In this section, we therefore look beyond the sheer fact of rising populations to uncover the institutional reasons for urban inequality. As described, inequalities are rooted in the colonial past, but also are reinforced by more recent institutional constraints and policy failures. In particular, we consider the failure to adequately address the complex and confused systems of land tenure that have enabled an elite minority to monopolize access to land and housing and forced a poor majority to rely on insecure and inadequate arrangements. We also address the shortcomings of urban governance, which have resulted in ever-larger populations congregating in areas of cities that lack even the most basic access to energy, sanitation, or transportation infrastructures.

The story of urban inequality is not uniformly gloomy, however. Chapter 11, which presents our summary and conclusions, notes recent initiatives to address unjust institutions, such as by simplifying systems of land tenure, and to improve service delivery to the poor, such as through programs to upgrade slums or reform local government.

The Colonial Legacy

Colonial legacies have contributed to spatially based welfare disparities in contemporary African cities. The populations of colonial Accra, Kampala, and Maputo were not large by present-day standards, but the colonial era created systemic inequalities. For example, the land use and settlement patterns of the colonial city reflected socioeconomic and racial divisions. In most African cities, the "standard of infrastructure in the neighborhoods inhabited by Europeans was many times higher than in African areas. ... Europeans tended to live in bungalows or villas in large plots along clean, shady streets. ... Africans tended to live ... along unplanned paths, enjoying few, if any, sanitary services" (Stren and Halfani 2001). In colonial Accra, most commercial activity and planned development were located near the port; African residents lived and worked in overcrowded areas outside of this central business area (Grant and Yankson 2003).

The divisions in Kampala were written into law and starker still. Colonial Kampala was divided into African, Asian, and European residential areas. Most of the city's African population lived in the Kibuga, an area subject to the authority of the king of Buganda, whereas Europeans and Asians lived in Kampala proper and were served by the municipal government. The separate systems of administration created de facto segregation between the Kibuga and Kampala in service delivery (Nilsson 2006). Roads, mosquito control, drainage, water supply, and sanitation were far inferior in the Kibuga compared with that in municipal Kampala (Nilsson 2006; Bryceson 2008). Because the municipality financed its services through taxes and fees, the divide had socioeconomic and racial ramifications. According to Elkan and van Zwanenberg (1975), "Life in the municipality (Kampala) was healthy but expensive, whereas in the Kibuga ... it was insanitary and cheap. ... Given the racial distribution of income, this led naturally to a racial distribution of residence."

Similarly, Maputo (then known as Lourenço Marques) was ruled under a trifurcated legal regime. The city was organized into separate areas for the African *indigenas, assimilados* (a small group of "Europeanized" Africans), and Europeans, with differentiated civil rights granted on the basis of both race and location. Confined to the periphery of the city, *indigenas* were barred from building houses from permanent materials. As Jenkins (2006) describes, this practice gave rise to a dualistic settlement pattern: "a gracious Southern European-style planned inner 'cement city' surrounded by the *'caniço'*" (in reference to the reeds from which many of the buildings were constructed). The monopolistic pattern of landownership indicated the extent of socioeconomic inequality: in 1965, 75 percent of private land was in the hands of just 11 large-scale landowners (Jenkins 2000).

By placing some areas under the jurisdiction of the traditional authorities while imposing European legal norms in others, colonial rulers compounded complex systems of tenure. In Accra, as elsewhere in Ghana, customary land tenure systems—whereby ownership was corporate and vested in a "stool," represented by the chiefs, or in a family—operated in parallel with the British conveyancing system (Gough and Yankson 2000). In Kampala, a 1900 agreement granted *mailo* land—a system of freehold land tenure—in perpetuity to the Bagandan majority. The original inhabitants of *mailo* land became tenants overnight, paying annual dues to the landowners. Although the colonial regime found these systems convenient, enabling indirect control of large territories, they created a complex legacy, contributing to inelastic land supply and cementing divisions between a landed elite and a landless city. The challenge of overcoming colonial legacies was made more difficult by the ambivalent attitudes of some newly independent governments toward the process of urbanization (see box 4.2).

Failure to Strengthen Systems for Land Delivery

The colonial period, then, resulted in the codification of a dual system of land tenure, leaving a complex legacy that has become only more confusing as cities have grown in physical size and population. Post-independence governments have generally been slow to respond to the challenging task of simplifying land tenure arrangements. In Accra, for example, the dual system of customary and formal land ownership has resulted in "persistent anarchy in the land market" (Gyimah-Boadi 2004). The city is rife with "grey areas" where two or more stools (chieftaincies) contest ownership (World Bank 2007b). With dispute resolution taking up to a decade, land acquisition through formal means is perceived to be a daunting task (Durand-Lasserve et al. 2007). Large public land holdings and "huge deficits in the policing, regulation,

Box 4.2

Postindependence Attitudes toward Urban Development

Since independence, national governments have displayed various attitudes toward the process of urbanization. In Ghana, starting with the Nkrumah government (1957–66) the country's leadership promoted Accra as the central growth pole of the national economy, improving the city's transportation network and making major infrastructure investments such as in the deepwater harbor at Tema (Grant and Yankson 2003).

By contrast, successive governments of independent Uganda tended to conceive of urban areas as "places of opportunity" that required little policy intervention, focusing instead on development in rural areas (Nuwagaba 2004). Under the rule of Idi Amin (1971–78), Kampala's economic health was subverted in pursuit of brutal ideological goals: tens of thousands of Ugandans were executed in the capital, and an estimated 80,000 ethnic Asian residents nationwide, owning as much as 90 percent of all businesses, fled the country. Only more recently (since 1986) has the government aimed its economic development policies at supporting commercial and industrial development in the Kampala region (Giddings 2009).

In Mozambique, the official stance of the ruling FRELIMO (Liberation Front of Mozambique) party toward urban development in the years following the country's independence was even more hostile. After independence, 150,000–200,000 of Maputo's Portuguese and assimilados residents, fearing persecution, fled. The government aimed its economic development policies at rural areas. In 1985, the state imposed Operation Production, whose expressed goal was to remove surplus urban workers (described as "parasitic") to the countryside. Under this policy, as many as 50,000 people were relocated from Maputo, and it is believed that many perished. It is only since adoption of the 1990 constitution that Mozambique had been a free-market economy, and Maputo is increasingly seen as an essential "engine of development" (Jenkins 2006).

Today, a "rural bias" in policy making persists in some countries. According to a 2008 United Nations Department of Economic and Social Affairs survey, 83 percent of African governments implement policies to reduce rural-to-urban migration, and 78 percent intervene to reduce migration to large urban agglomerations (UNDESA 2008). Although little panel data-based research is found in Africa, research from other areas suggests that restrictions on migration, which may consist of denial of services or slum evictions, result in maintaining surplus labor in rural areas and low agglomeration economies in urban areas, ultimately slowing the development of both rural and urban areas.

acquisition and use" of such land further stifle the market (Gyimah-Boadi 2004). The institutional impediments to efficient planning and the functioning of a land and housing market in Accra include over-lapping arrangements between different agencies, poor land manage-ment, cumbersome processes of titling, conveyancing and deeds registration, and inadequate mapping (World Bank 2002).

In Kampala, the development of an efficient land market has been hampered by the colonial legacy of *mailo* land. About 60–70 percent of the land in Kampala is owned under the *mailo* freehold system (World Bank 2008a, annex 1). This kind of tenure permits separating the owner-ship of land from the ownership of developments on land (World Bank 2009). Because most of the title-holding landowners do not have enough capital to develop their land, they rent or allow squatters to occupy it, usually without providing the most basic of services. Observers claim that the *mailo* system has resulted in a "land impasse" in Kampala (Augustus Nuwagaba, quoted by Rulekere 2006). Efforts to reform the system have only compounded the problems. For example, the 1995 constitution stated that tenants were to be compensated for the sale or development of *mailo* land, but this stipulation has had the effect of depressing demand, because any purchaser could face multiple compensation claims (Rulekere 2006). Leasehold land is in short supply; Giddings (2009) esti-mates that the acquisition of a public plot through leasehold arrangement can take up to five years.

In postcolonial Mozambique, FRELIMO (Liberation Front of Mozambique, which was the ruling party until 2009 and is currently the majority political party in the government) nationalized land and rented or abandoned housing. From 1975 to 1987, the state dominated all for-mal activity in urban land and housing supply. After 1987, market forces increasingly prevailed, although the 1997 Land Law and 2004 constitu-tion both assert that all land belongs to the state (Jenkins 2001; Malauene et al. 2005). Although the state remains in de jure control of land alloca-tion, it has not been able to keep pace with the demand for land and housing, particularly among Maputo's low-income groups. Cumbersome bureaucratic processes act as a disincentive for formal registration. Indeed, Malauene et al. (2005) identify more than 27 steps associated with registering land, 9 steps for requesting plans, and a further 28 steps for registering a building. And although formal access to land is nominally free, in practice, multiple fees must be paid to the Maputo Municipal Council. Among the most pertinent problems, observers find that the current legal framework, enshrined in the 1997 Land Law, is ill-suited for urban circumstances; the institutional and technical capacity is weak; land management instruments are lacking; and low-income groups tend to be unaware of their rights[4] (Jenkins 2001; Malauene et al. 2005; World Bank 2008b).Together, these factors add to the scope for arbitrary decision making and bribe taking among officials, which only act as further barriers to entry for the poor.

In each of the three cities, inadequate legal frameworks, weak dispute settlements, low institutional and technical capacities, lengthy registration processes, poor land management, and corruption have combined to create tight formal housing markets. In Accra, because of legal ambiguities such as lack of documentation and poor boundary definition, private parties are reluctant to invest in the existing housing stock. As a result, Accra qualifies as a "superstar city," in which a highly inelastic housing supply is pricing lower- and even middle-income groups out of the market (Buckley and Mathema 2007). One report calculates that the backlog of demand for formal housing units in Accra has reached 500,000, with an additional 14,000–16,000 units required each year (referenced by World Bank 2007b). In Kampala, the unwillingness of owners to sell land has led to "skyrocketing" prices (World Bank 2008a). Current land prices are from two to four times what they were in 2002, and the city has a deficit of housing units estimated at 100,000 (Giddings 2009). To take advantage of rising prices, the private sector has mainly engaged in high-value construction, with the hope of attracting rent from foreigners; meanwhile, housing for middle- and low-income groups remains in short supply (Nuwagaba 2004). Likewise, surveying the data for Maputo, Jenkins (2000) concludes that formal land and housing "of even a most basic standard" is unobtainable for the vast majority of low-income city dwellers.

National governments have not been blind to the urgent need to address land problems in their capital cities. In Accra, a Land Administration Pilot Project, initiated under the umbrella of a slum upgrading program in 1996, aimed to improve mapping capabilities and land titling administration. Other programs were directed at strengthening records management and establishing a small unit for the digital production of registry maps. However, a broader attempt to resolve the underlying issues of tenure has not been forthcoming (World Bank 2002). Uganda has experienced similar difficulties. As of 2009, the government of Uganda's comprehensive land policy review was in its fourth draft. The policy aims to "rationalize and simplify the complex tenure regimes." To this end, it recommends (1) that the *mailo* system of ownership be eliminated; (2) that freehold land, especially in urban areas, be converted into leasehold land; and (3) that customary tenure be formalized.[5] However, the current draft has generated opposition from landlords and the Buganda Kingdom (the largest *mailo* landlord); they view it as an attempt by the government to take away their land. According to Giddings (2009), "How fast the policy will move towards adoption, or how much compromise will be necessary given the resistance of the *mailo* owners, is therefore uncertain."

Constraints to Effective Urban Governance

The approach to governance in many African cities has had distinct phases. The minimalist state of the colonial period was usually replaced by a more bureaucratic approach in the post-independence era, and the structural adjustment programs of the 1980s sought to make unwieldy public services more nimble (Gyimah-Boadi 2004). By the early 1990s, many African cities were facing a "crisis of governance," manifested in the shortcomings of service delivery and severe spatially based inequalities (Stren and Halfani 2001). Decentralization programs aimed at devolving governmental functions and finances from the national to the district or municipal level were an attempt to alleviate this crisis by making governments more responsive to local needs.

Decentralization has been an official goal of all three of the countries featured here.[6] But administrative weaknesses have constrained the actual extent of the decentralization. A recent urban profile of Accra points to the dual allegiance of decentralized departments, nonconnectivity of departments, lack of transparency, overcentralization of administration, and functional duplication of public and parastatal agencies as just some of the obstacles to effective local governance at the city level (UN-Habitat 2009). The Maputo Municipal Council is constrained by a skills shortage (in 2005 only 1.5 percent of staff had a higher education and 7 percent had technical training), weak operational supervision, inadequate information systems, and poor budget management tools (World Bank 2006). Many of the obstacles to effective local governance in Kampala are tied up in the complex land tenure system. For example, the arduous bureaucratic procedures required to purchase a public plot of land only add to the incentives for corruption (see box 4.3).

The ability of local urban authorities to implement decisions has been further limited by the willingness of national governments to transfer the financial resources needed to match devolved responsibilities (United Cities and Local Governments 2007). Contrary to notions of an "urban bias," central governments tend to favor rural areas in the

Box 4.3

Corruption in Kampala

Councilors have demanded immediate investigations into Kampala City Council senior staff who have constantly failed to execute their duties, leading to construction of several illegal structures in the city. Makerere University Councilor, Mr Bernard Luyiga said the engineering and planning departments should be investigated over failure to realize the city plan. "We have several properties constructed in the road reserves while others have altered the approved plans. The two departments are primarily responsible and if there is any political influence, it should be exposed," he said.

Lubaga Division representative Mr Zachel Mberazze, said several roads and access lanes in the central business district have been blocked by illegal structures which has tainted council's image and worsened traffic congestion in the city.... The developments come after a Ministry of Works, Transport and Communication report recommended that the Inspector General of Government investigates the continuous sale of Kisenyi lane, a public utility to individuals....

The report signed by the MoW (Ministry of Works) Permanent Secretary Charles Muganzi says council senior staffs were responsible for the increasing city mess. "The ministry wants in-depth investigations conducted to establish the individuals who took part in the evil act of selling off three plots of land that were set aside as road reserve in Kisenyi parish, Kampala Central Division," the report, a copy of which Daily Monitor has obtained, reads in part. The report indicates that plots 215,239 and 203 on Block 12 Kafumbe Mukasa Road opposite Nakivubo Stadium, which were reserved as roads accessing the commercial area, were encroached on in November 2006. "It has been established that these plots had been planned as accesses to the planned commercial area. And all constructions on the said plot are illegal and being carried out in the wrong place," Mr Mungazi said. ... The MoW report also recommends disciplinary action against the KCC officials.

Source: Reprinted from Robert Mwanje, "Uganda: Councilors Want KCC Officials Punished Over Illegal Structure," *Daily Monitor,* October 21, 2009, http://allafrica.com/stories/200910210139.html.

distribution of funds. Ugandan policy makers' characterization of urban areas as "places of opportunity" has historically affected the design of policy and program interventions in favor of rural areas. As for Ghana, the World Bank (2007a) has noted that its urban District Assemblies are disfavored in the transfer of central funds. Also according to the World Bank (2006), municipalities in Mozambique receive only 1 percent of the national budget.

Meanwhile, cities' own revenue-generating capacities have been stymied by a high degree of informality—whether of land, property, or enterprise—as well as by poor administrative capacity (Durand-Lasserve et al. 2007). In 2001, the Accra Metropolitan Assembly estimated that it was able to benefit from less than one-third of its fiscal base. Only 5 percent of properties in Maputo are taxed, and the Maputo Municipal Council lacks an updated cadastre and other tools to increase property tax revenues. In addition, local fees and user charges are outdated and difficult to collect, and the laws governing municipal fiscal autonomy are very restrictive (World Bank 2006). Likewise, in Kampala outdated valuations, frequent property sales and exchanges, and inadequate title registration have limited the extent to which local authorities can levy property taxes (Fjeldstad 2006).

National and local authorities have recognized the urgent need to strengthen urban governance in order to deliver better and more equitable services to city dwellers. Accra has been implementing slum upgrading programs over the last two decades, and most recently the city turned its attention to revamping its collapsed mass transport system (UN-Habitat 2009). Slum upgrading has resulted in improved road paving, water, sanitation, solid waste removal, and street lighting in selected parts of the city. The first-generation projects were top-down initiatives designed and fully funded by the central government. A more recent environmental sanitation project adopted a much more participatory approach and engaged local government in both funding and implementation (World Bank 2002). These programs have led to markedly improved welfare indicators in the areas in which they have been implemented, and they also have stimulated local economic development (box 4.4). However, they have not yet been replicated on a large enough scale to lead to improvements in citywide welfare indicators (World Bank 2008a).

In Maputo, decentralization has become more meaningful by involving submunicipal officials and neighborhood structures in participatory planning and service assessments. For example, the Consultative Citizens' Report Card Survey described earlier has fed into a participatory process to formulate a 10-year development program for the city called ProMaputo. The first phase of ProMaputo recognizes that the municipal government has an extremely limited capacity to raise its own revenues and to provide its citizens with quality services. Therefore, the initial

Box 4.4

Slum Upgrading in Accra

In 1985, with World Bank support, the government of Ghana implemented a pilot infrastructure upgrading project in the East Maamobi community of Accra. The government's reaction upon completion of the scheme was favorable, and more schemes were initiated in 1988 under the Priority Works Project, in 1996 under the Urban 2 Project, and in 1997 under the Urban Environmental Sanitation Project (UESP).

The UESP was implemented in seven urban communities in Ghana, including three in Accra—Sukura, Old Teshie, and West Maamobi. The slum upgrading component of the UESP set cost-per-hectare limits and promoted community participation throughout the identification, planning, design, and implementation phases. Efforts were also made to engage local governments: they were required to contribute 11 percent of the capital costs and were responsible for managing implementation of the UESP.

Although they have not addressed social infrastructure such as health care clinics and schools, the upgrading schemes have improved environmental, sanitation, and economic conditions in the selected communities:

• Improved solid waste collection has reduced the accumulation of garbage in areas where children play and parents cook and clean their dishes and utensils.
• Improved drainage has led to reduced flooding in most areas, thereby slowing the spread of waterborne diseases.
• Paved streets and improved access to communities have resulted in a proliferation of small businesses and kiosks in areas that once were not economically viable.
• Upgrading has motivated individual households to invest more in improving their shelter structures.
• The introduction of street lighting in some areas has reduced the incidence of crime.

The benefits of upgrading extend beyond the specific areas upgraded. For example, people from the areas around Maamobi use the communal toilets, waste containers, and running water facilities in the upgraded areas. Because of the success of these programs, the government of Ghana and the World Bank are considering preparation of an urban upgrading project for the Greater Accra Metropolitan Area, which could set the stage for a national upgrading program (World Bank 2002).

focus is on improving governance, financial stability, and institutional capacity in order to provide a platform for subsequent sustainable improvements to service delivery (World Bank 2006).

In Kampala, after accusations of corruption and ineffectiveness were made against the Kampala City Council, Parliament passed a bill in November 2010 that provided for the administration of Kampala by the central government, although proposals to expand the official city limits and abolish the council were dropped. The new Kampala Capital City Authority to "oversee the delivery of quality services to the population" and the Metropolitan Physical Planning Authority to promote a new structure plan and to "ensure that land use in the City and metropolitan area follow designated plans, irrespective of the tenure of land." The Buganda Kingdom and some opposition groups had opposed the new law (Mpagi and Ssenkabirwa 2009, Namutebi and Bekunda 2010).

Conclusion

Cities in Sub-Saharan Africa are growing at an extraordinarily fast pace, and they continue to attract migrants to the economic opportunities and greater amenities they offer. In the three capitals discussed in this part of the report, poverty levels are lower and the overall living standards, as measured by access to social and infrastructure services, are better than those in rural areas, although the degree of disparity varies considerably.

But urbanization also has its "dark side" (Spence, Annez, and Buckley 2009), manifested in the prevalence of slums and the absence of decent shelter or basic services for those who dwell in them. Colonial histories, a complex mix of traditional, colonial, and postcolonial land tenure systems, the resultant dysfunctional land markets, and weak governance all have a role to play in the stark spatial inequalities found in Accra, Kampala, Maputo, and many other African cities.

As noted in WDR 2009, historical evidence indicates that such inequalities will persist longer than the rural-urban welfare gaps, diminishing only at the more advanced stages of development. But this finding does not mean that national and urban governments should not take action to alleviate urban inequalities. Failure to invest sufficiently in infrastructure in rapidly growing cities results in congestion, crime, pollution, and social tension, which, in turn, undermine the potential benefits of agglomeration.

The policies needed to address these spatial inequalities are discussed briefly in chapter 11, this report's summary and conclusions. Here, it is worth noting that not all policies to address urban inequalities will target the city. *WDR 2009* emphasizes the importance of framing the policy debate on cities in the context of the overall rural-urban transformation as well as regional economic growth. For example, introducing better services in rural areas will reduce "push factors" for people whose primary reason for moving to cities is to access better amenities. And policies to promote regional integration would enable larger agglomeration economies and opportunities for job creation (box 4.5).

Indeed, for anyone designing policies it is better to think about costs and benefits along the rural-urban continuum rather than in distinctly rural or urban spaces. For large cities in particular, the success of all these policies rests on improving coordination between the national, municipal, and local levels of government. Responsibilities are often transferred down to local governments that lack the resources or the capacity to address the problems of a metropolitan region. It is hardly surprising,

---

Box 4.5

Promoting Agglomeration through Regional Integration

Recent work by Collier and Page (UNIDO 2009) suggests that because of Africa's political fragmentation and many landlocked countries, urban welfare and economic growth would benefit greatly from policies that promote regional integration. They argue, consistent with *WDR 2009*, that bigger cities have the potential to generate greater economies of scale.

Simulating a merger of 10 African countries, Collier and Venables (2008), cited in UNIDO (2009), conclude that if each country had one city of 10 million, after the merger 6 of the 10 cities would increase in size and thus in productivity. Four cities would shrink, although, depending on the extent of integration, their losses could be compensated through income redistribution.

Collier and Page (UNIDO 2009) conclude that "small low-income countries are at a massive disadvantage with regard to industrialization," but they also acknowledge that the current trend away from vertical integration of industries may make city size less critical. However, other factors, such as an adequate concentration of good-quality infrastructure in a limited physical space, thereby creating what Collier refers to as "islands of protected governance," are critical for encouraging agglomeration economies even in a "sea of corruption."

Sources: UNIDO (2009) and Collier's presentation of the UNIDO report at the World Bank, February 23, 2010.

then, that the one city that concurrently implemented spatially neutral institutions, connective infrastructure, and targeted interventions with success was Singapore, a city-state. And even if lines of authority and responsibility between various levels of government are clarified, national governments must take on more responsibility for financing the urban transformation (Spence, Annez, and Buckley 2009). The task of ensuring that the bright lights of the city are not just an illusion is not purely a technical question but one of political will and public pressure.

Notes

1. Accra Metropolitan Assembly, http://ama.ghanadistricts.gov.gh.
2. The population estimate for Maputo in 2009 was 1.1 million, but because Maputo and Matola are adjacent municipalities, their combined population estimate of over 1.8 million provides a better measure of the size of the metropolitan area.
3. UN-Habitat, http://www.unhabitat.org/content.asp?cid=3294&catid=460& typeid=13&subMenuId=0.
4. The World Bank (2008b) finds that only 15 percent of urban households have any knowledge of how to obtain a land title under the current law.
5. Republic of Uganda, Ministry of Lands, Housing and Urban Development, "Drafting the National Land Policy, Emerging Issues for Discussion," May 2007; cited by Giddings (2009).
6. Ghana's Local Government Act of 1993 charged District Assemblies with ensuring the development of basic infrastructure, the provision of sanitary conditions and education services, and protection of the environment. Since passage of Uganda's 1997 Local Government Act, the Kampala City Council has had responsibility for ensuring economic development and service delivery in the capital, although the recently passed Kampala Capital City Bill has changed the allocation of responsibilities. Also in 1997, Mozambique passed a municipal legislation package that established 33 urban local governments with limited but autonomous powers and democratically elected mayors and assemblies. In accordance with the legislation, Maputo's Municipal Assembly is responsible for land use, basic water and sanitation services, urban roads, solid waste management, and the municipal environment.

References

Adjasi, C. K. D., and K. A. Osei. 2007. "Poverty Profile and Correlates of Poverty in Ghana." *International Journal of Social Economics* 34 (7): 449–71.

Arndt, C., R. James, and K. Simler. 2006. "Has Economic Growth in Mozambique Been Pro-Poor?" *Journal of African Economies* 15 (4): 571–602.

Aryeetey, E., and A. McKay. 2007. "Ghana: The Challenge of Sustained Poverty Reduction." In *Delivering on the Promise of Pro-Poor Growth*, ed. T. Besley and L. Cord. Washington, DC: World Bank and Palgrave Macmillan.

Bryceson, D. 2008. "Creole and Tribal Designs: Dar es Salaam and Kampala as Ethnic Cities in Coalescing Nation States." Crisis States Working Papers Series 2, London School of Economics, U.K.

Buckley, R., and A. Mathema. 2007. "Is Accra a Superstar City?" Policy Research Working Paper 4453, World Bank, Washington, DC.

Collier, P., and A. J. Venables. 2008. "Trade and Economic Performance: Does Africa's Fragmentation Matter?" Paper prepared for the Annual World Bank Conference on Development Economics, Cape Town, South Africa, June 9–11, 2008.

Durand-Lasserve, A., E. Fernandes, G. Payne, and C. Rakodi. 2007. "Social and Economic Impacts of Land Titling Programs in Urban and Peri-Urban Areas: A Review of the Literature." Study funded by the government of Norway following the World Urban Forum in Canada, June 2006.

Elkan, W., and R. van Zwanenberg. 1975. "How People Came to Live in Cities in Colonialism in Africa." In *The Economics of Colonialism*, Vol. 4, ed. P. Duignan and L. H. Gann, 655–72. Cambridge, U.K.: Cambridge University Press.

Fjeldstad, O-H. 2006. "Local Revenue Mobilization in Urban Settings in Africa." CMI Working Papers, Chr. Michelsen Institute, Bergen, Norway. http://www.cmi.no/publications/file/2338-local-revenue-mobilization-in-urban-settings-in.pdf.

Ghana Statistical Service. 2007. "Pattern and Trends of Poverty in Ghana, 1991–2006." Accra.

Giddings, S. 2009. "The Land Market in Kampala and Its Effect on Settlement Patterns." International Housing Coalition, Washington, DC.

Gough, K., and P. Yankson. 2000. "Land Markets in African Cities: The Case of Peri-Urban Accra, Ghana." *Urban Studies* 37 (13): 2485–500.

Grant, R., and P. Yankson. 2003. "City Profile: Accra." *Cities* 20: 65–74.

Grest, J. 2006. "Urban Governance, State Capacity and the Informalization of Urban Management in Maputo: Some Thoughts on Poverty, Informalization and Survival in the City." Notes for "GDRI: Governing Cities in Africa; Law, Local Institutions and Urban Identities since 1945. Regional Workshop: South African Cities," Stellenbosch, South Africa, November 16–17.

Gyimah-Boadi, E. 2004. "The Search for a Developmental Public Service in Ghana: Challenges and Prospects." Paper presented at the Public Services Commission 7th Annual Lecture, Accra, Ghana, May 19.

Jenkins, P. 2000. "Urban Management, Urban Poverty and Urban Governance: Planning and Land Management in Maputo." *Environment and Urbanization* 12 (1): 137–52.

———. 2001. "Strengthening Access to Land for Housing for the Poor in Maputo, Mozambique." *International Journal of Urban and Regional Research* 25 (3): 629–48.

———. 2006. "Image of the City in Mozambique: Civilization, Parasite, Engine of Growth or Place of Opportunity?" In *African Urban Economies: Viability, Vitality or Vitiation?* ed. D. Bryceson and D. Pots. New York: Palgrave Macmillan.

Kessides, C. 2006. *The Urban Transition in Sub-Saharan Africa: Implications for Economic Growth and Poverty Reduction.* Washington, DC: Cities Alliance.

Kilroy, A. 2007. "Intra-Urban Spatial Inequality: Cities as 'Urban Regions.'" Background paper, *World Development Report 2009,* World Bank, Washington, DC.

Malauene, D., A. Chilundo, B. Cau, and M. Mubai. 2005. "Land Registration in Maputo and Matola Cities, Mozambique." International Institute for Environment and Development, London.

Maputo City Council. 2005. "Municipal Score Card Survey Urban Services Provision." Maputo, Uganda.

Maxwell, D., C. Levin, M. Armar-Klemesu, M. Ruel, S. Morris, and C. Ahiadeke. 2000. "Urban Livelihoods and Food and Nutrition Security in Greater Accra, Ghana." Research Report 112, International Food Policy Research Institute, Washington, DC.

Mpagi, C. M., and A. Ssenkabirwa. 2009. "Cabinet Stuck Over Kampala Expansion." *Daily Monitor* (Kampala), July 13. http://www.monitor.co.ug/.

Namutebi, J., and Bekunda, C. 2010. "House Passes Kampala Takeover Bill." *New Vision Online,* 3 Nov. 2010. http://www.newvision.co.ug/D/8/13/736999

Nilsson, D. 2006. "A Heritage of Unsustainability: Reviewing the Origin of the Large Scale Water and Sanitation System in Kampala, Uganda." *Environment and Urbanization* 18 (2): 369–85.

Nuwagaba, A. 2004. "Understanding the Causes of Increased Urban Poverty in Uganda: The Case of Kampala and Mbale." Background paper, World Bank Uganda Poverty Assessment, World Bank, Washington, DC.

Nyakaana, J. B., H. Sengendo, and S. Lwasa. 2005. "Population, Urban Development and the Environment in Uganda, the Case of Kampala City and Its Environs." Makerere University, Kampala, Uganda.

Rulekere, G. 2006. "Land Tenure Policies Complicating Development in Kampala." April 24. http://www.ugpulse.com.

Spence, M., P. Annez, and R. Buckley, eds. 2009. *Urbanization and Growth.* Commission on Growth and Development. Washington, DC: World Bank.

Stren, R., and M. Halfani. 2001. "The Cities of Sub-Saharan Africa: From Dependency to Marginality." In *Handbook of Urban Studies*, ed. R. Paddison, 466–85. London: Sage Publications.

Tuffour, J. A., and J. Apallo. 2005. "Inequality and Social Welfare in Ghana in the 1990s." Working paper 2005-01, Department of Economics, St. Francis Xavier University, Nova Scotia, Canada.

UNDESA (United Nations Department of Economic and Social Affairs). 2008. *World Population Policies 2007.* New York: UNDESA. http://www.un.org/esa/population/publications/wpp2007/Publicationindex.htm.

UN-Habitat. 2002. *Expert Group Meeting on Urban Indicators, Secure Tenure, Slums and Global Sample of Cities.* Nairobi: United Nations Human Settlements Programme. Urban Secretariat and Shelter Branch in close collaboration with United Nations Statistic Division and the Cities Alliances. http://www.citiesalliance.org/ca/sites/citiesalliance.org/files/expert-group-meeting-urban-indicators%5B1%5D.pdf.

———. 2008. *State of the World's Cities 2008/9: Harmonious Cities.* Nairobi: United Nations Human Settlements Programme.

———. 2009. *Ghana: Accra Urban Profile.* Nairobi: United Nations Human Settlements Programme.

UNIDO (United Nations Industrial Development Organization). 2009. *Industrial Development Report 2009. Breaking In and Moving Up: New Industrial Challenges for the Bottom Billion and the Middle-Income Countries.* Vienna: UNIDO.

United Cities and Local Governments. 2007. *Decentralization and Local Democracy in the World. First Global Report.* Barcelona: United Cities and Local Governments.

United Nations. 2010. *World Urbanization Prospects: The 2009 Revision.* Department of Economic and Social Affairs, Population Division. New York: United Nations.

World Bank. 2002. *Upgrading Low Income Settlements, Country Assessment Report Ghana.* Washington, DC: World Bank.

———. 2006. "Program Appraisal Document on a Proposed Credit in the Amount of SDR 20 Million (USD 30 Million Equivalent) to the Republic of Mozambique for ProMaputo: The Maputo Municipal Development Program." Report 37530-MZ, World Bank, Washington, DC.

———. 2007a. "Ghana Meeting the Challenge of Accelerated and Shared Growth: Country Economic Memorandum." Report 40934-GH, World Bank, Washington, DC.

———. 2007b. "Republic of Ghana Urban Development and Economic Growth." World Bank, Washington, DC.

———. 2008a. "Africa's Urbanization for Development: Understanding Africa's Urban Challenges and Opportunities." Working Paper 45298, World Bank, Washington, DC.

———. 2008b. "Beating the Odds: Sustaining Inclusion in a Growing Economy. A Mozambique Poverty, Gender and Social Assessment." Report 40048-MZ, World Bank, Washington, DC.

———. 2008c. *World Development Report 2009: Reshaping Economic Geography.* Washington, DC: World Bank.

———. 2009. "Uganda: Legal and Judicial Sector Study Report. Legal Vice Presidency." Report 49701, World Bank, Washington, DC.

PART II

Managing the Rural-Urban Transformation: Examples from South Asia

CHAPTER 5

Pathways Out of Poverty: Managing the Rural-Urban Transformation in South Asia

Rural areas are home to three-quarters of the poor in developing countries, and most of the rural poor are directly or indirectly dependent on agriculture for their livelihood.[1] Lifting this mass of people out of poverty will entail two interrelated processes: (1) shifting employment from agriculture, where labor productivity tends to be low, to the higher-productivity nonagriculture sectors; and (2) increasing the concentration of people and economic activities in urban areas. Not surprisingly, as described in the overview and chapter 1 to this report, policy challenges for managing these two transformation processes were at the center of the 2008 and 2009 editions of the *World Development Report (WDR)*.

World Development Report 2008: Agriculture for Development places agricultural growth and transformation of the rural economy at the heart of a strategy for inclusive economic development (World Bank 2007). *World Development Report 2009: Reshaping Economic Geography* considers the challenges of transformation at three different geographical levels: urbanization at the local level, rural-urban disparities at the national level, and regional integration at the international level (World Bank 2008). Both *World Development Reports* note that the process of rural-urban transformation is geographically uneven.

Part II of this report sheds further light on the texture of transformation in five countries in South Asia: Bangladesh, India, Nepal, Pakistan, and Sri Lanka. Each of these countries is at a different stage in the transformation process. Of the five, only Nepal is still a predominantly agricultural country where urbanization is at an incipient stage. The other four countries are "transforming" or "urbanizing," although, as indicated by the *WDR 2009* agglomeration index, urbanization levels are much higher in India and Pakistan than in Sri Lanka and Bangladesh. Intracountry differences are even more striking. For example, the Kathmandu Valley in Nepal is nearly fully urbanized, with a poverty incidence of 3.4 percent. By contrast, the eastern hill region of Nepal is almost entirely dependent on agriculture and has a poverty incidence of 43 percent. The interdependence of rural and urban transformation is acknowledged in both *WDRs*. But the reports tend to put greater emphasis on the impact of urbanization on rural development ("neighborhood effects" in the parlance of *WDR 2009*) than on the impact of rural policies and institutions on urban development. In practice, urbanization depends on the flow of goods, capital, and people from rural areas. Interventions in rural, lagging, or agricultural spaces can create significant distortions and spillovers in urban, leading, or nonagricultural spaces, and vice versa. The chapters that follow thus aim to explore how the rural-urban transformation process is shaped by the policies, institutions, and initial conditions *across space*. Among other things, we consider the extent of distortions and spillovers between rural and urban areas. For example, how do agrarian institutions such as land laws shape the rural-urban transformation process? How does proximity to urban centers affect nonfarm rural activities? And what are the push and pull factors shaping migration decisions?

Much of part II of this report is structured around country-level case studies for three reasons. First, because of the high degree of intracountry differences just noted and documented in much greater detail in chapter 6, the country is the most appropriate unit of analysis. Second, as shown in the *WDRs*, a country's stage of rural-urban transformation is determined by a complex interaction of history, policies, and institutions. A case study approach enables us to investigate the specific policies and institutions that matter in a particular country context—land laws, for example, may be a binding constraint in one country, whereas in another, uneven infrastructure and services may be the most pertinent issue. Third, data availability is inevitably an important consideration in selecting case study topics.

The case studies demonstrate how the various policies and institutions in countries in South Asia have led to differences in the level and pace of rural-urban transformation. For example, relative to that of other countries in the region, the provision of infrastructure in Nepal remains weak, in part because of the terrain. As a result, for most of the Nepalese the nearest urban center with a population of 100,000 or more is on average more than eight hours away, limiting the mobility of workers from rural to urban areas. By contrast, Sri Lanka has historically pursued a policy of equitable provision of infrastructure that should have aided the mobility of labor. And yet, because of restrictions on agricultural land transactions in Sri Lanka, relative to that of some East and South Asian countries (such as India and the Republic of Korea), the pace of transformation from an agriculture-based economy to a nonagriculture-based one has been rather slow.

This part of the report is organized as follows. Chapter 6 provides country-level diagnostics that document sectoral employment and the income pattern across the five countries. The distribution of economic activities is then paired with information on population density and poverty to identify the stages of urbanization and geographic transformation. Chapter 7 identifies some of the principal institutional and policy constraints affecting the rural-urban transformation in South Asia, including economic policies, factor markets, access to social services, and infrastructure development.

Chapters 8–10 focus on specific country cases. Chapter 8 considers the effects of unequal land distribution in Pakistan and the land market restrictions on rural-urban transitions in Sri Lanka. Chapter 9 looks at two aspects of rural-urban transformation drawn from case studies of Bangladesh: (1) the impact of infrastructure and urban access on shifts from agricultural to nonagricultural employment in rural areas; and (2) the role of agglomeration economies, amenities, and infrastructure in the location choice of manufacturing firms. Chapter 10 concludes this part by shedding some light on the role of infrastructure, amenities, and income in determining the flow of migrants across regions of Nepal.

Chapter 11 summarizes both parts of this report, including the key findings from case studies, and draws some policy lessons.

Note

1. Part II of this report was produced by a team led by Forhad Shilpi and composed of Brian Blankespoor, Toru Nishiuchi, Daan Struyven, Dana

Thomson, Emily Schmidt, Wei Xiao, and Haomiao Yu. It was prepared under the supervision of Marisela Montoliu Munoz. Katy Hull edited an earlier version of this part of the report.

References

World Bank. 2007. *World Development Report 2008: Agriculture for Development.* Washington, DC: World Bank.

———. 2008. *World Development Report 2009: Reshaping Economic Geography.* Washington, DC: World Bank.

CHAPTER 6

Patterns of Rural-Urban Transformation in South Asia

Despite considerable achievement in poverty reduction during the last decade, the differences in living standards across regions, and across rural and urban areas, remain substantial in South Asian countries. The widening gaps in living standards have increased social and political tensions. Managing the rural-urban transformation to ensure more inclusive economic development has thus become an important consideration among policy makers in South Asian countries.

As discussed at the outset of this report, the 2008 and 2009 editions of the *World Development Report* categorize countries (or areas) according to their stage of sectoral or geographical transformation (World Bank 2007, 2008). The typologies in *WDR 2008*—"agriculture-based," "transforming," and "urbanized"—are predicated on the contribution of agriculture to economic growth and the percentage of the poor residing in rural areas. The typologies in *WDR 2009*—"1-D," "2-D," and "3-D"—are based on measures of economic "density," the "distance" of the poor from areas of economic density, and the presence of "divisions."

In this chapter, we employ similar typologies to assess patterns of rural-urban transformation in South Asia. We begin by examining the extent to which the poor are located in economically lagging or rural areas and the relative contribution of agriculture to economic growth and employment.

We then consider various measures of urbanization in each country before addressing the contribution of nonfarm activities (whether urban or rural) to growth and poverty reduction.

Poverty Incidence and Geographical Distribution

The South Asian region is home to 1.4 billion people, 72 percent of whom reside in rural areas. Of the half-billion poor, about 389 million (75 percent of the total) live in rural areas. But living standards vary widely across countries. The per capita gross domestic product of Sri Lanka ($1,074) is almost four and a half times higher than that of Nepal ($243)—see table 6.1.[1] In Bangladesh, the consumption of 40 percent of the population falls below the official poverty line; in Sri Lanka, almost 85 percent of the population lives above the poverty line.[2]

Most of the South Asian countries saw substantial growth in their GDP from 1998 to 2007 (table 6.1). The annual average GDP growth between 1998 and 2007 was the highest in India (7.2 percent) and lowest in Nepal (3.6 percent). The slower population growth during this period translated into healthy growth in per capita income in India and Sri Lanka (higher than 4 percent). The income growth was associated with a substantial reduction in the incidence of poverty, but in many cases an increase in inequality as well. Thus almost all of the South Asian countries experienced a nearly 10 percentage point or more decline in the poverty headcount ratio during the last decade, but the Gini coefficient of distribution of per capita consumption expenditure increased considerably in India (from 0.29 in 1993 to 0.35 in 2005), Sri Lanka (from 0.32 in 1991 to 0.40 in 2006), and Nepal (from 0.34 in 1995 to 0.41 in 2003).

Table 6.1   Poverty, Inequality, and Economic Growth, South Asia

	GDP per capita (constant 2000 US$, 2006)	Annual average growth, 1998–2007 (%)		Poverty headcount ratio (%)	Gini coefficient of per capita consumption expenditure
		GDP	Per capita income		
Bangladesh	419	5.7	3.7	40.0 (2005)	0.31 (2005)
India	637	7.2	5.6	27.5 (2005)	0.35 (2005)
Nepal	243	3.6	1.5	30.9 (2003)	0.41 (2003)
Pakistan	630	5.1	2.7	29.2 (2004)	0.30 (2004)
Sri Lanka	1,074	5.0	4.3	15.2 (2006)	0.40 (2006)

Sources: World Bank Development Data Platform (DDP), http://go.worldbank.org/DNBRRS9TB0, and various poverty assessments.

Intracountry differences in living standards are even more striking. Figure 6.1 plots the poverty headcount ratios for the leading and lagging regions within Bangladesh, Nepal, Pakistan, and Sri Lanka. The leading regions are Western Province in Sri Lanka, Sindh in Pakistan, Kathmandu in Nepal, and the eastern region in Bangladesh. The lagging regions are Uva Province in Sri Lanka, Balochistan in Pakistan, the rural eastern hills in Nepal, and the western region in Bangladesh. According to the estimates for 2007, the incidence of poverty in Western Province of Sri Lanka was only 8 percent compared with 27 percent in Uva Province. In Nepal, the estimates of headcount ratios for 2004 show even starker differences: only 3.3 percent in the capital city, Kathmandu, but 42.9 percent in the rural eastern hills. Box 6.1 describes the location of the poor relative to areas of economic density in each of the countries.

Contribution of Agriculture to Growth and Employment

In the South Asian region as a whole, agriculture remains the most important employer of the labor force. Even in Sri Lanka, the least poor country in the region, agriculture accounts for 34 percent of total employment (table 6.2). The importance of agriculture is much greater in Nepal, where it employs more than 90 percent of the labor force. Consistent with its contribution to employment, agricultural growth

Figure 6.1   Poverty Headcount Ratio in Lagging and Leading Regions, South Asia

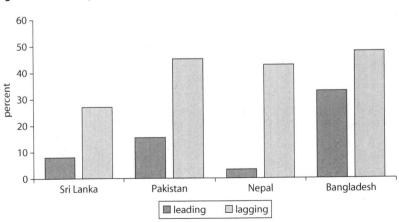

Source: World Bank staff estimates based on latest poverty assessments.
Note: For years from which data were taken, see table 6.1.

Box 6.1

Economic Density versus Density of the Poor

Comparisons of the locations of areas of high economic density with areas of high density of the poor reveal three patterns.

First, and not surprising, economic activities are much denser in urban areas than in rural areas. Although urban poverty rates are lower, higher population density implies that the number of poor can be large in the more urbanized areas. These areas include Western Province in Sri Lanka, Punjab in Pakistan, the eastern region of Bangladesh, the Kathmandu Valley in Nepal, and the western region of Uttar Pradesh, India.

Second, countries have remote regions with a high density of the poor. These regions include the western part of Bangladesh, Central Province of Sri Lanka, the eastern part of Nepal, and a large part of India such as Bihar, Orissa, and part of Uttar Pradesh. Some of these regions are also home to ethnic minorities and a large share of the lower castes, who face considerable barriers to moving.

Third, some relatively isolated areas have a higher incidence of poverty than less isolated areas, but are sparsely populated. These areas include Balochistan in Pakistan, the far western region in Nepal, Uva Province in Sri Lanka, and tribal areas in India.

Table 6.2   Selected Indicators for Contribution of Agriculture to Economy and Rural Poverty, South Asia

	Share of agriculture in		Contribution of agriculture to GDP growth (%, 1992–2001)	Rural poverty headcount ratio (%)	Share of poor in rural areas (%)
	GDP (%, 2006)	Employment (%, 2006)			
Bangladesh	20	51	13.3	43.8 (2005)	82.2
India	18	60	9.6	28.1 (2005)	73.7
Nepal	35	93	32.1	34.6 (2003)	95.3
Pakistan	20	45	12.0	20.6 (2008)	80.0
Sri Lanka	12	34	7.1	15.7 (2006)	79.2

Sources: World Bank Development Data Platform (DDP), http://go.worldbank.org/DNBRRS9TB0, and various poverty assessments.

had the strongest poverty-reducing effect in India from 1960 to 1990 (Ravallion and Datt 1996).

But the role of agriculture in GDP is diminishing (table 6.2). Its contribution to economic growth is greatest in Nepal, accounting for 35 percent of GDP in 2006. During the same period, its contribution was (close to) 20 percent in Bangladesh, India, and Pakistan, but only 12 percent in Sri Lanka. The average annual growth in agriculture in these countries was just above 2.5 percent compared with more than 5 percent growth in overall GDP. In India, Bangladesh, and Sri Lanka, the contribution of agriculture to overall GDP growth has declined (figure 6.2). During the 1980s, agriculture's contribution to growth was about 20 percent in two of the five countries—India and Nepal. Therefore, in the 1980s these two countries would have fit into the *WDR 2008* category "agriculture-based." Since 2001, only Nepal, where agriculture has contributed more than 30 percent to GDP growth, still qualifies as an agriculture-based economy. The other countries in the region are best described as "transforming."

In all of the South Asian countries, the incidence of poverty is much higher in rural areas than in urban areas. For example, in Nepal in 2003 the incidence of poverty in rural areas was three and a half times as high as that in urban areas—34.6 percent and 9.6 percent, respectively (tables 6.2 and 6.3). The rural-urban gap is small only in India, where there is a 2.3 percentage point difference between rural and urban poverty. As is typical in both agriculture-based and transforming economies, the majority of the poor still lives in rural areas in all five countries. The share of rural poor in total poor ranges from 74 percent in India to 95 percent in Nepal.

Figure 6.2   Contribution of Agriculture to GDP Growth, South Asia

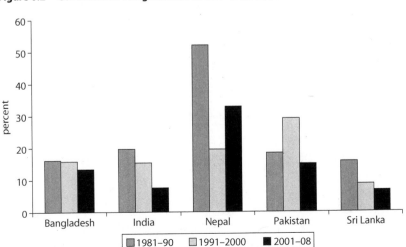

Source: World Bank Development Data Platform (DDP), http://go.worldbank.org/DNBRRS9TB0.

Table 6.3   Selected Urbanization Indicators, South Asia

	Population density per km² (2006)	% of population in urban areas (2006)	Agglomeration index (%, 2000)	Annual growth in urban population (%)	Poverty incidence in urban areas
Bangladesh	1,198	25	48.0	3.5 (1995–2005)	28.4 (2005)
India	378	28	52.4	2.6 (1993–2000)	25.8 (2005)
Nepal	198	15	26.0	6.5 (1995–2003)	9.6 (2003)
Pakistan	206	34	53.6	3.1 (1998–2004)	10.1 (2008)
Sri Lanka	310	38	38.2	1.1 (1995–2006)	6.7 (2006)

Sources: World Bank Development Data Platform (DDP), http://go.worldbank.org/DNBRRS9TB0; World Bank 2008; and various poverty assessments.

Intracountry differences in employment structure and poverty incidence reveal that even within a transforming country, some regions have agriculture-based economies. The intracountry differences in employment and income structure, like those for living standards, are starker than cross-country differences. For example, in Western Province of Sri Lanka, less than 10 percent of the economically active population is employed in agriculture (figure 6.3). Outside Western Province, agriculture accounts for at least one-third of total employment, with its share rising as high as 66 percent in Uva Province, the poorest, where agriculture accounts for 44 percent of the province's GDP. These patterns hold true in other countries as well. For example, in Nepal 81 percent of the labor force is employed in agriculture in the rural eastern hills compared with 21 percent in the urban Kathmandu Valley.

Urbanization, Nonagricultural Activities, and the Rural-Urban Transformation

Level of urbanization is a key factor in determining the urbanization strategy for development. Historically, the Gangetic floodplains have supported a high-density population. A great number of urban centers—both large and small—are located in these floodplains and in the coastal areas. Among South Asian countries, India alone has 27 cities with a population of more than 1 million and 3,700 smaller cities and towns.[3] Bangladesh, another country located in the Gangetic plain, has three cities with a population of more than 1 million and 154 smaller cities and towns.

The urban populations of all South Asian countries have experienced considerable growth during the last decade (table 6.3). The highest

Figure 6.3   Agriculture's Contribution to GDP and Employment, Sri Lanka

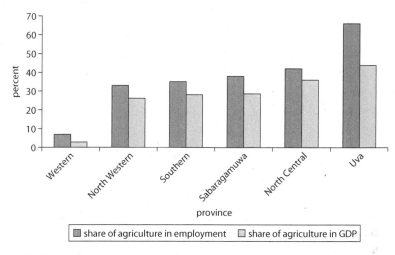

Source: World Bank staff estimate based on Household Income and Expenditure Survey, 2002.

growth took place in Nepal (6.5 percent), followed by Bangladesh (3.5 percent), and Pakistan (3.1 percent). These urban growth rates exceeded overall population growth rates (2.0 percent in Bangladesh, 2.3 percent in Nepal, 2.2 percent in Pakistan, and 0.8 percent in Sri Lanka). The urbanization rate computed from national statistics—which, of course, vary from country to country—ranges from 35 percent in Pakistan and Sri Lanka to 15 percent in Nepal.

Because the national definition of *urban area* varies from country to country, the comparative measure provided by the agglomeration index in *WDR 2009* is useful. The index measures level of urbanization based on the density of population and distance to centers of human settlement of 50,000 or more.[4] According to this index, the urban share of population is 48 percent in Bangladesh, 52 percent in India, and 54 percent in Pakistan. In Nepal, only about 26 percent of population can be regarded as living in urban-like settlements. Both national statistics on urbanization and the agglomeration index suggest that Bangladesh, India, Pakistan, and Sri Lanka are rapidly urbanizing. In Nepal, urbanization is incipient. That said, the level of urbanization in any of the five countries is subject to considerable variations. Although overall urbanization is incipient in Nepal, some of its regions are urbanizing rapidly. In the central hill region, which includes the Kathmandu Valley, the urban share of population is about 40 percent, and Kathmandu Valley itself is almost fully urbanized. In Pakistan, one of the most urbanized countries in South Asia, the urban share of population is only about 13 percent in the northwestern frontier province.

The contribution of urbanization to economic growth cannot be discerned precisely because GDP is reported by sector, not location, and a large portion of nonfarm activities are located outside urban areas. But recent World Bank poverty assessments indicate substantial growth in consumption in urban areas. As noted, the incidence of poverty is lower in urban areas than in rural areas in all South Asian countries. The poverty trends during the last decades indicate a larger decline in urban poverty than in rural poverty in all countries except India, where the rural-urban gap was small initially. In Nepal, urban poverty declined by 52 percent (from 21.6 to 9.6 percent) between 1995–96 and 2003; rural poverty declined by 21 percent over the same time period. Similar patterns are found in Bangladesh, Pakistan, and Sri Lanka.

In recent decades, urbanization has been found to reduce poverty in rural areas as well. Cali and Menon (2009) report that urbanization had a strong, robust effect on rural poverty reduction in post-1991 India. This poverty-reducing effect of urbanization remains significant even after controlling for rural-to-urban migration and reclassification of rural areas. The World Bank's 2009 poverty assessment of India finds the linkage between urban growth and rural poverty reduction to be strongest for smaller cities and towns. For Bangladesh, Shilpi (2008) finds a stronger spillover of urban growth to poverty reduction in surrounding rural areas.

Rural Nonfarm Activities and the Rural-Urban Transformation

Because GDP growth is reported by sector, not location, it is not possible to provide a precise breakdown of the relative contribution of nonagricultural activities to growth in urban and rural areas. Growth in nonfarm activities in urban areas appears to have made a significant contribution to overall growth in those areas, and rural areas have also undergone a sectoral shift from farm to nonfarm activities. The contributions of rural nonfarm activities to rural employment and household income are significant (figure 6.4), ranging from about a third in Nepal and Pakistan to more than half in Sri Lanka and Bangladesh.[5] The larger contribution of nonfarm activities to income relative to employment in most countries suggests that, on average, these activities provide a higher labor return than farming. For example, in Bangladesh the incidence of poverty is lower

Figure 6.4   Contribution of Rural Nonfarm Sectors to Rural Income and Employment, South Asia

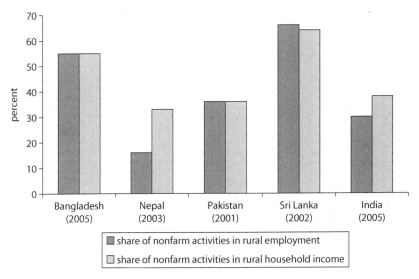

Source: Various poverty assessments.

among rural households with access to nonfarm employment than those depending purely on agriculture (World Bank 2004). For India, Foster and Rosenzweig (2003) report that growth in nonfarm activities in rural areas reduced inequality significantly, and the impact of nonfarm employment growth on poverty reduction was larger than that of agricultural productivity growth.

According to employment data, a large fraction of nonfarm activities are located in rural areas. For example, in Pakistan the share of rural areas in total employment is 50 percent in the manufacturing sector and 47 percent in the service sector. The share of rural areas in total nonagricultural employment is much higher in Bangladesh, about 66 percent. Even in a predominantly agricultural country—Nepal—more than half of those employed in nonfarm activities live in rural areas.

Conclusion

The evidence from South Asian countries demonstrates clearly that countries are at different stages of the rural-urban transformation. There are substantial differences in the level and pace of urbanization, in agriculture's contribution to growth and employment, and in the importance of the rural nonfarm sector in income and employment generation. Despite these differences, Bangladesh, India, Pakistan, and Sri Lanka can be grouped broadly as transforming and rapidly urbanizing countries. Nepal remains the only country in which agriculture is still the mainstay of the economy and urbanization is at the incipient stage.

Intracountry differences in the pattern of rural-urban transformation are, however, much starker than cross-country differences. Within each country, regions range from agriculture based to highly urbanized. In terms of distribution of the poor and of economic density, and the presence of barriers to mobility, regions in these countries fit all combinations of density, distance, and division suggested by *WDR 2009*. The presence of such differences implies a need for examining the challenges of rural-urban transformation on a much finer geographical scale.

The large intracountry variations in the pattern of rural-urban transformation are somewhat surprising. As *WDR 2009* observes, divisions and distances within a country are likely to be smaller than those at the international level because of the presence of national borders, currencies, and macroeconomic policies. But this is not true for most South Asian countries. However, both *WDRs* also emphasize that observed patterns of economic transformation are outcomes of underlying policies, institutions, and initial conditions. In the next chapter, we explore both the intra- and intercountry differences in policies, institutions, and initial conditions.

Notes

1. At purchasing power parity, the per capita GDP is $1,340 in Bangladesh, $2,740 in India, $1,040 in Nepal, $2,570 in Pakistan, and $4,210 in Sri Lanka.

2. At a $1.25 per day poverty line, the incidence of poverty is 50 percent in Bangladesh (2005), 44 percent in rural India and 36 percent in urban India (2004), 55 percent in Nepal (2003), 22 percent in Pakistan (2004), and 14 percent in Sri Lanka (2002).

3. Census of India, 2001. http://censusindia.gov.in.

4. The population density has to be at least 150 persons per square kilometer, and distance has to be less than or equal to one hour of travel time from the center of a city or town of at least 50,000 people.

5. Because the definitions of *rural area* and *urban area* are different across countries, the shares of nonfarm sectors in employment and income are not strictly comparable across countries.

References

Cali, M., and Carlo M. 2009. "Does Urbanisation Affect Rural Poverty? Evidence from Indian Districts." Spatial Economics Research Centre Discussion Paper 14, London School of Economics, U.K.

Foster, A., and M. Rosenzweig. 2003. "Agricultural Development, Industrialization and Rural Inequality," Brown University, Providence, RI.

Ravallion, M., and G. Datt. 1996. "How Important to India's Poor Is the Sectoral Composition of Economic Growth?" *World Bank Economic Review* 10 (1): 1–25.

Ravallion, M., and D. van de Walle. 2008. "Does Rising Landlessness Signal Success or Failure for Vietnam's Agrarian Transition?" *Journal of Development Economics* 87 (2): 191–209.

Shilpi, F. 2008. "Migration, Sorting and Regional Inequality: Evidence from Bangladesh." Policy Research Working Paper 4616, World Bank, Washington, DC.

World Bank. 2004. *Bangladesh: Promoting the Non-Farm Sector in Bangladesh.* Report 29719-BD, World Bank, Washington, DC.

———. 2007. *World Development Report 2008: Agriculture for Development.* Washington, DC: World Bank.

———. 2008. *World Development Report 2009: Reshaping Economic Geography.* Washington, DC: World Bank.

CHAPTER 7

Policies, Institutions, and Initial Conditions

As shown in chapter 6, South Asian countries are at different stages of the rural-urban transformation. The key indicators of transformation—such as the incidence and geographical distribution of poverty, the contribution of agriculture to employment and income, and levels of urbanization—vary considerably within and across countries. As argued in the 2008 and 2009 editions of the *World Development Report*, rural-urban transformations are influenced by policies and institutions (World Bank 2007, 2008b). Although any policy could conceivably affect transformation, in this chapter we focus on the major levers identified by the *WDR*s: economic policies, land and labor market institutions, investments in human capital in the form of health and education policies, and investments in physical capital in the form of connective infrastructure.

Economic Policies

During the decades after their independence, South Asian countries implemented distortive trade and exchange rate policies. Although economic reforms in subsequent decades reduced distortions, liberalization progressed at an uneven pace across countries. Sri Lanka led the way, implementing major trade and exchange rate reforms as early as 1977.

India, by contrast, lagged behind until a balance-of-payments crisis kick-started a wave of reform in 1991. Bangladesh, Nepal, and Pakistan also liberalized their economies during the early 1990s. The liberalization packages typically included a reduction in, or even the elimination of, quantitative restrictions on trade, a reduction in tariff rates and simplification of tariff structures, and rationalization of exchange rate regimes. As shown in figure 7.1, the average tariff rates in Bangladesh, India, and Pakistan were between 47 and 56 percent during the early 1990s; by 2006 the rate had fallen to 15 percent or below in all South Asian countries.

In almost every country in South Asia, reforms in the agriculture sector lagged far behind monetary and trade policy reforms. Agricultural policies in South Asian countries have been shaped by the desire to ensure food self-sufficiency, resulting in trade restrictions, price support, generous input subsidies, and public investments in irrigation and research and extension systems. Figure 7.2 presents the average tariff on agricultural products in each country. The average tariff rate protecting the agriculture sector in India in 2004–05 was about 40 percent—almost four times the level of India's average industrial tariff and among the highest in the world. A comparison of figures 7.1 and 7.2 reveals a similar skew toward agricultural tariffs for Bangladesh and Sri Lanka.

Figure 7.1   Average Tariff Rate (Unweighted), South Asia

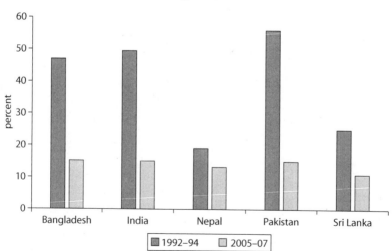

Source: United Nations Conference on Trade and Development (UNCTAD) TRAINS database.

Figure 7.2   Average Tariff Rate on Agricultural Products, South Asia

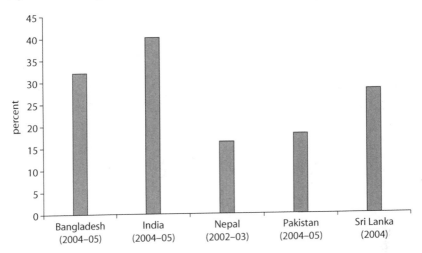

Source: Anderson and Martin 2009.

In addition to tariff protection, India and Sri Lanka have provided agricultural subsidies for power and fertilizers, among other investment and subsidy schemes. In India, the total subsidies were estimated to be about $7.8 billion in 2004, with much of it in the form of electricity subsidies for rice and wheat crops (Pursell, Gulati, and Gupta 2007). In 2006, fertilizer subsidies in Sri Lanka were doubled from about $40 million to $80 million, and they rose even further after the world price spike in 2007.

Recent estimates of the nominal rate of assistance (NRA) to farmers demonstrate the extent of total agricultural support (Anderson and Martin 2009). During the early 1990s, the NRA was negative in Bangladesh, Pakistan, and Sri Lanka, signifying implicit taxation of farmers' incomes (figure 7.3). By the early 2000s, the NRA had become positive in all three countries and substantial in India (15.8 percent) and Sri Lanka (9.5 percent). These levels of NRA would translate into a subsidy per farmer of $4 in Pakistan, $5 in Bangladesh, $40 in Sri Lanka, and $57 in India.

The implicit subsidization of agriculture in recent years has protected farmers' incomes in India and Sri Lanka. But subsidization has also come with a cost. Most of the subsidies went to two subsistence crops—rice and wheat—which deterred farmers from diversifying into high-value crops such as fruits, vegetables, and livestock products. High spending on

Figure 7.3   Nominal Rate of Assistance, South Asia

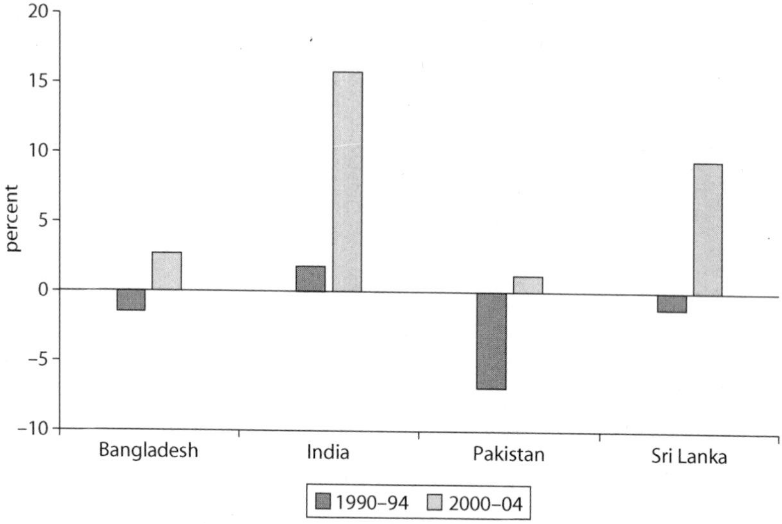

Source: Anderson and Martin 2009.

subsidies has also been at the expense of investments in other rural infrastructure such as roads (World Bank 2006).

Factor Markets: Land and Labor

Land market institutions can have far-reaching effects on the rural-urban transformation by altering incentives to invest or to move from rural to urban areas. Even though all countries in South Asia have instigated some form of land reform, the pace of implementation has been uneven. India has been a leader, particularly in the area of tenancy reform. By contrast, Pakistan has not yet dealt with its feudal landownership system in some provinces such as Sindh.

Government interventions have focused on three main areas of the land markets. First, ceiling legislation has been a common feature of land reform in almost all South Asian countries. This legislation allows governments (and states in India) to expropriate land held by private owners in excess of ceilings and to transfer it to poor farmers and landless agricultural workers. Ceilings vary from country to country and across states in India—from 15 acres in the Indian state of Tamil Nadu and about 20 acres in Bangladesh to 500 acres of irrigated (and 1,000 acres of unirrigated) land in Pakistan. But in spite of de jure ceilings, implementation has been slow in all countries, with the practice of subdivision enabling landowners to avoid expropriation. As a result, substantial inequality in the distribution of landownership remains, particularly in Pakistan. *WDR 2008* estimates the Gini coefficient of landownership distribution to be 0.61 in Pakistan, 0.48 in Bangladesh, and 0.45 in India (World Bank 2007).

Second, almost all countries have tenancy legislation aimed at improving tenure security and limiting rents. Legal provisions differ across countries (and states in India) in terms of conditions for permitting tenancy, the maximum rent ceilings, and the types of property rights awarded to tenants. But the actual implementation of tenancy laws has been slow and weak in most counties, with the exception of some states in India such as West Bengal. Many landlords were able to evict tenants in anticipation of the laws coming in effect, and even long-term tenants remain vulnerable to eviction despite the legislation. When effectively enforced, however, such as in West Bengal, tenancy laws have significant positive effects on farm productivity (Banerjee, Gertler, and Ghatak 2002).

Third, governments in South Asian countries have also intervened in the land sales markets, restricting the sale and subdivision of land. For example, in Sri Lanka large tracts of land came under government ownership after enactment of the Crown Lands Encroachment Ordinance, and these were subsequently distributed to landless farmers under the Land Development Ordinance (LDO). Recipients of LDO land have the right to occupy and cultivate the land in perpetuity, subject to restrictions imposed on sale, leasing, and mortgaging, and to conditions related to abandoning or failing to cultivate the land. In India, the government maintains laws that restrict the sale of land from tribals to nontribals, and some states impose subdivision restrictions to prevent fragmentation of holdings below a minimum size. Sri Lanka and some Indian states have also imposed restrictions on the conversion of agricultural land to nonagricultural use, even at the urban periphery.

Labor market institutions can have major effects on rural-urban transformations through their impacts on job creation, firm size, and sectoral transformation, among other factors. In most South Asian countries, labor market regulations apply primarily to the larger formal sector firms (for example, those in India having more than 20 workers and those in Bangladesh having 10). The regulations typically stipulate the minimum hours of work, minimum wages, the right of association, and safety and health standards. All countries also have rules for termination of workers and dispute resolution. In India, no less than 45 central laws and 170 state statutes deal with labor market issues ranging from industrial relations to social security and insurance. In Sri Lanka, the Termination of Employment Act makes it virtually impossible to fire workers who have been employed for more than six months for reasons other than serious and well-documented disciplinary problems. In India, terminations have to be approved by the state authority. The cost of firing is highest in Sri Lanka, worth about 178 weeks of salary (figure 7.4). Compared with the difficulty of firing, the hiring of workers presents few or no problems in Bangladesh, India, and Sri Lanka. By contrast, the difficulties of hiring and firing are almost equally large in Nepal and Pakistan.

Because labor regulations tend to "bite" only in the larger formal sector firms, their impact is uneven across sectors. Of all countries in the region, India has been best documented. There, regulations have caused the loss of 30–40 percent of formal manufacturing jobs (Ahsan and Pages 2007). According to Besley and Burgess (2004), amendments of the Industrial Disputes Act in a pro-worker direction lowered output, employment, investment, and productivity in formal manufacturing firms and increased urban poverty. Aghion, Burgess, and Redding (2008) find there was higher output growth in pro-employer states than in pro-worker states after deregulation of License Raj in India in 1991. Ahsan and Pages (2007) report that an increase in redundancy cost increases

Figure 7.4   Difficulty of Hiring and Redundancy Costs, South Asia

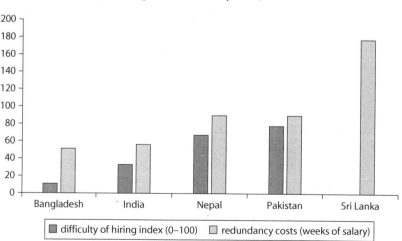

Source: Doing Business database, http://www.doingbusiness.org/; World Bank (2007).

salaries for employed workers, but lowers employment, output, and investment, and increases the share of informal work. The higher cost of labor disputes reduces salaries for employed workers, and also leads to lower employment, lower output, lower investment, and a higher share of informal work. These regulations, by dissuading firms from taking advantage of economies of scale, may have slowed down the transition from farm to nonfarm jobs and from informal to formal jobs.

Human Capital Endowments

Human capital endowments are important determinants of urbanization and economic growth. Examples are the health and education status of South Asian countries (table 7.1). The cross-country differences in health indicators are quite substantial. Sri Lanka ranks highest in per capita health care expenditure, access to improved sanitation, and infant survival rates, among other measures of health. The per capita health care expenditure is lowest in Bangladesh. The number of physicians to the population varies between 1 to 5,000 persons in Nepal to 1 to 1,400 in Pakistan. In Bangladesh, India, and Nepal, less than 30 percent of the population has access to improved sanitation facilities. As a result of these disparities in health care inputs, life expectancy varies between 65.7 years in Bangladesh and 74.0 years in Sri Lanka. Cross-country differences in infant mortality rates are even more striking. The probability of an infant dying at birth is more than six times higher in Pakistan (7.8 percent) than in Sri Lanka (1.2 percent).

In education, gender differences in gross enrollment rates have been eliminated in all countries except Pakistan, where women remain at a significant disadvantage. Bangladesh lags behind India and Sri Lanka in terms of average years of schooling (8 years in Bangladesh versus 10 in India), primary school completion rates (56.3 percent in Bangladesh versus 96.2 percent in Sri Lanka), and adult literacy (53.5 percent in Bangladesh versus 90.8 percent in Sri Lanka). Indeed, adult literacy remains a challenge in all countries except Sri Lanka, with almost half of all adults in Nepal and Pakistan and one-third in India classified as illiterate. But even in Sri Lanka, challenges remain. Two-thirds of primary school graduates in Sri Lanka lack basic language and math skills (World Bank 2006).

Intracountry differences in access to schools and health facilities are somewhat less striking. In Nepal, a country with difficult terrain, a typical rural household lives within 15 minutes of a school and half an hour

Table 7.1   Selected Human Development Indicators, South Asia

	Year	Bangladesh	India	Nepal	Pakistan	Sri Lanka
Health indicator						
Physicians (per 1,000 persons)	2004	0.26	0.60	0.21	0.74	0.55
Health expenditure, total (% of GDP)	2006	3.2	3.6	5.1	2.0	4.2
Health expenditure per capita (current US$)	2006	12	29	17	16	62
Access to improved sanitation (% population)	2006	36	28	27	58	86
Life expectancy (years)	2007	65.7	63.4	66.3	66.2	74
Infant mortality (per 1,000 live births)	2006	52	57	46	78	12
Education indicator						
Expected years of schooling	2006	8.0	10.0	8.9	6.5	—
Gross enrollment (% of school-age population)	2006[a]	103	112	126	84	108
Gross enrollment: male (% of school-age population)	2006[a]	101	114	129	94	108
Gross enrollment: female (% of school-age population)	2006[a]	105	109	123	73	108
Primary school completion rate, total (% of relevant age group)	2006	56.3	85.7	76.0	61.8	96.2
Adult literacy (% of population aged 15+)	2007	53.5	66.0	56.5	54.2	90.8

Sources: World Bank Development Data Platform (DDP), http://go.worldbank.org/DNBRRS9TB0; Food and Agriculture Organization (FAO) nutrition country profiles; United Nations Children's Fund (UNICEF), http://unicef.org; and Human Development Index Database.
Note: — = not available.
a. Estimates for Bangladesh are for 2004.

of a hospital (table 7.2). In the Mid-Western Region, however, both schools and hospitals are marginally less accessible. At the other end of the spectrum, Sri Lanka is renowned for its equitable provision of health and education services across different regions, as depicted in figure 7.5. Most Sri Lankans live within 30 minutes of a health facility, 1.4 kilometers of a basic health clinic, and 4.8 kilometers of a government-sponsored free health care facility (World Bank 2010). Access to schools is similarly equitable across regions in Sri Lanka. Intracountry differences in access to health care and education are also small in Bangladesh and Pakistan.

Table 7.2   Access to Education and Health Care Facilities in Rural Areas: Nepal, 2003

	Median hours	Mean hours	Standard error hours
Travel time to nearest school			
Eastern	0.17	0.31	0.02
Central	0.17	0.34	0.03
Western	0.17	0.25	0.02
Mid-Western	0.25	0.37	0.05
Travel time to nearest hospital			
Eastern	0.50	0.78	0.08
Central	0.50	0.76	0.08
Western	0.50	0.94	0.15
Mid-Western	0.75	0.97	0.11

Source: World Bank staff estimates, Nepal Living Standards Survey (NLSS), 2003.

The only exception to this general pattern is India, where health and education indicators are much worse in the lagging regions. In 2000, for example, 52.77 percent of children were malnourished in the low-income states versus 29.33 percent in the northeastern special category states.[1] In the low-income states, only 6.41 percent of villages have access to high schools compared with 25.00 percent in the higher-income states. Similarly, female adult literacy varies between 39 percent in the low-income states and 67 percent in the northeastern special category states.

But relatively equitable access to health care facilities and schools across regions within a country (with the exception of India) does not translate into equal quality of service. In Sri Lanka, school performance is worst in the northern and eastern provinces. In Bangladesh, at 74 percent, the absentee rate for doctors in rural primary health clinics is very high (Kremer et al. 2005). And in poor neighborhoods of Delhi, qualified public doctors render worse care than unqualified private sector doctors (Das and Hammer 2005). The inequalities in the quality of health care and education have both spatial and socioeconomic dimensions. Over 33 percent of public spending on health care in India is enjoyed by the richest 20 percent of the population, while less than 10 percent goes to the poorest consumption quintile (World Bank 2006). The quality of education received by the lowest consumption decile of Indian students is much worse than that of the topmost decile (Das and Zajonc 2008).

Figure 7.5   Access to Health Care Facilities, Sri Lanka

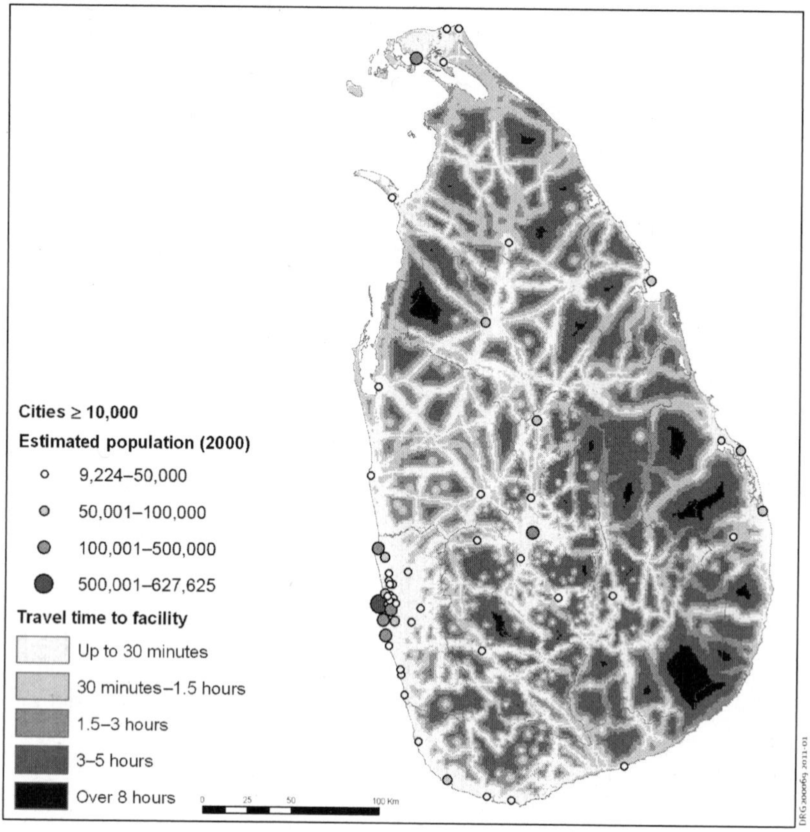

Cities ≥ 10,000
Estimated population (2000)
o   9,224–50,000
o   50,001–100,000
◉   100,001–500,000
●   500,001–627,625
Travel time to facility
☐   Up to 30 minutes
☐   30 minutes–1.5 hours
☐   1.5–3 hours
☐   3–5 hours
☐   Over 8 hours

Source: World Bank 2010.

Connective Infrastructures

As indicated in *WDR 2009*, by reducing the distance between human settlements and centers of economic density, connective infrastructure is a
crucial means of easing rural-urban transformations (World Bank 2008b).
In this section, we address the intra- and intercountry differences in roads,
power, and communications.

Road densities in most of the South Asian countries fare well by
international standards (figure 7.6). Bangladesh, India, Pakistan, and
Sri Lanka have more than 1 kilometer of road for each square kilometer
of area. Road density per capita is highest in Sri Lanka, which has
5 kilometers of road per 1,000 inhabitants; India has 3 kilometers of road

Figure 7.6   Road Density, South Asia

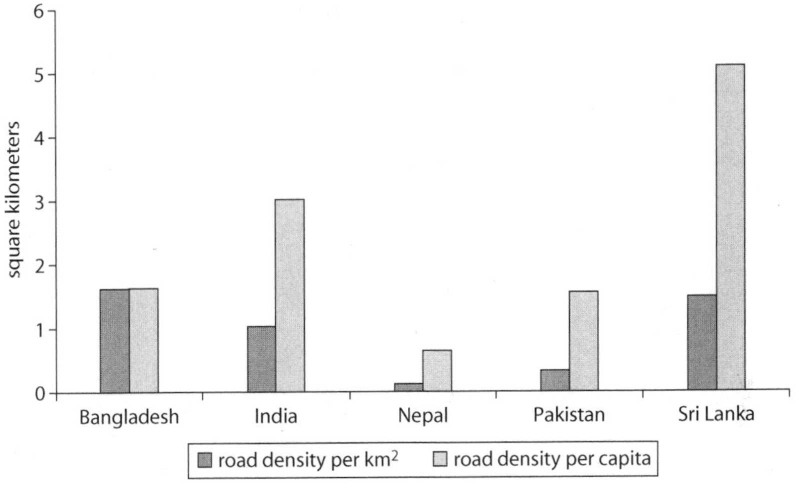

Source: World Bank Development Data Platform (DDP), http://go.worldbank.org/DNBRRS9TB0.

per 1,000 inhabitants. By contrast, the transport network in Nepal remains one of the weakest because of the country's difficult terrain, and road density is only about half a kilometer per 1,000 inhabitants. The share of paved roads differs significantly across countries, ranging from 9.5 percent in Bangladesh (2002–06) to 81.0 percent in Sri Lanka (2003)—see table 7.3.

Road density alone does not measure accessibility, because it reveals nothing about road quality or the extent to which roads are connecting villages to markets and urban centers (rather than other villages). Even in Sri Lanka, which has the highest share of paved roads, road quality is an issue. As measured by the International Roughness Index (IRI), roads in Sri Lanka are poor, with only 2 percent of national roads of sufficient quality to support traffic volumes. Estimates of travel times by road to cities of 100,000 or more are available for all countries except India. The average travel time is about 1.7 hours in Bangladesh, 2.4 hours in Pakistan and Sri Lanka, and 8.2 hours in Nepal (table 7.3).

Intracountry differences in remoteness are even more striking. Road quality tends to be much poorer and accessibility much lower in the less wealthy and more rural regions. Some regions of Nepal (figure 7.7) and Pakistan are 38 hours or more away from a city of 100,000 or more.

Table 7.3   Selected Infrastructure Indicators, South Asia

	Year	Bangladesh	India	Nepal	Pakistan	Sri Lanka
Travel time to cities of 100,000 persons or more						
Average (hours)	2009	1.69	—	8.24	2.38	2.37.
Minimum (hours)	2009	0.01	—	0.37	0.02	0.02
Maximum (hours)	2009	10.3	—	38.2	44.5	15.2
Telephone lines (per 100 persons)	2007	0.7	3.5	2.5	3.0	13.7
Cell phones (per 100 persons)	2007	21.7	20.8	11.6	38.7	39.9
Rail lines (km)	2005	2,855	63,465	—	7,791	1,200
Roads (10,000 km)	2003–06	24 (2003)	332 (2006)	2 (2004)	26 (2006)	10 (2003)
Paved roads (% of all)	2002–06	9.5 (2003)	47.4 (2002)	56.9 (2004)	65.4 (2006)	81.0 (2003)
Access to electricity (%)	2000	20.4	43.0	15.4	52.9	62.0

Sources: World Bank staff estimates (travel time); all others, World Bank Development Data Platform (DDP), http://go.worldbank.org/DNBRRS9TB0.
Note: — = not available.

Because of Nepal's difficult terrain, the average travel time to a paved road is 4.87 hours and to a commercial bank 3.49 hours, in contrast to 0.18 hours and 0.35 hours, respectively, in urban areas. Even in Sri Lanka, some remote locations are more than 15 hours away from the nearest large town (figure 7.8), and roads are narrower and bumpier off main routes and in rural areas than on major national routes and in Colombo. Although road densities are high and travel times are shorter in Bangladesh, regions within the country remain cut off from each other because of the lack of bridges on larger rivers.

There are also substantial differences in access to electricity (table 7.3). In 2000 the share of households with access to electricity was 62.0 percent in Sri Lanka, and then dropping to 52.9 percent in Pakistan,

Figure 7.7   Travel Times, Nepal

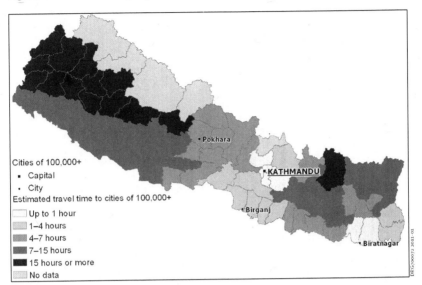

Sources: District boundaries: MapLibrary; travel times: estimates by World Bank based on data from Nepal Living Standard Survey, 2003; cities: Global Rural-Urban Mapping Project (GRUMP); 2000 population estimates, Center for International Earth Science Information Network (CIESIN), Columbia University.

43.0 percent in India, 20.4 percent in Bangladesh, and 15.4 percent in Nepal. Power shortages are a critical concern for firms; more than 75 percent of the firms in Bangladesh (and almost 40 percent of those in India, Pakistan, and Sri Lanka) perceive power shortages to be a major obstacle. In Bangladesh, resolution of power shortages would add two percentage points to economic growth (World Bank 2008a). Intracountry differences in access to power are also very significant. In India, 99 percent of the villages in the higher-income states (but only 69 percent of those in low-income states) have access to power.[2] In Kathmandu, Nepal, nearly all households in urban areas have access to electricity in contrast to one-quarter of rural residents.

Access to a landline phone is very limited in all countries, ranging from 13.7 percent of households in Sri Lanka to 0.7 percent in Bangladesh. Cell phone penetration rates in 2007 were 11.6 percent in Nepal, 20.8 percent in India, 21.7 percent in Bangladesh, 38.7 percent in Pakistan, and 39.9 percent in Sri Lanka (table 7.3). In Nepal, of the 3,919 village development committees, more than 1,000 do not have any telephone link.

Figure 7.8   Travel Times, Sri Lanka

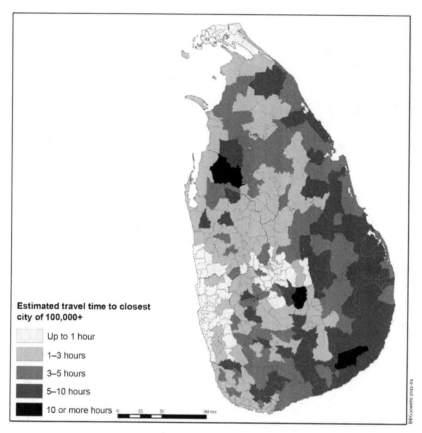

Estimated travel time to closest
city of 100,000+

- Up to 1 hour
- 1–3 hours
- 3–5 hours
- 5–10 hours
- 10 or more hours

Sources: District and Divisional Secretariat Divisions: MapLibrary; travel times: estimates by World Bank based on road network; cities: Global Rural-Urban Mapping Project (GRUMP); 2000 population estimates, Center for International Earth Science Information Network (CIESIN), Columbia University.

Conclusion

Our preliminary analysis suggests that, as indicated by *WDR 2008* and *WDR 2009*, policies and institutions will have a profound effect on the pace and shape of rural-urban transformations. In South Asia, macroeconomic policies and human capital investments vary across countries, but are relatively uniform within countries. Land and labor institutions, however, as well as connective infrastructure, tend to vary both across countries and within countries. In the chapters that follow, we present in-depth results from case studies focusing on the role of institutions and connectivity in determining some key processes of the rural-urban transformation.

Notes

1. The low-income states are Bihar, Chattisgarh, Jharkhand, Orissa, Rajasthan, Uttar Pradesh, and Madhya Pradesh. The northeastern special category states are Arunchal, Assam, Manipur, Megalaya, Mizoram, Nagaland, and Tripura.

2. The higher-income states are Goa, Haryana, Maharashtra, Punjab, and Tamil Nadu. The group of low-income states includes Bihar, Chattisgarh, Jharkhand, Orissa, Rajasthan, Uttar Pradesh, and Madhya Pradesh.

References

Aghion, P., R. Burgess, and S. Redding. 2008. "The Unequal Effects of Liberalization: Evidence from Dismantling the Licence Raj in India." *American Economic Review* 98 (4): 1397–1412.

Ahsan, A., and C. Pages. 2007. "Are All Labor Regulations Equal? Assessing the Effects of Job Security, Labor Dispute, and Contract Labor Laws in India." Policy Research Working Paper 4259, World Bank, Washington, DC.

Anderson K., and W. Martin. 2009. *Distortions to Agricultural Incentives in Asia.* Washington, DC: World Bank.

Banerjee A., P. Gertler, and M. Ghatak. 2002. "Empowerment and Efficiency: Tenancy Reform in West Bengal." *Journal of Political Economy* 110 (2): 239–80.

Besley, T., and R. Burgess. 2004. "Can Labor Regulation Hinder Economic Performance? Evidence from India." *Quarterly Journal of Economics* 119 (1): 91–134.

Das, J., and J. Hammer. 2005. "Which Doctor? Combining Vignettes and Item Response to Measure Clinical Competence." *Journal of Development Economics* 78 (2): 348–83.

Das J., and T. Zajonc. 2008. "India Shining and Bharat Drowning: Comparing Two Indian States to the Worldwide Distribution in Mathematics Achievement." Policy Research Working Paper 4644, World Bank, Washington, DC.

Kremer, M., N. Chaudhury, F. H. Rogers, K. Muralidharan, and J. Hammer. 2005. "Teacher Absence in India: A Snapshot." *Journal of the European Economic Association* 3 (2–3): 658–67.

Pursell, G., A. Gulati, and K. Gupta. 2007. "Distortions to Agricultural Incentives in India." Agricultural Distortions Working Paper 34, World Bank, Washington, DC.

World Bank. 2006. *Can South Asia End Poverty in a Generation?* South Asia Region Unit. Washington, DC: World Bank.

———. 2007. *World Development Report 2008: Agriculture for Development.* Washington, DC: World Bank.

————. 2008a. *Harnessing Competitiveness for Stronger Inclusive Growth. Bangladesh Second Investment Climate Assessment.* Washington, DC: World Bank.

————. 2008b. *World Development Report 2009: Reshaping Economic Geography.* Washington, DC: World Bank.

————. 2010. "Sri Lanka: Connecting People to Prosperity." Draft report of South Asian Poverty Reduction and Economic Management Unit, World Bank, Washington, DC.

CHAPTER 8

Land Market Institutions and the Rural-Urban Transformation

Access to land is a key determinant of a household's economic well-being and social status. The institutions that govern land rights can influence people's incentives to invest in productivity improvements and determine their access to credit and public services. The impact of land institutions can extend beyond household welfare to the long-term path and pace of economic transformation. In this chapter, we use case studies to explore the impact of two fundamental land market institutions on the rural-urban transformation. First, we look at the effects of inequality of landownership on rural and urban employment patterns and wages in Pakistan. Second, we consider the impact of restrictions on land market transactions on the rural-urban transformation in Sri Lanka.

Impact of Land Inequality: The Existing Evidence

The unequal distribution of land is a major source of income inequality and higher incidence of poverty in rural areas in most developing countries (World Bank 2007c). Landownership inequality affects productivity and growth through two principal mechanisms. First, it can induce a higher incidence of share tenancy, which tends to depress investment in land improvement and newer technology. For example, Jacoby and

Mansuri (2008) find that in Pakistan, investments are lower in leased land than owned land.

Second, landownership inequality tends to cement the position of rural elites, who may be incentivized to hamper investments in public institutions. For example, Banerjee and Iyer (2002) report that the colonial Zamindari system in India compounded inequalities in land distribution and created an entrenched landlord elite, even after the abolition of the Zamindari system itself. This development resulted in lower agricultural investment and productivity and lower public investments in health, education, and agricultural technology in districts dominated by landlords. Indeed, according to Galor, Moav, and Vollrath (2009), land inequality has a significant negative effect on public investment in education at the state level in the United States. They argue that, because education facilitates the movement of workers from the agriculture to nonagriculture sectors, landowners have an incentive to limit public investment in education.

The negative influence of land inequality on public education suggests that transitions from farm to nonfarm occupations are likely to be slower in countries and areas with higher land inequality. The ultimate effect of landownership on the transformation from agricultural to nonagricultural activities is complex, because it affects not only income distribution and access to credit but also savings and investment. The evidence summarized in box 8.1 suggests that the impact of land inequality on the pattern and pace of occupational transformation is likely to be nonlinear, depending on the extent of inequality itself.

Land Inequality and Occupational Transitions in Pakistan

Among the South Asian countries, Pakistan has the most unequal distribution of agricultural land. According to the 2000 agricultural census, the Gini coefficient of the landownership distribution is 0.66. The Pakistan Social and Living Standards Measurement Survey (PSLM), 2004–05, cites the coefficient as higher still, 0.77. There are, however, differences in the distribution of landownership across provinces, and the Gini coefficient is particularly high in Punjab (0.76) and Balochistan (0.78). Unequal distribution of land is cited as a major source of income inequality in rural Pakistan. Adams and Alderman (1992) find that between a third and three-quarters of income inequality in rural areas can be attributed to high inequality in landownership. Regression-based decompositions of income inequality also confirm the key role of land inequality in determining rural income inequality

Box 8.1

Inequality and the Evolution of Occupational Structure: Theoretical Insights

Banerjee and Newman (1993) contend that the distribution of wealth affects the employment composition of an economy and vice versa. In their model, because of capital market imperfections, people can borrow only limited amounts. As a result, occupations that require higher levels of investment are beyond the reach of poor people, who choose instead to work for wealthier employers. Depending on the labor market conditions and on their wealth, other agents become self-employed in low-scale production or remain idle. The structure of occupation in an economy determines how much people save and how much risk they bear.

These factors give rise to a new distribution of wealth in a dynamic setting. In a static equilibrium, high inequality is associated with more wage work and lower wages, and thus greater poverty. In a dynamic setting, the degree of inequality determines the economy's growth path. When the distribution of initial wealth is highly unequal (with a large number of poor, a smaller middle class, and a minority of highly affluent people), the economy may converge to stagnation because of low wages and thus low savings and demand. When inequality is not so extreme and there is a sizable middle class, the economy may converge to a prosperous equilibrium. The inequality in this case forces poorer agents to become workers and over time allows large-scale industrial production. When inequality in wealth distribution is only moderate and very few poor people are available to participate in wage work, the economy converges to an equilibrium where self-employment in smaller business enterprises predominates.

(Naschold 2009). But empirical evidence on the impact of land inequality on occupational transitions in Pakistan is sparse.

To investigate the impact of land inequality on occupational structures and wages in Pakistan, we run regressions on several rounds of the Labor Force Survey data from Pakistan. The empirical analysis presents several challenges. First, the unobserved location characteristics that may have affected wage distribution can be correlated with the distribution of land. Second, there may be reverse causality, because occupation structure may affect savings and investment and thus land distribution. The empirical methodology used to deal with these problems is elaborated in Shilpi (2009) and omitted here for the sake of brevity. In this chapter, we present the main results of the empirical analysis.

For employment patterns, our regressions indicate that the relationship between landownership inequality and employment structure is nonlinear (table 8.1). Except for manufacturing employment and nonagricultural self-employment, the index of land inequality and its squared term are jointly statistically significant. The estimated coefficients suggest a concave relationship between land inequality and employment in nonfarm self-employment, wage work in agriculture, and services employment. Thus when inequality is low, self-employment in farming predominates. As inequality increases, more and more people engage in off-farm work. At a very high level of inequality, people revert to self-employment in farming.[1] The pattern is reversed only for employment in public services.

Like land inequality, education is an important determinant of participation in nonfarm activities. An education level higher than or equal to middle school increases significantly the probability of participation in nonfarm self-employment and services employment (both private and public). Education between the primary and middle school levels also improves the rate of participation in nonfarm self-employment relative to self-employment in agriculture. As expected, those who are engaged in agricultural wage work lack primary-level education. The manufacturing sector also seems to attract mainly those who lack primary-level education.

Regression results also suggest a concentration of activities in and around cities. The farther the distance to urban centers with a population of 100,000 or more, the greater is the negative effect on participation in manufacturing and services activities. This finding indicates a geographical concentration of wage employment in nonfarm activities in and around large urban centers. The metropolitan and urban dummies are also significant, pointing to a concentration of nonagricultural activities in those areas. Manufacturing activities are concentrated in and around metropolitan cities (but not in smaller towns and cities) and are also more prevalent in areas with better access to electricity. By contrast, services are concentrated in smaller cities and towns, in addition to metropolitan areas.

The employment patterns in urban areas are also found to be responsive to land inequality in surrounding rural areas.[2] When the analysis is repeated for the rural subsample (61 percent of the sample), urban subsample (13 percent), and metropolitan subsample (26 percent), the results are similar to those for the full sample for rural areas. In urban areas, land inequality has significant nonlinear effects on self-employment in nonfarm activities only. Self-employment in the nonagriculture sector is by far the largest employment category in smaller urban cities and towns,

Table 8.1 Employment Choice of Individuals, Pakistan: Marginal Effects from Multinomial Logit Regressions

	Self-employment		Wage employment		
	Nonagriculture	Agriculture	Manufacturing	Service	Public service
Index of land inequality	0.027 (1.71)	0.015 (3.27)**	0.01 (0.67)	0.02 (2.73)**	-0.013 (2.65)**
Land inequality squared	-0.003 (1.39)	-0.002 (3.28)**	-0.002 (1.08)	-0.002 (2.40)*	0.002 (2.85)**
Log (distance)	0.001 (0.84)	0.000 (1.53)	-0.003 (2.82)**	-0.002 (2.76)**	0.001 (1.85)
Middle school and up	0.025 (3.15)**	-0.018 (6.41)**	-0.105 (13.53)**	0.036 (8.02)**	0.098 (22.39)**
Primary to middle school	0.077 (9.25)**	-0.019 (7.82)**	-0.035 (4.62)**	0.007 (1.51)	0.025 (5.71)**
Phone in workplace (yes = 1)	0.254 (5.82)**	-0.028 (1.37)	-0.211 (5.08)**	0.081 (5.19)**	-0.004 (0.31)
Household has electricity	0.141 (3.36)**	-0.034 (2.60)**	0.169 (4.27)**	0.001 (0.05)	-0.048 (4.07)**
Urban (yes = 1)	0.174 (8.75)**	-0.022 (3.58)**	-0.014 (0.71)	0.047 (5.47)**	0.036 (5.81)**
Metro (yes = 1)	0.216 (9.96)**	-0.024 (4.46)**	0.155 (7.51)**	0.104 (10.50)**	0.057 (7.15)**
Number of observations	45,023	45,023	45,023	45,023	45,023

Source: World Bank staff estimates based on Pakistan Labor Force Survey, 2005–06.
Note: Robust *t*-statistics are in parentheses. All regressions included province dummies and other household- and individual-level controls.
*p < .05.
**p < .01.

accounting for 42 percent of all employment. The nonlinear effect implies that self-employment in nonagricultural activities in smaller towns and cities is low when land inequality in the surrounding rural areas is small, but rises with an increase in inequality, and eventually falls as inequality becomes extreme. In metropolitan areas, a similar concave relationship between manufacturing employment and land inequality is observed. By contrast, private employment in services in metropolitan areas is not very responsive to land inequality in the surrounding rural areas.

We also analyze the average growth in employment in different activities from 1999 to 2005.[3] The results suggest faster growth of total employment in areas near large urban centers and in areas with higher land inequality. The impact of land inequality is significantly negative only for growth in manufacturing employment. The negative impact of land inequality on this growth may seem puzzling when considered in the light of overall employment growth in the same areas. However, it is possible that areas with higher land inequality may experience lower growth in demand for manufacturing goods. This result seems to suggest that large landowners are spending a large share of their income on goods produced outside the local area.

And what is the impact of land inequality on real wages? Our regression results indicate that inequality of ownership has a significant negative effect on wages in agriculture and manufacturing (table 8.2). The negative effect of land inequality on wages is expected because areas with a higher concentration of ownership of agricultural lands are likely to face an increasing supply of labor. For wage growth, the regression results suggest a significant negative effect of land inequality on the growth of manufacturing wages only.

The negative effect of inequality on both manufacturing employment and wage growth may seem puzzling at first. The regression results in table 8.1 show clearly that manufacturing employs mainly uneducated and unskilled workers in semiurban and urban areas. But distance to large urban centers does not matter much for wages (except in services) once provincial dummies are included in the regressions (table 8.2). Combined, these results suggest that workers are mobile across locations, at least within the province. Thus manufacturing employment may decline locally in areas with high land inequality, but mobility of workers also ensures an overall downward pressure on wages for unskilled workers, particularly in manufacturing activities.

Indeed, land inequality, education, and infrastructure are all important drivers of wages. Education commands a sizable premium in all types of

Table 8.2   Real Wages, Pakistan: Individual-Level Instrumental Variable Regressions, Labor Force Survey, 2005–06

	Log of real wages in		
	Agriculture	Manufacturing	Services
Index of land inequality	−0.225 (2.30)*	−0.101 (5.34)**	−0.043 (1.31)
Log (distance)	−0.006 (0.72)	−0.003 (1.03)	0.011 (2.31)*
Middle school and up	0.166 (2.13)*	0.107 (4.95)**	0.327 (8.64)**
Phone in workplace (yes = 1)	0.198 (0.41)	−0.081 (0.70)	0.615 (4.63)**
Urban (yes = 1)		−0.025 (0.77)	0.118 (2.22)*
Metro (yes = 1)		0.032 (0.98)	0.317 (5.90)**
Number of observations	1,325	9,608	3,875

Source: World Bank staff estimates based on Pakistan Labor Force Survey, 2005–06.
Note: Robust *t*-statistics are in parentheses. All regressions included province dummies and other household- and individual-level controls.
*p < .05.
**p < .01.

wage work (table 8.2). The premium for an above-middle school education is greatest in service activities. Workers with education above primary school but below the middle school level command a substantial premium in manufacturing and services activities. Among workers with different levels of education, only those with a higher than secondary education experienced positive growth in wages. Wages in agriculture and services grew at a faster rate in areas with more urbanized services, such as better access to phones. But manufacturing wages declined in more urbanized settings because of the increased supply of labor from rural migrants. To the extent that investment in education and infrastructure are adversely affected by land inequality, as argued by Banerjee and Iyer (2002) and Galor, Moav, and Vollrath (2009), the regression results in tables 8.1 and 8.2 underestimate the adverse effect of land inequality.

Impact of Land Market Restrictions: The Existing Evidence

The restrictions on land market transactions common in developing countries (World Bank 2003) have been shown to affect sectoral and spatial transformation. Hayashi and Prescott (2008) find that during 1855–1940, agricultural employment remained nearly unchanged in Japan, despite very large rural-urban income disparity. They argue that the prewar patriarchy forced the designated heirs to stay in agriculture. This informal barrier to labor mobility caused misallocation of labor across activities, depressing per capita output by about a third. The introduction of partible inheritance after the war led to a mass exodus from rural areas, a sharp change in employment patterns, and an increase in per capita income. Yang (1997) argues that the inalienability of land rights under the household responsibility system in China increased migration costs, slowing sectoral transformation. Removal of the control in 1988 was followed by a surge in migration, although most rural-to-urban migrants were "floating populations" whose families remained in rural areas to retain the households' land earnings.

Overall, the existing evidence suggests that the removal of land market restrictions increases long-term investment in agriculture, improves participation in nonfarm activities, and generally allows land-poor households to gain better access to land (box 8.2).

Land Market Restrictions and Rural-Urban Transitions in Sri Lanka

Among South Asian countries, land market restrictions are perhaps the most stringent in Sri Lanka. The Crown Lands Encroachment Ordinance of 1840 transferred all lands without private title to the state. Under the Land Development Ordinance (LDO) of 1935, the government introduced a system of protected tenure: private recipients of LDO land had the right to occupy and cultivate the land in perpetuity subject to restrictions imposed on sale, leasing, and mortgaging, and to conditions related to abandoning or failing to cultivate the land. Although subsequent amendments have weakened some conditions on mortgages and transfers, the basic provisions of unitary succession and a ban on the subdivision of plots and land rental remain largely intact. Restrictions on LDO leases are strict by South Asia standards, but they are similar to those found in pre-reform China, in Vietnam, and in many African countries where commons are still an important source of agricultural land.

Figure 8.1 shows the incidence of LDO leases in Sri Lanka. The percentage of land under the LDO is much lower in the urbanized Western Province than elsewhere in the country. LDO land is particularly prevalent in North Central Province.

Our empirical analysis seeks to uncover the impact of LDO restrictions on the pace of sectoral transformation in Sri Lanka. As discussed in chapter 7, Sri Lanka implemented a broad-based economic liberalization

Box 8.2

Evidence on the Effects of Land Reforms

Tenancy reforms. Tenancy laws attempt to increase tenure security by registering sitting tenants and by establishing limits on the amount of rent to be paid. According to Banerjee, Gertler, and Ghatak (2002), successful implementation of such reforms in West Bengal, India, resulted in a significant increase in agricultural productivity. Looking at Pakistan, Jacoby and Mansuri (2008) report an increase in investment in land improvement measures by share tenants with an increase in tenure security. By contrast, Deininger, Jin, and Nagarajan (2008) find that in India, tenancy restrictions tend to reduce the demand for and supply of rental contracts, limiting the ability of the poor and landless to acquire land through such contracts. However, Deininger, Jin, and Nagarajan (2009) find that tenancy and other land reforms (including redistribution of land) in India have a positive effect on a household's investment in human capital and the growth of income, consumption, and nonland assets.

Liberalization of land sales and rental markets. In 1993 Vietnam distributed land use certificates known as red books. Red books came with the rights to sell, rent, mortgage, and bequeath land. They led to a vibrant land lease and sales market, allowing transfers of land to more productive users (Markussen, Tarp, and Van den Broeck 2009). Do and Iyer (2008) find that this reform had a positive and significant impact on long-term agricultural investments and on the time devoted to nonfarm activities. Meanwhile, Ravallion and van de Walle (2008) observe that land reforms increased the incidence of landlessness. Rising rural landlessness has been a benign, even positive, factor in the process of aggregate poverty reduction, because farm households have taken up new opportunities in the labor market, and the landless have experienced a higher rate of poverty reduction relative to the rest of the population. In China, the liberalization of land tenure arrangements increased the share of households participating in land rental arrangements from 2.3 percent to 9.4 percent in 2000. Benjamin, Brandt, and Rozelle (2000) report that the rental market shifted land to more productive and land-poor producers, with positive implications for both efficiency and equity.

Land titling. Clear and secure titles to land are important for the conversion of land from one use (or user) to another. Evidence from rural land titling programs in Andra Pradesh, India, suggests that a proper title increases land value by 15 percent (World Bank 2007a). Although evidence from recent land titling programs in urban slums shows that titling has little impact on households' access to land, it demonstrates a significant positive effect on women's labor market participation and hours of work (Galiani and Schargrodsky 2005; Field 2007).

Figure 8.1   Area under Land Development Ordinance (LDO) Restrictions, Sri Lanka

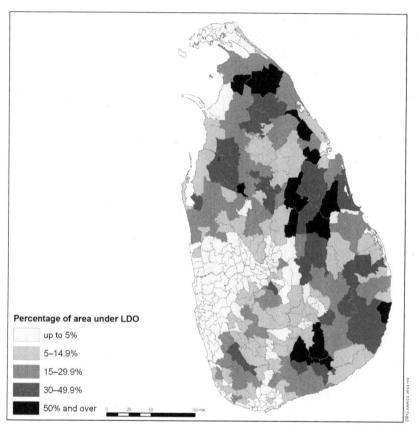

Percentage of area under LDO
- up to 5%
- 5–14.9%
- 15–29.9%
- 30–49.9%
- 50% and over

Source: World Bank staff estimates based on agriculture census of Sri Lanka, 1998.

and industrial deregulation program in 1977, almost a decade and a half earlier than India (although agriculture still receives considerable government support in the form of input subsidies and trade protection). The country is also renowned for its equitable provision of education, health care, and other social services to its citizens regardless of their location. Yet in spite of this largely favorable policy environment, the pace of sectoral transformation has been relatively slow. In 1960 agriculture's share of total employment was about 56 percent in Sri Lanka, 60 percent in the Republic of Korea, and 78 percent in Indonesia. Today, those shares stand at 44 percent, 9 percent, and 44 percent, respectively (figure 8.2). Even

Figure 8.2   Agriculture's Share in Total Employment, Selected Countries in Asia

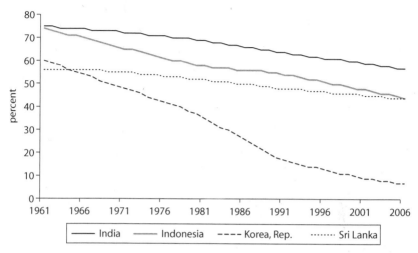

Source: World Bank Development Data Platform (DDP), http://go.worldbank.org/DNBRRS9TB0.

India experienced a faster decline in agriculture's share of employment and income during this period.

Comparatively, the regional pattern in Sri Lanka indicates a higher level of sectoral transformation in Western Province, the wealthiest of the provinces, and a much higher dependence on agriculture in other provinces (table 8.3). In the wealthy western region, 44 percent of the population is employed in services and 26 percent in manufacturing. Only 12 percent is employed in agriculture (including both farmers and wage laborers). At the other end of the spectrum, in Uva Province, the poorest of the provinces, 34 percent are farmers, and another 30 percent are agricultural wage laborers. Manufacturing employment accounts for only 6 percent of the provincial labor force.

Using a regression-based model, we examined the impact of LDO restrictions on sectoral employment and wages in Sri Lanka. The econometric details are reported in a background paper by Shilpi (2010). This section summarizes the main results.

The empirical analysis indicates that LDO restrictions have slowed the pace of transition out of agriculture. Estimates from the regression model show that the percentage of area under LDO leases has had a significant negative impact on the probability of participation in all types of non-agricultural employment (table 8.4). The direct effect of distance to the

Table 8.3   Sectoral Employment Shares in Sri Lanka, 2002

| | Percentage of total employment | | | | |
| | Self-employment | Wage employment | | | |
Province	Agriculture	Nonfarm	Agriculture	Manufacturing	Services
Western	8	18	4	26	44
Central	15	12	29	12	32
Southern	21	15	20	18	26
North Western	21	16	11	21	31
North Central	33	13	18	8	27
Uva	34	8	30	6	22
Sabaragamuwa	18	13	20	17	32
Sri Lanka	18	15	16	18	34

Source: World Bank staff estimates based on Household Income and Expenditure Survey, 2002.

Table 8.4   Effects of the Land Development Ordinance (LDO) on Employment Choice, Sri Lanka

| | Employment in | | | |
	Self-employment, nonagriculture	Wage agriculture	Wage manufacturing	Wage services
Percent area under LDO	−0.183	0.238	−0.162	−0.224
	(3.23)***	(3.91)***	(2.40)**	(2.29)**
Travel time to large city	−0.004	0.014	−0.018	−0.007
	(1.03)	(4.22)***	(4.00)***	(1.42)
Area LDO*travel time	0.027	−0.029	0.047	−0.037
	(1.75)*	(1.62)	(2.17)**	(1.42)
Education level (year)	0.002	0.013	0.039	−0.018
	(0.31)	(1.70)	(4.56)***	(1.59)
Number of observations	24,123	24,123	2,4123	24,123

Source: World Bank staff estimates based on Household Income and Expenditure Survey, 2002.
Note: Robust z-statistics are in parentheses. All regressions include a large number of individual, household, and location controls and a district-level fixed effect.
*$p < .10$.
**$p < .05$.
***$p < .01$.

nearest large city is negative and significant for nonfarm self-employment and wage employment in manufacturing.

The interaction of LDO and distance is also statistically significant for all activities except services (table 8.4). For wage employment in manufacturing and self-employment in nonfarm enterprises, the probability of participation in these activities declines with the increase in land under

LDO restrictions. The interaction effect is positive. This finding implies that the impact of the LDO is more negative in locations that have better market access; in more remote places, LDO restrictions have a much smaller adverse effect.

In contrast with nonfarm employment, the effects of LDO restrictions and distance are positive for agricultural wage labor. The result implies that relative to self-employment in farming, participation in agricultural wage labor is higher in areas with higher LDO restrictions. The higher incidence of agricultural wage labor probably stems from the lease restrictions on LDO land, which impede those residents with larger farms from leasing land out and force those with inadequate land to turn to agricultural labor for supplementary income.

In addition to keeping a larger proportion of people dependent on agriculture, land market restrictions tend to keep them poorer because they earn less per unit of labor (table 8.5). The coefficient of land under the LDO is negative and statistically highly significant for agricultural and services wages. For manufacturing wages, it is negative but statistically significant at the 10 percent level. The magnitude of the estimated coefficients implies the largest negative effect of the LDO on services wages, followed by agricultural and then manufacturing wages. The results suggest that the interaction of the proportion of area under the LDO and

Table 8.5   Market Access, Land Tenure Arrangement, and Income, Sri Lanka

	Log (real annual wage)		
	Agriculture	Manufacturing	Services
Percent area under LDO	−3.213	−1.304	−9.000
	(4.79)***	(1.90)*	(2.50)**
Travel time to large city	−0.292	−0.067	−0.057
	(6.26)***	(1.60)	(1.00)
Area LDO*travel time	0.867	0.501	3.034
	(4.42)***	(2.12)**	(2.36)**
Education level (year)	0.009	0.047	0.076
	(2.54)**	(14.53)***	(21.49)***
Number of observations	3,350	3,804	7,444

Source: World Bank staff estimates based on Household Income and Expenditure Survey, 2002.
Note: Robust z-statistics are in parentheses. All regressions include a large number of individual, household, and location controls and a district-level fixed effect.
*p < .10.
**p < .05.
***p < .01.

travel time to a large city has a positive and statistically significant effect on all wages (table 8.5). The effect of the share of land under the LDO thus depends on access to large urban centers and vice versa. This interaction effect implies a larger negative effect of the LDO in locations with better access to urban centers. Wages are lower in a location with a higher proportion of land under the LDO compared with a location that is equidistant from an urban center but has a lower proportion of land under the LDO.

Our empirical analysis thus suggests that employment in locations with severe land regulations is less diversified toward nonfarm activities in manufacturing and services, and that those employed in nonfarm labor earn much less on average. These results are quite remarkable because we already control for much of the agglomeration externalities related to urbanization and increased density through district-level fixed effects. The regressions also control for differences in service provision across districts.

As in Pakistan, our empirical results indicate that level of education is an important determinant of employment structure and wages in Sri Lanka. According to table 8.5, education yields a significant premium in services and manufacturing. The employment choice estimation reported in table 8.4 indicates that higher education significantly improves the probability of securing a job in the manufacturing sector. Surprisingly, higher education has little effect on securing a job in services, although its return is highest in service activities. As in most developing countries, service activities in Sri Lanka comprise both low- and high-skill jobs. Low-skill service jobs seem to be more prevalent than high-skill ones, causing access to service jobs to be nonresponsive to education level on average.

Summary of Case Studies and Policy Implications

The empirical analysis for Pakistan demonstrates that inequality in the distribution of land has forced a large portion of the population to seek off-farm employment, thereby depressing wages, particularly in agriculture and manufacturing. The effect is not confined to rural areas. Self-employment in smaller cities and towns and manufacturing in metropolitan areas are also affected. The adverse effect on wages stifles savings, investment, and demand, forcing more and more workers into subsistence (self-employment) work. The impact of land inequality on the growth of employment and wages suggests an exodus of workers from areas high in land inequality to urban areas, where they are absorbed into self-employment (in smaller cities and towns) and unskilled jobs in manufacturing (in metropolitan areas). As a result, land inequality has a significant negative effect on real wage growth in manufacturing.

Our results suggest that by improving the access of the poor to land, Pakistan can ensure smoother and faster sectoral transformation and a significant reduction in income inequality. Three major attempts at redistributive land reform in Pakistan have failed, the most recent in 1977. Land reform has neither political support nor the backing of Islamic religious authorities. As noted by a World Bank report, any attempt to enact redistributive land reform would have to create a win-win situation (World Bank 2007b). Policy measures to increase access to land could include: greater access to credit to enable the poor to purchase land, land taxation to minimize the holding of land for speculative purposes, and measures to improve the efficiency of land sales and rental markets. Land purchase schemes that include grant components for the poorest landless households is another option, although the fiscal costs could limit the scale of such an operation.

The empirical analysis for Sri Lanka indicates that an increase in the incidence of LDO leases is associated with lower nonfarm employment diversification. Areas with a higher percentage of land under the LDO have disproportionately more people dependent on agricultural wage labor. The finding that nonfarm enterprise income also declines with an increase in land under the LDO points to the negative effect of mortgage restrictions on the development of credit markets. The limited expansion of nonfarm enterprises in these areas means that wages for all types of workers have been depressed in areas with a higher incidence of LDO leases. Thus, although LDO leases have created a middle-class peasantry in Sri Lanka, they seem to have lowered the income prospects for agricultural workers, who are among the poorest in rural areas.

Because LDO leases are quite secure, they should not depress long-term investment in land. The rental restrictions can nevertheless create productivity inefficiency if they restrict the transfer of land from inefficient to efficient producers, although, in practice, informal leases are quite prevalent in LDO areas (PSIA 2008). Moreover, any productive inefficiency created by the LDO restrictions in agriculture has been mitigated by massive public investment in irrigation schemes and other infrastructure development projects. As a result of these generous investments, today land productivity in many settlement areas is much higher than that in the rest of the country. However, sales restrictions are found to reduce the value of LDO lands by 15–25 percent (PSIA 2008). Relaxing leasing and sales restrictions on land under the LDO is likely to have positive effects on rural incomes, poverty reduction, and longer-term structural transformation in Sri Lanka.

Finally, in both countries land reforms would have to be complemented with investment in human capital, because higher levels of education would help the poor to secure better nonfarm employment. In the medium to long run, the modernization of Pakistan and Sri Lanka's manufacturing and services sectors will depend on the availability of a highly skilled labor force.

Notes

1. This pattern of private employment is consistent with the prediction of Banerjee and Newman (1993).

2. These results are provided in the background paper by Shilpi (2009).

3. These results are omitted for the sake of brevity.

References

Adams, R., Jr., and H. Alderman. 1992. "Sources of Income Inequality in Rural Pakistan: A Decomposition Analysis." *Oxford Bulletin of Economics and Statistics* 54 (4): 591–608.

Banerjee A., P. Gertler, and M. Ghatak. 2002. "Empowerment and Efficiency: Tenancy Reform in West Bengal." *Journal of Political Economy* 110 (2): 239–80.

Banerjee, A., and L. Iyer. 2002. "History, Institutions, and Economic Performance: The Legacy of Colonial Land Tenure Systems in India." *American Economic Review* 95 (4): 1190–213.

Banerjee, A. V., and A. F. Newman. 1993. "Occupational Choice and the Process of Development." *Journal of Political Economy* 101 (2): 274–98.

Benjamin, D., L. Brandt, and S. Rozelle. 2000. "Aging, Well-being, and Social Security in Rural North China." *Population and Development Review* 26: 89–116.

Deininger, K., S. Jin, and H. K. Nagarajan. 2008. "Efficiency and Equity Impacts of Rural Land Rental Restrictions: Evidence from India." *European Economic Review* 52 (5): 892–918.

———. 2009. "Land Reforms, Poverty Reduction, and Economic Growth: Evidence from India." *Journal of Development Studies* 45 (4): 496–521.

Do, Q.-T., and L. Iyer. 2008. "Land Titling and Rural Transition in Vietnam." *Economic Development and Cultural Change* 56 (April).

Field, E. 2007. "Entitled to Work: Urban Property Rights and the Labor Supply in Peru." *Quarterly Journal of Economics* 122 (4): 1561–602.

Galiani, S., and E. Schargrodsky. 2005. "Property Rights for the Poor: Effects of Land Titling." Business School Working Papers, Universidad Torcuato Di Tella, Buenos Aires.

Galor, O., O. Moav, and D. Vollrath. 2009. "Inequality in Landownership, the Emergence of Human-Capital Promoting Institutions, and the Great Divergence." *Review of Economic Studies* 76 (1): 143–79.

Hayashi, F., and E. C. Prescott. 2008. "The Depressing Effect of Agricultural Institutions on the Prewar Japanese Economy." *Journal of Political Economy* 116 (4): 573–632.

Jacoby, G., and G. Mansuri. 2008. "Land Tenancy and Non-Contractible Investment in Rural Pakistan." *Review of Economic Studies* 75 (3): 763–88.

Markussen, T., F. Tarp, and K. Van den Broeck. 2009. "The Forgotten Property Rights: Restrictions on Land Use in Vietnam." Discussion Paper 09-21, Department of Economics, University of Copenhagen.

Naschold, F. 2009. "Microeconomic Determinants of Income Inequality in Rural Pakistan." *Journal of Development Studies* 45 (5): 746–68.

PSIA (Poverty and Social Impact Analysis). 2008. *Land Reforms in Sri Lanka: A Poverty and Social Impact Analysis.* Washington, DC: World Bank.

Ravallion, M., and D. van de Walle. 2008. "Does Rising Landlessness Signal Success or Failure for Vietnam's Agrarian Transition?" *Journal of Development Economics* 87 (2): 191–209.

Shilpi, F. 2009. "Land Inequality and Occupation Choice: Evidence from Pakistan." World Bank, Washington, DC.

———. 2010. "The Effect of Land Market Restrictions on Employment Pattern and Wages: Evidence from Sri Lanka." World Bank, Washington, DC.

World Bank. 2003. *Land Policies for Growth and Poverty Reduction.* New York: Oxford University Press.

———. 2007a. *India: Land Policies for Growth and Poverty Reduction.* New Delhi: Oxford University Press.

———. 2007b. "Pakistan: Promoting Rural Growth and Poverty Reduction." South Asia Region, Sustainable and Development Unit, Report 39303-Pk, World Bank, Washington, DC.

———. 2007c. *World Development Report 2008: Agriculture for Development.* Washington, DC: World Bank.

Yang, D. 1997. "China's Land Arrangements and Rural Labor Mobility." *China Economic Review* 8 (2): 101–15.

CHAPTER 9

Geographical Linkages and the Rural-Urban Transformation

As described in chapter 8, land market policies intended for rural areas have implications for the urban labor market. In this chapter, we address the issue of geographical spillovers along the entire rural-urban continuum by considering at three principal questions. First, how important are small towns and cities in the national economic landscape? Second, looking especially at Bangladesh, does urbanization affect employment patterns in rural areas? And, third, what areas—metropolitan, periurban, smaller cities, or rural—are more attractive to emerging firms?

Poverty, Urbanization, and Employment Structure along the Rural-Urban Continuum

In most developing countries, the rural-urban differences in economic structure and poverty incidence are well documented, but evidence on the economic structure of cities of different sizes is still very sparse. Here we provide evidence on poverty, population, and employment patterns along the rural-urban continuum in selected South Asian countries.

Evidence from these countries reveals that the incidence of poverty is highest in rural areas, followed by smaller towns and cities, and lowest in metropolitan areas. For example, the poverty incidence in Bangladesh is about 26 percent in metropolitan areas, about 38 percent in periurban areas and smaller cities, and 43 percent in rural areas (figure 9.1).[1]

A similar pattern is observed in Pakistan (figure 9.2). In India, 43 percent of people residing in smaller towns are poor compared with 32 percent in medium-size cities and 20 percent in metropolitan cities. Although poverty rates are lower in the larger metropolitan cities, they

Figure 9.1   Poverty Headcount Ratio: Bangladesh, 2004–05

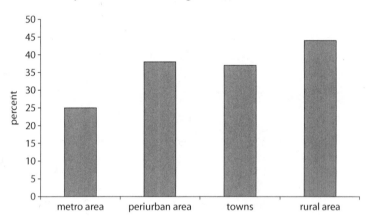

Source: World Bank staff estimates based on Household Income and Expenditure Survey, 2004–05.

Figure 9.2   Poverty Headcount Ratio: Pakistan, 2004–05

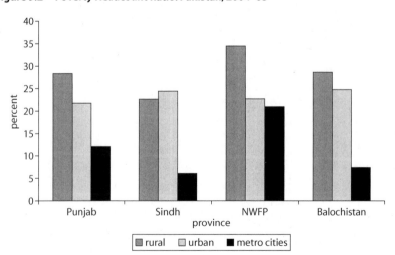

Source: World Bank staff estimates based on Pakistan Social and Living Standard Measurement Survey, 2004–05.
Note: NWFP = North West Frontier Province.

are typically home to high inequalities. For example, child and infant mortality rates are highest among the poor in large cities in India (World Bank 2011).

Differences in access to services mirror poverty incidence. The percentage of households with access to electricity for lighting is highest in metropolitan areas in both Bangladesh and Pakistan (figures 9.3 and 9.4). In Bangladesh, 76 percent of households in metropolitan areas have access to electricity compared with only one-third of households in peri-urban areas and smaller towns.[2] Although the disparity in electricity access between metropolitan cities and smaller towns in Pakistan ("urban" in figure 9.4) is much smaller, substantial disparities remain in access to piped water and telephones.

More than 200 cities and towns dot Bangladesh and Pakistan. And yet urbanization in both of these countries is dominated by a few large metropolitan cities. Two metropolitan cities with a population of more than 1 million—Dhaka and Chittagong—account for 43 percent of Bangladesh's urban population. In Pakistan, eight cities with a population of more than 1 million account for 58 percent of the urban population. Another 24 percent of the urban population in Pakistan resides in 48 cities with populations of 100,000 to 1 million.[3]

The pattern of urbanization in South Asian countries indicates two stylized facts. First, rural areas continue to account for a large share of

Figure 9.3   Access to Services: Bangladesh, 2000

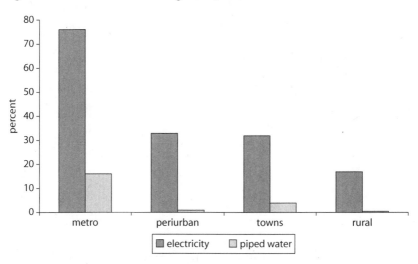

Source: Staff estimate based on population census of Bangladesh, 2000.

Figure 9.4   Access to Services: Pakistan, 2004–05

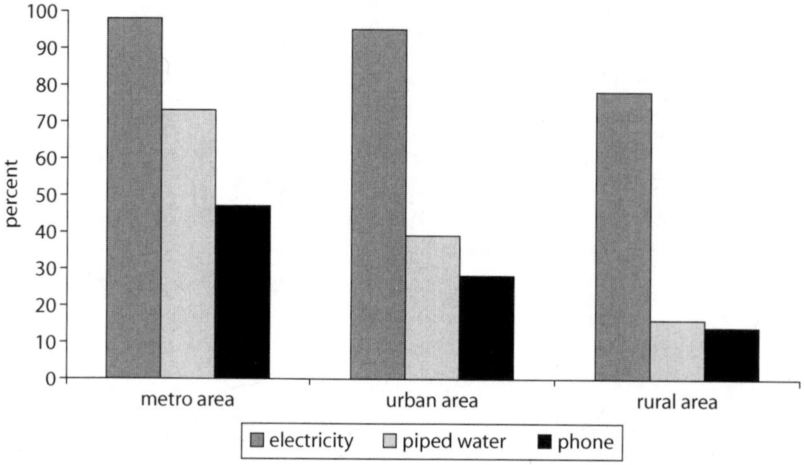

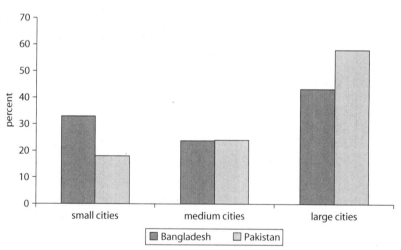

Source: World Bank staff estimates based on Pakistan Social and Living Standard Measurement Survey, 2004–05.

Figure 9.5   Percentage of Urban Population in Small, Medium, and Large Cities, Bangladesh and Pakistan

Source: World Bank staff estimates based on population censuses.

population and therefore employment, even in the nonfarm sector. For example, nearly half of all manufacturing activities in each country are located in the rural areas of Bangladesh, Nepal, and Pakistan. Thus employment transition in rural areas will remain critical for the overall rural-urban transformation. Second, consistent with the weaker provision of services, smaller towns and cities are not always able to attract manufacturing activities. Rural or periurban areas in close proximity to larger urban markets may be better placed strategically to attract manufacturing activities.

These two issues are analyzed in detail in the following case studies using data from Bangladesh, where the growth of the nonfarm sector is particularly critical to national development. At 1,148 persons per square kilometer, the population density in Bangladesh is among the highest in the world. With the margin of cultivation almost exhausted and cropping intensity approaching its physical limit, agriculture is unable to offer additional employment opportunities. The bulk of the 1 million or so annual new entrants into the labor force will have to be absorbed into the nonfarm activities in both rural and urban areas.

The first case study presents evidence on the relative importance of farm and urban linkages to the growth of rural nonfarm employment. The second case study analyzes the relative importance of agglomeration economies, infrastructure provision, and spatial spillovers in determining the location decisions of manufacturing firms across the rural–urban continuum.

Case Study 1: The Rural Employment Pattern and Urban Linkages

The existing evidence highlights two observations about the pattern of nonfarm development in rural areas of developing countries. First, the growth of nonfarm activities is often driven by growth in agricultural productivity, at least at the initial stage (Haggblade, Hazell, and Dorosh 2006), because of production, consumption, and labor market linkages between the farm and nonfarm sectors. Second, a large share of nonfarm activities is located in and around towns and cities (Renkow 2006) because of the demand and supply side interlinkages between rural and urban areas (von Thünen 1966; Fuijta, Krugman, and Venables 1999).

A background study undertaken for this chapter considers the relative strength of farm and urban linkages in determining nonfarm employment in Bangladesh (Deichmann, Shilpi, and Vakis 2009). Here we summarize the main findings.

Proximity to large cities is an important determinant of the nature of nonfarm activities in a region. The probability of employment in high-return wage work is greater the closer a person is to a large metropolitan city such as Dhaka or Chittagong (table 9.1). The probability of self-employment is lower for those people living farther from urban centers,

Table 9.1   Urban Access, Cash Crop Potential, and Nonfarm Employment in Bangladesh: Multinomial Logit Results

Dependent variable = type of nonfarm occupation	Regression		
	Wage employment		
	Low return	High return	Self-employment
Distance to major cities (log)	0.01	−0.04	−0.015
	(1.44)	(2.71)**	(1.47)
Distance*crop suitability	−0.006	−0.006	−0.008
	(4.64)**	(1.93)	(3.58)**
Distance to towns (km)	0.001	−0.001	0.001
	(0.73)	(1.41)	(1.92)

Source: Deichmann, Shilpi, and Vakis 2009.
Note: All regressions include individual characteristics (gender, education, age), household characteristics (size, landownership, asset ownership, electricity connection), village characteristics (whether village has electricity, nongovernmental organization programs, credit programs, markets), distance to town, and an intercept term as regressors. Robust z-statistics are in parentheses.
*$p < .05$.
**$p < .01$.

although the estimated effect is not statistically significant. In contrast to the important influence of metropolitan areas, access to smaller rural towns (with populations of about 5,000) exerts little influence on nonfarm activities.

The effect of agricultural potential also depends on how far a village is from urban centers. The results suggest that better-paying wage employment and self-employment in the nonfarm sector are more likely for those living closer to urban centers. Those who are living farther away from such centers are less likely than those living closer to be in well-paid nonfarm jobs if they are living in areas with greater agricultural potential.

Low-return wage work, which pays less than or equal to the median agricultural wage of a region, appears to have no significant relationship to access to urban centers. These jobs seem to cater to local demand and are distributed almost evenly over geographical space.

Lack of connectivity is not only likely to depress growth in agricultural productivity and diversification in areas with higher agricultural potential but also to discourage the growth of higher-paying nonfarm activities in those areas. The empirical results highlight the need for improved connectivity in Bangladesh between regions with higher agricultural potential (such as the northwestern region) and urban centers to stimulate growth in high-return wage employment and self-employment in nonfarm activities. In the second case study, we further examine the pattern of location of nonfarm activities over the entire rural–urban continuum.

Case Study 2: Agglomeration, Spillover, and Location of Nonfarm Activities

Nonfarm activities in developing countries are often clustered in a few locations because of either the natural endowments or the agglomeration economies available at those locations (Krugman 1991; Henderson 1997; Fujita, Krugman, and Venables 1999). Agglomeration economies arise through knowledge and information sharing, economies of scale, and better matching of workers and jobs. Concentration also increases competition, incentivizing firms to make productivity-enhancing investments. However, a greater concentration of activities in an area can lead to congestion, pollution, and transport and services bottlenecks. Without adequate investment in infrastructure and service provision, the diseconomies from congestion can more than offset agglomeration economies, choking off the further growth of nonfarm activities in that area.

The regression results presented in the preceding section suggested a concentration of rural nonfarm activities in proximity to large urban centers—the Dhaka and Chittagong metropolitan areas—in Bangladesh. In this section, in considering the location pattern of nonfarm activities across the rural–urban continuum, we classify areas according to four categories: (1) metropolitan areas (Dhaka, Chittagong, Rajshahi, Khulna, Barisal, and Sylhet); (2) periurban areas consisting of the *upazillas* (subdistricts) bordering the six metropolitan cities; (3) small towns—the district headquarters (*sadar upazillas*); and (4) rural areas—the rest of the country. As noted, these four areas differ markedly in terms of their connectivity to major markets and access to services.[4]

The empirical analysis focuses on firms that employ 10 or more people. These firms account for more than a third of total nonfarm employment in Bangladesh.

The existing evidence indicates that nonfarm activities are highly localized in metropolitan and periurban areas (figure 9.6). According to the 2006 economic census, metropolitan areas account for 43 percent of total employment in firms of 10 or more, followed by rural areas (24 percent) and periurban areas (23 percent). Even within metropolitan areas, activities are clustered in Dhaka and Chittagong. Dhaka alone accounts for 72 percent of total employment and 81 percent of total firms located in metropolitan areas, with Chittagong a distant second (23 percent of employment and 12 percent of firms).

However, diseconomies of congestion have led to a decline in number of nonfarm firms in metropolitan areas as firms have moved to periurban and rural areas. Between 2000 and 2006, employment in metropolitan

Figure 9.6   Shares of Nonfarm Employment and Enterprises by Area: Bangladesh, 2006

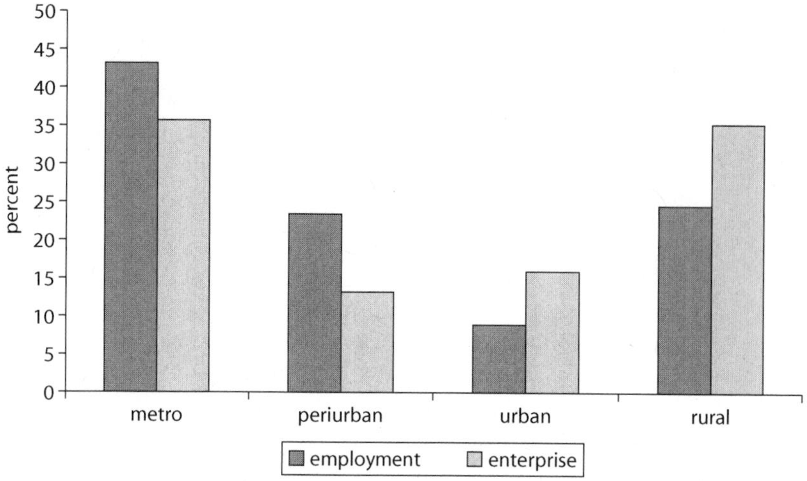

Source: World Bank staff estimates based on economic census of Bangladesh, 2006.

areas remained flat, and the number of firms declined by an annual rate of 2.5 percent (figure 9.7). This decline in the number of firms in metropolitan areas is not surprising in view of the high land prices, congestion, and pollution in those cities, particularly Dhaka. In contrast with metropolitan areas, rural and periurban areas experienced substantial increases in both employment and number of firms (5.2 percent and 1.8 percent, respectively, in rural areas and 4.4 percent and 2.5 percent in periurban areas). Small towns, by contrast, experienced only slight growth in employment and number of firms.

The estimates of Ellison and Glaeser's (1997) concentration index show that only two industries—textile and wearing apparel—display a high degree of concentration in Bangladesh.[5] These industries are, however, the two most important in terms of their contribution to nonfarm employment. Manufacturing of food and beverages, tobacco, and nonmetallic mineral products display intermediate levels of concentration. The rest of the two-digit industries show very low levels of concentration, and hotels and restaurants are the least-concentrated activity in Bangladesh.

To ascertain the relative importance of infrastructure provision and agglomeration forces in determining the dynamics of the clustering of nonfarm activities, we analyze the location decisions of manufacturing

Figure 9.7   Annual Percentage Growth in Nonfarm Employment and Enterprises: Bangladesh, 2000–06

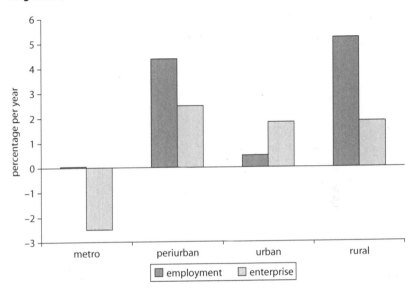

Source: World Bank staff estimates based on economic censuses of Bangladesh, 2000 and 2006.

start-ups using unit record data from the 2000 and 2006 economic censuses. The analysis has been carried out at the two-digit industry and *upazilla* levels.[6] The empirical methodology is described in the background paper by Shilpi (2009). Here we summarize the main results.

Urbanization, as measured by population density and the percentage of urban households in a location, has a significant and positive role in attracting start-ups to a location (table 9.2). Because the regression included dummies to capture any systematic differences in investment climate constraints across regions, the percentage of urban households in a location can be taken as a summary measure of the availability of urban services such as sanitation, garbage disposal, and infrastructure. These results therefore indicate that firms prefer locations with better urban services.

The regression results in table 9.2 reveal that the degree of competition measured by the number of firms per capita in an activity at a given location has a consistently positive and statistically significant effect on firm start-ups in all four regions. These results indicate that competition attracts more productive entrants to a location that already has a concentration of that activity, which is consistent with the observations of Porter (1990). But the interaction of the competition index with firm size has a negative

Table 9.2   Agglomeration Economies and Start-up Firms' Location, Bangladesh

	Metropolitan areas	Periurban areas	Towns	Rural areas
Urbanization economies				
Log (population)	0.301	0.301	0.301	0.301
	(3.81)**	(3.81)**	(3.81)**	(3.81)**
% of household urban	0.008	0.008	0.008	0.008
	(5.67)**	(5.67)**	(5.67)**	(5.67)**
Agglomeration economies				
Specialization index (SI)	1.64	1.29	0.86	2.829
	(1.32)	(2.79)**	(1.44)	(9.17)**
SI*firm size (FS)	0.03	0.03	0.006	0.004
	(1.98)*	(8.61)**	(1.66)	(3.10)**
Competition index (CI)	0.005	0.003	0.003	0.001
	(11.36)**	(31.55)**	(10.71)**	(52.66)**
CI*firm size (FS)	2.0E–05	–1.0E–05	–5.0E–05	–4.5E–06
	(3.85)**	(8.29)**	(3.72)**	(10.47)**
Diversity index (DI)	0.24	0.28	–0.02	0.025
	(4.03)**	(8.29)**	(1.10)	(2.03)*
DI*firm size (FS)	0.003	–8.0E–04	2.0E–04	7.8E–5
	(0.75)	(1.84)	(1.04)	(0.88)

Source: World Bank staff estimates based on economic census of Bangladesh, 2006.
*$p < .05$.
**$p < .01$.

sign for all areas except metropolitan. Thus larger firms prefer locations with a relatively lower density of competitors in the case of periurban areas, rural areas, and smaller towns.

Specialization economies are measured by a location's share of total employment for an activity. The results indicate that start-ups in periurban and rural areas seek out locations with an existing clustering of similar activities. In these areas, the positive externality from locating near similar firms outweighs congestion costs. But in metropolitan areas, congestion costs seem to neutralize the positive externalities from specialization; the regression results suggest no statistically significant effect of specialization on the entry of firms. Not surprisingly, specialization has only a very weak effect in attracting new entrants in smaller towns, which are typically home to a range of activities.

The geographical concentration of various types of activities in a location allows knowledge transfers across firms and makes complementary services available. Our regression results show that the diversity index (measured by the inverse of log of the Herfindahl index of employment concentration) has a positive effect on an entrant's location choice only in metropolitan and periurban areas.

The regression results suggest positive spillovers from the major metropolitan growth poles of Dhaka and Chittagong (table 9.3). The market size in growth poles is measured by the total population of the closest growth pole divided by the distance from an *upazilla* to that growth pole. The influence of market size of the growth poles is positive and statistically significant in all areas except for small towns. Specialization in growth poles has a positive and significant effect on firm entry in metropolitan and periurban areas, and on the entry of larger firms in rural areas. Firms are more likely to choose a location that has better access to markets and firms in growth poles.

By contrast, the regression results indicate that, in medium-size cities, access to markets and specialization have only a weak effect on firm entry. Larger firms are more likely to start up in small towns if the nearest medium-size town has a larger market size and a concentration of firms

Table 9.3   Spillover and Start-up Firms' Location, Bangladesh

	Metropolitan areas	Periurban areas	Towns	Rural areas
Spillover from growth poles				
Market size (MS)	2.90E–06	1.50E–06	1.20E–07	1.62E–06
	(13.34)**	(9.87)**	(0.55)	(10.67)**
Specialization (SP)	9.95	6.17	–3.88	3.29
	(7.27)**	(5.08)**	(1.41)	(1.71)
MS*firm size (FS)	1.3–E–11	3.60E–09	9.60E–10	3.23E–09
	(0.01)	(3.86)**	(0.62)	(3.39)**
SP*FS	–0.035	–0.012	–0.0026	–0.01
	(2.60)**	(0.85)	(0.07)	(0.46)
Spillover from city of size >100,000				
Market size (MS)	2.28E–06	1.81E–06	–1.56E–06	–1.50E–06
	(3.80)**	(5.56)**	(1.83)	(0.67)
Specialization (SP)	7.55	2.27	2.56	34.48
	(2.51)*	(1.42)	(0.90)	(2.51)*
MS*firm size (FS)	–2.73E–09	–2.33E–09	6.85E–08	–5.00E–08
	(0.37)	(0.91)	(2.80)**	(1.52)
SP*FS	–0.09	–0.035	0.3	0.02
	(1.11)	(4.39)**	(3.62)**	(0.27)

Source: World Bank staff estimates based on economic census of Bangladesh, 2006.
*$p < .05$.
**$p < .01$.

in the same activity. And market size in the nearest medium-size town appears to have a positive effect on start-ups in metropolitan and periurban areas. Specialization in the nearest medium-size cities encourages entry into rural and metropolitan areas, but it discourages entry by larger firms in periurban areas. These results suggest that specialization in medium-size cities positively influences firm start-ups in small towns and rural areas. But medium-size towns also pull some large firms away from periurban areas.

Agglomeration economies have a significant positive effect on the productivity of firms located outside of metropolitan areas. The regression based on the Non-Metro Investment Climate Survey (NMICA 2007) shows that the index of specialization has a statistically significant and positive effect on productivity. Similar to our findings for the enterprise start-ups, competition has a statistically significant and positive effect on productivity (table 9.4). The index representing diversity has no significant impact on productivity. The proximity to markets in growth poles influences the productivity of enterprises significantly and positively. By contrast, specialization in growth poles and in the closest medium-size towns seems to affect productivity negatively. When the effects of all different types of specialization variables are evaluated at their mean values, the regression coefficients imply a positive influence of specialization on firm productivity. By survey design, the selected locations in the

Table 9.4   Productivity and Spatial Externality in Bangladesh: Regression Results from Non-Metro Investment Climate Survey Sample

	Coefficient	t-statistic
Specialization index	4.125	(2.62)**
Competition index	0.001	(3.23)**
Diversity index	0.055	(0.28)
Market size of nearest growth pole	6.86E–07	(4.12)**
Specialization of nearest growth pole	–1.502	(2.15)*
Market size of nearest city of population >100,000	1.43E–07	(0.91)
Specialization of nearest city of population >100,000	–4.353	(2.60)**
Log (area)	0.121	(1.37)
Log (population)	0.128	(1.31)
% urban	0.002	(1.04)

Source: World Bank staff estimates based on Non-Metro Investment Climate Survey, 2008.
*$p < .05$.
**$p < .01$.

NMICA 2007 survey are close to urban markets, which may explain why the regression indicates the absence of a substantial effect of own population on firm-level productivity.

Overall, our results suggest that the growth of nonfarm activities, particularly manufacturing activities, outside the two main metropolitan areas of Dhaka and Chittagong will be important for broad-based growth and structural transformation in Bangladesh. Although these two cities manifest the highest level of clustering in the country, according to the regression results the congestion costs already outweigh the benefits of agglomeration. These results are consistent with the evidence of extremely high real estate prices, severe traffic congestion, pollution, and lack of basic urban services in these cities. Although investment in urban services and reforms in urban management may improve the overall investment climate in metropolitan areas, they are unlikely to relax the land constraint imposed by rivers, particularly in the case of Dhaka.[7] Compared with Dhaka and Chittagong, other areas—particularly periurban and rural areas close to metropolitan cities—offer many advantages: cheaper land and labor and little or less congestion. The provision of urban services and maintenance of basic infrastructure in periurban areas would enable further clustering of nonfarm activities.

Smaller towns and cities fare poorly in terms of accessibility to larger urban markets and the provision of services. Whereas periurban areas are within 45 kilometers of four major metropolitan areas (Dhaka, Chittagong, Khulna, and Rajshahi), the smaller towns are on average 160 kilometers away and rural areas 190 kilometers away. The provision of services in smaller towns is comparable to that in periurban areas, and yet smaller towns suffer from lack of connectivity. As a result, these towns and cities have not been able to attract enough specialized activities. Connecting these locations to markets can help the clustering of firms, allowing agglomeration economies to take hold.

Notes

1. The definitions of metropolitan versus smaller cities and towns differ across countries. In Bangladesh, the six administratively defined metropolitan cities are included in the metro sample, whereas in Pakistan, the 14 largest cities are considered metropolitan areas (populations of more than 300,000).

2. Similarly, there are disparities in access to electricity across cities of different sizes in India, although the difference is not as stark as in Bangladesh (World Bank 2008).

3. In contrast to Bangladesh and Pakistan, more than 70 percent of India's urban population lives in medium-size and smaller cities and towns (population of less than 1 million).

4. Bangladesh is administratively organized into 64 districts and more than 480 *upazillas* (subdistricts).

5. The Ellison and Glaeser (1997) concentration index was estimated for all International system of Industry Classification (ISIC) two-digit industries using economic census data.

6. Bangladesh has 484 *upazillas*. Each of the areas specified here—metropolitan cities, periurban areas, smaller towns and cities, and rural areas—consists of many *upazillas*.

7. Expansion of Dhaka city is constrained by the presence of several rivers to the east and south of the city.

References

Deichmann, U., F. Shilpi, and R. Vakis. 2009. "Urban Proximity, Agricultural Potential and Rural Non-farm Employment: Evidence from Bangladesh." *World Development* 37 (3): 645–60.

Ellison, G., and E. L. Glaeser. 1997. "Geographic Concentration in U.S. Manufacturing Industries: A Dartboard Approach." *Journal of Political Economy* 105: 889–927.

Fujita, M., P. Krugman, and A. J. Venables. 1999. *The Spatial Economy: Cities, Regions and International Trade.* Cambridge, MA: MIT Press.

Haggblade, S., P. Hazell, and P. Dorosh. 2006. "Sectoral Growth Linkages between Agriculture and the Rural Nonfarm Economy." In *Transforming the Rural Nonfarm Economy,* ed. S. Haggblade, P. Hazell, and T. Reardon, chap. 7. Baltimore: Johns Hopkins University Press.

Henderson, J. V. 1997. "Externalities and Industrial Development." *Journal of Urban Economics* 42: 449–70.

Krugman, P. 1991. "Increasing Returns and Economic Geography." *Journal of Political Economy* 99: 483–99.

Porter, M. 1990. *The Competitive Advantage of Nations.* New York: Free Press.

Renkow, M. 2006. "Cities, Towns and the Rural Nonfarm Economy." In *Transforming the Rural Nonfarm Economy,* ed. S. Haggblade, P. Hazell, and T. Reardon, 183–98. Baltimore: Johns Hopkins University Press.

Shilpi, F. 2009. "Agglomeration and Location Choice of Rural Enterprises: Evidence from Bangladesh." World Bank, Washington, DC.

von Thünen, J. H. 1966. *Isolated State: An English Edition of Der Isolierte Staat.* Oxford, U.K.: Pergamon Press.

World Bank. 2008. "Harnessing Competitiveness for Stronger Inclusive Growth: Bangladesh Second Investment Climate Assessment." Report No. 56635, Washington, DC.

———. 2011. *Persepectives on Poverty in India: Stylized Facts from Survey Data.* Washington, DC: World Bank.

CHAPTER 10

Labor Mobility and the Rural-Urban Transformation

Chapter 8 examined the impacts of agrarian institutions on the transition from agricultural to nonagricultural activities. Chapter 9 then considered two more dimensions of the rural-urban transformation: sectoral transformation in rural space and the determinants of firms' decisions to locate in smaller towns, or rural, periurban, or metropolitan areas. In this chapter, we consider an additional process associated with the rural-urban transformation: migration of workers from rural to urban areas.

Rural-to-urban migration has contributed significantly to the rapid urbanization of South Asia. Migrants to urban areas are made up of those in search of better living standards—"pull" migrants—and those who have been forced out of rural areas by a lack of job opportunities, poor public services, or natural or human-produced disasters—"push" migrants. Pull migrants frequently are well educated and skilled, raising concerns about a "brain drain" from the area of origin. However, recent evidence suggests that such concerns are misplaced. Migration benefits not only the migrants themselves but also those left behind (Clemens and McKenzie 2009). Moreover, migration helps to moderate the differences in living standards between destination and origin areas (box 10.1).

In addition to facilitating regional convergence of living standards, migration plays a critical role in the reorganization of people and activities

Box 10.1

The Recent Evidence on Migration: A Selected Review

Recent studies argue that simply comparing the earnings of migrants and non-migrants overestimates returns to migration (Gabriel and Schmitz 1995; Dahl 2002; Akee 2006). For example, McKenzie, Gibson, and Stillman (2006) show that ignoring the self-selection of migrants would lead to an overestimation of the gains from migration by 9–82 percent. Despite this selection issue, migration tends to benefit the migrant workers. Beegle, de Weerdt, and Dercon (2008) report that in Tanzania, the poverty rate among those who moved out of Kagera region dropped by 23 percentage points compared with a 12 percentage point drop among those who moved within the region and a 4 percentage point drop among those who did not move.

Recent literature also highlights the role of networks in the migration process. Carrington, Detragiache, and Vishwanath (1996) argue that the presence of a large migrant population in the place of destination reduces migration costs and generates path dependence. Likewise, Munshi (2003) finds that interpersonal networks play a significant role in helping Mexican migrant workers in the United States. Using data on refugees resettled in various parts of the United States, Beaman (2006) reveals a more complex story: an influx of refugees initially over-whelms the network as it struggles to provide job-relevant information, but in the longer term, the network has a positive effect as new migrants find their way into employment. Meanwhile, Munshi and Rosenzweig (2005) find that in India, strong mutual assistance networks in the place of origin discourage migration.

Work migrants often send remittances home, either on a regular basis or to deal with external shocks. These remittances often improve the living standards of nonmigrants and help them to invest (Adams 1997; Woodruff 2001; Lokshin, Bontch-Osmolovski, and Glinskaya 2007; Beegle, de Weerdt, and Dercon 2008). For some countries, they also constitute a significant source of foreign exchange and play an important macroeconomic role. Returning migrants may also invest some of the proceeds from migration into self-employment at home (e.g., McCormick and Wahba 2001; Mesnard and Ravallion 2001).

over geographical space. For one to understand how the spatial pattern of population distribution, and thus urbanization, will evolve, it is important to identify factors that influence migrants' choices of destination. The prospect of earning better wages is perhaps the most frequently cited explanation for the selection of destination. But other factors may influence migration decisions as well, such as the provision of services or ease of assimilation at the destination (Lall, Timmins, and Yu 2009).

Although recent literature has focused on four main issues—returns to migration, the role of networks, remittances, and return migration (box 10.1)—in this chapter we use the case of Nepal to investigate the determinants of migration. We begin by considering the extent of migration across South Asian countries before focusing on Nepal's experience. In Nepal, the bulk of migration is internal—from rural to urban areas—rather than to other countries. Our empirical analysis uncovers the motivation for migration within Nepal, considering the relative importance of infrastructure, provision of services, incomes, and social networks in migrants' decisions.

Internal Migration in South Asia

Historically, many regions of the Indian subcontinent experienced substantial seasonal migration. Reliable estimates of migration flows across regions during recent years are, however, difficult to obtain because internal migration (both temporary and permanent) remains a sparsely researched topic.

Estimates based on recent population censuses suggest the presence of substantial differences in migration rates among countries. When migrants are defined as those who are living in areas different from their place of birth, about 30 percent of India's population, 20 percent of Sri Lanka's, 15 percent of Nepal's, and 9 percent of Pakistan's can be classified as migrants.[1]

Evidence from censuses also suggests an acceleration of migration rates during recent years. In India and Sri Lanka, about 20 percent of migrants moved during the four years before the census. In Nepal, about one-third of migrants moved during those years.

In Nepal, Pakistan, and Sri Lanka, more than 60 percent of migration is from rural to urban areas. In India, rural to rural migration accounts for the bulk (53 percent) of all migration. Moreover, in India, most migration takes place within the province or state; only 14 percent of migrants moved to a state different from their birth state.

Women and men migrate at different paces, and for different reasons, in these countries. In India, women are more mobile than men— constituting more than 70 percent of all migrants. In Nepal, women make up just over half of all migrants. Nearly three-quarters of South Asian women migrate because of marriage. Work migration among women is minuscule in India (about 2 percent) and small in Nepal (22 percent). By contrast, men migrate principally because of work. Among all male migrants, more than a third migrated for work in India. The share is much higher in Nepal (54 percent) and Sri Lanka (45 percent). Among adult males, nearly 70 percent moved for work in Nepal.

The pace of work migration has picked up in recent years in most South Asian countries. The evidence suggests that these migrants are often better educated than those left behind. For example, in Sri Lanka, of households moving in the country, the proportion of people with an O-level education or above is much higher among the heads of migrant households than among those who remained in the district of origin (World Bank 2010). A similar pattern is also true for Nepal.

Internal Work Migration in Nepal

Home to the Himalayas, Nepal remains one of South Asia's remotest countries. The mountain and rural hills regions in Nepal offer few earning opportunities because of their difficult geography and lack of physical infrastructure. For households in these regions, temporary and permanent migration has been an important livelihood strategy. For centuries, people migrated to the Terai plains and adjacent areas in India during off-seasons to supplement their income. This migration continues to this day.

According to a World Bank poverty assessment (World Bank 2006), remittances received by households from both internal and external migrants have been important in reducing the incidence of poverty in Nepal. Between 1995–96 and 2003–04, the poverty headcount ratio declined from 42 percent to 31 percent. A simulation exercise conducted by Lokshin, Bontch-Osmolovski, and Glinskaya (2007) indicates that if remittances had remained at their 1995–96 level, then the incidence of poverty in 2003–04 would have been about 3.9 percentage points higher. In other words, more than a third of the 11 percentage point decline in the poverty headcount ratio between 1995–96 and 2003–04 in Nepal was attributable to higher remittances.

Although both internal and external migration are important in Nepal, we focus on the movement and motivation of internal migrants, who constitute the majority of Nepali migrants. According to the population census sample survey data (2001), about a fifth of adult workers in Nepal are migrant workers. The same census data also indicate that almost 70 percent of adult working-age male migrants move in search of new job opportunities.

Figures 10.1 and 10.2 display the out- and in-migration of male adult workers in Nepal estimated from census data. The districts of origin are distributed widely across the country (figure 10.1). By contrast, a small number of destination districts receive a disproportionate number of work migrants (figure 10.2). A comparison of figures 10.1 and 10.2 indicates a movement of migrants from the hill and mountain districts toward the Terai plains and urban hill areas.

Compared with native workers, migrant workers are on average younger and better educated. About 40 percent of migrants are in the age 20–30 group compared with 19 percent of the native population (figure 10.3). Three-quarters of migrant workers compared with 40 percent of nonmigrants are aged 40 or younger. And nearly half of migrants have education above the secondary level compared with 12 percent of nonmigrants (figure 10.4).

This higher level of education of migrants improves their access to salaried jobs. About 64 percent of migrants are employed in salaried jobs compared with 25 percent of nonmigrants (figure 10.5). Agriculture—the main occupation for nonmigrants—employs just 13 percent of migrants.

Figure 10.1   Out-migration of Workers by District: Nepal, 2001

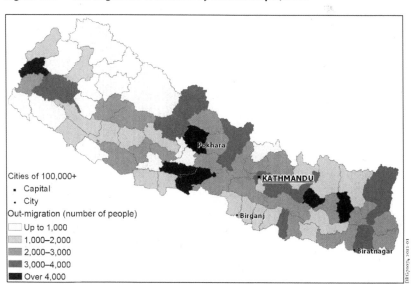

Source: World Bank staff estimates based on population census of Nepal, 2001.

Figure 10.2   In-migration of Workers: Nepal, 2001

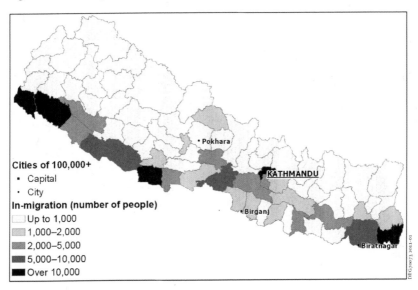

Source: World Bank staff estimates based on population census of Nepal, 2001.

Figure 10.3   Migrants and Nonmigrants by Age Category, Nepal

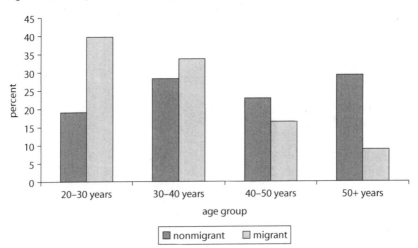

Source: World Bank staff estimates based on population census of Nepal, 2001.

Figure 10.4   Education Level of Migrants and Nonmigrants, Nepal

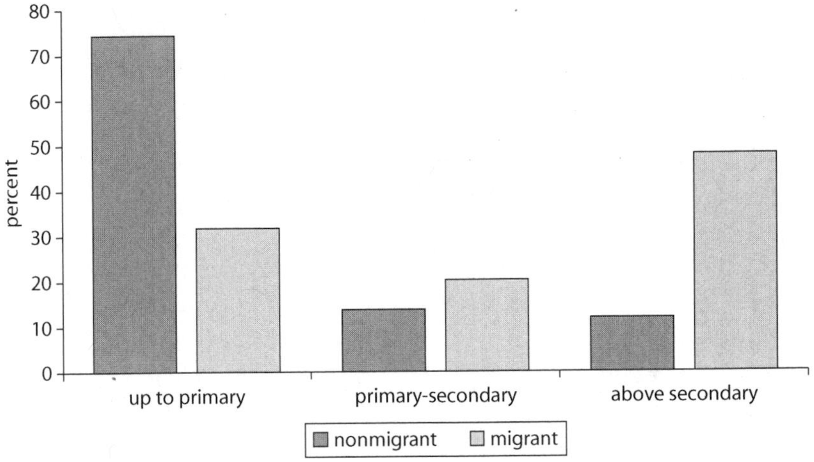

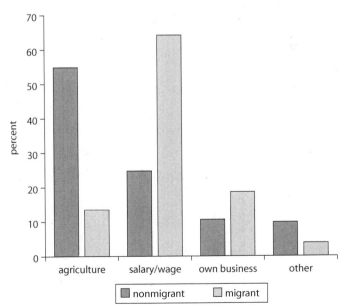

Source: World Bank staff estimates based on population census of Nepal, 2001.

Figure 10.5   Employment of Migrants and Nonmigrants, Nepal

Source: World Bank staff estimates based on population census of Nepal, 2001.

Migration rates for adult males vary across ethno-linguistic groups. For example, Brahmins (high-caste Hindus) constitute 11.7 percent of adult male nonmigrant workers but 34.5 percent of adult male migrants (table 10.1). And migration propensity is much higher among people speaking the Nepali language (74 percent among migrants versus 45.3 percent among nonmigrants).

The characteristics of migrants' destinations differ substantially not only from those of their origin but also from those of other potential destinations. Table 10.2 reports the location characteristics of the actual destination compared with those of alternative destinations.[2] All estimates in table 10.2 are relative to the district of origin. The consumption and housing price premiums in the actual destination district is positive relative to those in the district of origin. The average housing price premium is higher in alternative destinations compared with that in the district of origin. More important, consumption and housing price premiums in the actual destination were significantly higher than those in the alternative destinations in 1995–96. The actual destinations also offered lower rice prices and better services (faster travel times to banks and more paved roads) compared with those in both the origin and alternative destinations. The distance to the actual destination from the district of origin

Table 10.1   Ethnic Profile of Migrants and Nonmigrants (Adult Males), Nepal
percent

	Migrants	Nonmigrants (adult males)
Ethnicity		
Brahmin	34.5	11.7
Chhetri	21.5	15.6
Newar	7.4	7.9
Tharu	3.1	6.7
Magar	6.1	6.0
Tamang	4.2	5.9
Other	23.2	46.2
Language		
Nepali	73.9	45.3
Maithili	6.2	13.2
Bhojpuri	1.3	7.3
Newar	4.4	6.1
Tharu	2.0	5.8
Tamang	3.7	5.5
Other	8.5	16.8

Source: World Bank staff estimates based on population census of Nepal, 2001.

Table 10.2   Comparing Actual Destination and Alternative Destinations of Migrants, Nepal

	Mean in actual destination	Mean in alternative destinations	Difference in mean	
			t-statistic	Significance
Consumption				
Average consumption expenditures (log)	0.075	−0.047	−33.587	***
Differential in log consumption due to education and language	0.009	0.012	0.907	
Prices and services				
Log of rice price	−0.088	0.021	47.577	***
Housing price premium (log)	0.377	0.210	−12.188	***
Travel time to nearest paved road	−0.745	0.104	79.624	***
Travel time to nearest bank	−0.373	0.092	71.245	***
Population and distance				
Population density	0.281	−0.033	−86.063	***
Log (population)	0.329	−0.208	−73.980	***
Elevation in meters	−0.316	0.167	56.973	***
Ethno-caste similarity index	−0.042	−0.060	−13.660	***
Language similarity index	−0.123	−0.101	7.429	***
Religion similarity index	0.008	−0.016	−13.706	***
Distance (thousand km)	0.116	0.278	115.060	***

Source: Fafchamps and Shilpi 2008.
Note: All figures are relative to the district of origin.
***$p < .01$.

was also smaller than those to the alternative destinations. Migrants also chose locations with larger populations, higher rates of urbanization (measured by population density), and lower elevation.

Social distance is measured by the proportion of individuals who share the same language, religion, and ethno-caste group as the migrant.[3] In terms of social proximity, migrants on average face a population in their actual destination and alternative destinations that is more different from them in both language and ethno-caste than in their district of origin. A different pattern is observed for religion; if anything, migrants are more likely to encounter someone of their religion in their district of destination than in their district of origin. The actual destination appears to be more diverse than alternative destinations in the language spoken but less diverse in religion and ethno-caste similarity measures.

Destination Choice of Migrants

To understand what attracts a migrant to a particular location, we performed a regression analysis to ascertain the relative roles of income, services, and physical and social distances in the internal migration process in Nepal. We used an unusually detailed database from the sample survey of Nepal's 2001 population census. The sample survey covers 11 percent of Nepal's population, providing information on 2.5 million individuals (520,624 households). We focused our analysis on adult household heads (older than age 20) who migrated to seek work opportunities only. In the sample survey are some 16,850 such persons, representing about 70 percent of all adult male migrant household heads. The robustness of the empirical analysis is checked by estimating the regressions for the all adult male household heads sample.

The empirical methodology involves several steps, including strategies to guard against reverse causality, as elaborated in the background paper by Fafchamps and Shilpi (2009). Here we summarize the principal findings.

Table 10.3 reports the estimation results from a sample of adult male work migrants and all adult male migrants. The distance variable measures the distance between the district of origin and the district of potential destinations, including the actual destination. This distance is a proxy for migration cost. In both regressions (male work migrants and all male migrants), distance has the expected negative sign and is strongly significant. This finding implies that migrants tend to move to a location that is closer to their district of origin than other potential locations.

The average log consumption in table 10.3 is defined as the difference in average consumption (log) between the district of origin and the districts of potential and actual destinations.[4] Similarly, the consumption differential stemming from education and language measures the education and language premium in the districts of potential destinations relative to the district of origin. The regression coefficients of both of these terms are positive. The coefficient of the education and language premium is highly significant and has a much larger magnitude. The regression results suggest that migrants do respond to income (and thus consumption) differentials and choose a destination that provides higher average consumption than alternative destinations. In particular, migrants choose destinations that offer larger returns to their skills.

The coefficients of population density and log of population are positive and strongly significant in both regressions, indicating that migrants

Table 10.3   Consumption and Choice of Migration Destination: Male Migrants, Nepal

	Adult male work migrants		All adult male migrants	
	Coefficient	t-statistic	Coefficient	t-statistic
Average consumption expenditures (log)	0.331*	1.753	0.433**	2.105
Log consumption differential due to education and language	0.533***	6.330	0.614***	7.197
Prices and services				
Log of rice price	−4.492***	−6.809	−4.173***	−6.016
Housing price premium (log)	0.428***	7.314	0.409***	5.905
Travel time to nearest paved road	−0.770***	−8.297	−0.831***	−8.431
Travel time to nearest bank	0.276	1.569	0.335	1.589
Elevation (1,000 meters)	−0.512***	−3.149	−0.553***	−2.978
Population				
Population density	0.947***	7.316	1.019***	7.356
Log (population)	0.268**	2.099	0.357***	2.669
Social distance				
Ethno-caste similarity index	0.749***	2.607	0.794***	2.921
Language similarity index	1.486***	8.037	1.622***	8.812
Religion similarity index	−0.443	−1.416	−0.744**	−2.265
Distance				
Distance (km, hundreds)	−9.932***	−13.425	−10.62***	−13.481
Log-likelihood		−47,880.35		−66,980.53
Number of observations		1,072,804		1,555,740
Pseudo R^2		0.289		0.314

Source: Fafchamps and Shilpi 2008.
Note: Fixed effect conditional legit estimation. Standard errors are corrected for clustering across district of origin.
*$p < .10$.
**$p < .05$.
***$p < .01$.

move to locations that already have high concentrations of people. Because population tends to concentrate in areas with agglomeration economies and higher economic densities, this result suggests that the pull of opportunities in urban areas is quite important in attracting migrants to those locations.

The regressions included indicators of services. Access to facilities such as schools, hospitals, and markets is measured by travel time to a paved road. Access to financial services is represented by the travel time to a bank. Elevation provides an indication of the difficulty of transporting goods and people. The cost of living is measured by the price of rice and the housing price premium; the latter also provides an indication of public goods (such as air quality and congestion) that are not included directly as regressors in the estimation. The results in table 10.3 show that all but one of the coefficients (travel time to a bank) are highly significant. Migrants choose destinations that have much better access to schools, hospitals, and markets, as measured by travel to a paved road. The coefficient of elevation is negative, implying that, on average, migrants choose destinations where it is easier to transport goods and people. The regression coefficient implies that housing costs are higher in the destination district than in alternative destinations, indicating that migrants also value public goods and services that are unobservable in regressions. Finally, conditional on the housing price premium and other services, migrants choose destinations where rice prices—an important measure of the cost of living in Nepal—are lower than in alternative destinations.

Conditional on other regressors, the ethno-caste and language proximity indexes are significant, with positive signs (table 10.3). This finding implies that the social proximity between the migrant and the population of the destination district is higher than that in alternative destinations. The religion proximity index is, however, not significant in the work migrants' sample.[5] Taken together, these results suggest that, conditional on the material benefits of migration, migrants prefer to move to a destination where they can integrate more easily and possibly use networks to access jobs and housing.

To provide a sense of the importance of different factors in determining migration destination, we estimate the relative magnitude of a one standard deviation change in each regressor, keeping other regressors unchanged. The absolute values of these magnitudes are shown in figure 10.6. The most important regressor in terms of magnitude is distance. Migrants strongly prefer a nearby destination. The second most important factor is the cost of living (measured by the price of rice). Factors related to access to services (travel time to the nearest road and housing price premium) also have relatively strong effects on destination choice. Among different measures of social proximity, the language similarity index has the largest relative impact. The effect of consumption variables on migration destination is smaller in magnitude. For example, a one standard deviation increase in anticipated relative consumption has an effect on destination that corresponds to a third of the effect of a one standard deviation in the housing price premium, and one-sixth of a one standard deviation in the log of the price of rice.

Figure 10.6   Effects of Regressors on Destination Choice (Absolute Values), Nepal

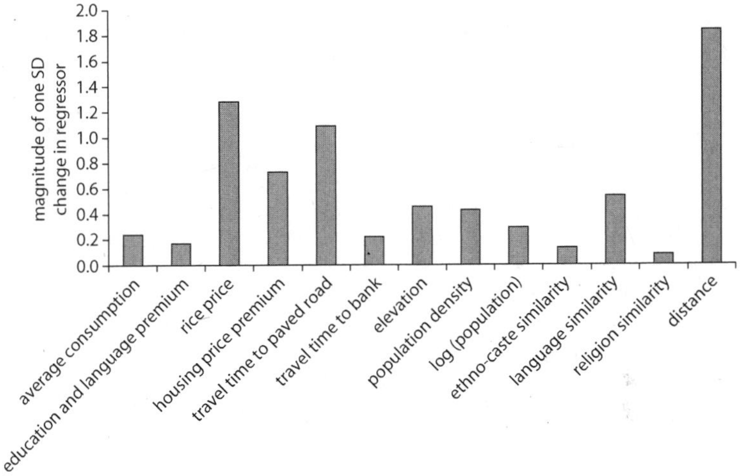

Source: Fafchamps and Shilpi 2008.
Note: SD = standard deviation.

Evidence from other developing countries underscores the role of services in attracting migrants to a location. Econometric estimations based on data from Sri Lanka find that migration decisions in the 1990s were influenced by district-level differences in access to well water and electricity, particularly for the less educated (World Bank 2010). Analysis of migration decisions in Brazil suggests that there, too, migrants are attracted to locations based on the quality of public goods and services offered, and poorer migrants are willing to accept lower wages to access better services (box 10.2).

The importance of physical and social distances in migrants' destination choices implies that migration flows are likely to be more vibrant across locations that are in close proximity. Thus smaller cities and towns can become important destinations for migrants from surrounding areas. But the growth of these cities and towns, according to the earlier empirical results, will depend on the availability of services. Investment in services in smaller towns and cities (or migrants' districts of origin) can relieve congestion pressure from metropolitan cities while reducing rural-urban gaps in economic well-being.

The costs and benefits of such investment programs, however, have to be weighed against the costs and benefits of providing services in larger cities. For example, investments in infrastructure in remote districts may prove to be prohibitively expensive, and investments in metropolitan

Box 10.2

Migrating to Economic Density in Brazil: Rational Decisions or Bright Lights?

Economists have long argued that migration decisions are motivated by the possibility of earning higher wages. But because many migrants do not find jobs after moving, this attraction may be irrational.

Recent empirical evidence from four decades of Brazilian census data is enlightening. Working-age men migrated not only to look for better jobs but also to gain better access to basic public services such as piped water, electricity, and health care. These findings indicate that results from models of migration behavior that focus only on a migrant's desire to move in search of better jobs can be biased because places with better public services also have more job opportunities. Firms like to locate where workers would like to live. By ignoring the importance of public services, some econometric estimates may overstate a migrant's willingness to move in response to wage differences.

For determination of how much public services matter, a rich set of data on public services at the municipality level was combined with individual records from Brazil's census to evaluate the relative importance of wage differences and public services in a migrant's decision to move. Predictably, wage differences are the main factor influencing migration choices. For the better-off, basic public services are not important in the decision to move. But for the poor, differences in access to basic public services matter. In fact, poor migrants are willing to accept lower wages to achieve access to better services. For example, a Brazilian minimum wage worker earning R$7 an hour was willing to pay R$420 a year to have access to better health services, R$87 for a better water supply, and R$42 for electricity.

Source: World Bank 2008, based on Lall, Timmins, and Yu 2009.

areas could help to reinforce preexisting agglomeration economies. Our findings suggest that, provided a rigorous cost-benefit analysis is performed, geographically targeted investments in public services could ease the rural-urban transition process.

Notes

1. In Bangladesh, the migration data needed for a comparison with other South Asian countries are not available. The estimate for Sri Lanka includes those who migrated because of conflicts in part of the country.

2. Alternative destinations consist of all districts other than districts of birth and actual destination.

3. The construction of social distance variables is described in the background paper by Fafchamps and Shilpi (2009). These indexes are in practice similar to the ethno-linguistic fractionalization measure common in the growth literature.

4. The income estimates from developing countries such as Nepal are notoriously weak because of the predominance of self-employment. Relative to income data, consumption data are of better quality. For this reason, we present the results using consumption measures. Regression estimates using income measures can be found in the background paper by Fafchamps and Shilpi (2009).

5. For the sample of adult male migrants, the coefficient of the religion similarity index is negative and statistically significant. This finding indicates that work migrants tend to choose urban destinations that are more diverse in religion.

References

Adams, R. 1997. *Remittances, Investment, and Rural Asset Accumulation in Pakistan*. Washington, DC: International Food Policy Research Institute.

Akee, R. K. Q. 2006. "Deciphering Immigrant Self-Selection: New Evidence from a Developing Country." Kennedy School of Government, Harvard University, Cambridge, MA.

Beaman, L. A. 2006. "Social Networks and the Dynamics of Labor Market Outcomes: Evidence from Refugees Resettled in the US." Department of Economics, Yale University, New Haven, CT.

Beegle, K., J. de Weerdt, and S. Dercon. 2008. "Migration and Economic Mobility in Tanzania: Evidence from a Tracking Survey." Policy Research Working Paper 4798, World Bank, Washington, DC.

Carrington, W. J., E. Detragiache, and T. Vishwanath. 1996. "Migration with Endogenous Moving Costs." *American Economic Review* 86 (4): 909–30.

Clemens, M. A., and D. McKenzie. 2009. "Think Again: Brain Drain." *Foreign Policy*, October 22.

Dahl, G. B. 2002. "Mobility and the Return to Education: Testing a Roy Model with Multiple Markets." *Econometrica* 70 (6): 2367–420.

Fafchamps, M., and F. Shilpi. 2008. "Determinants of Choice of Migration Destination." Policy Research Working Paper 4728, World Bank, Washington, DC.

———. 2009. "Isolation and Subjective Welfare: Evidence from South Asia." *Economic Development and Cultural Change* 57 (4): 641–83.

Gabriel, P. E., and S. Schmitz. 1995. "Favorable Self-Selection and the Internal Migration of Young White Males in the United States." *Journal of Human Resources* 30 (3): 460–71.

Lall, S., C. Timmins, and S. Yu. 2009. "Connecting Lagging and Leading Regions: The Role of Labor Mobility." Brookings-Wharton Papers on Urban Affairs, 151–74, Brookings Institution, Washington, DC.

Lokshin, M., M. Bontch-Osmolovski, and E. Glinskaya. 2007. "Work-Related Migration and Poverty Reduction in Nepal." Policy Research Working Paper 4231, World Bank, Washington, DC.

McCormick, B., and J. Wahba. 2001. "An Econometric Model of Temporary International Migration and Entrepreneurship." Department of Economics, University of Southampton, Southampton, U.K.

McKenzie, D., J. Gibson, and S. Stillman. 2006. "How Important Is Selection? Experimental vs. Non-Experimental Measures of the Income Gains from Migration." IZA Discussion Paper 2087, Institute for the Study of Labor, Bonn.

Mesnard, A., and M. Ravallion. 2001. "Is Inequality Bad for Business? A Nonlinear Empirical Model of Entrepreneurship." ARQADQ, University of Toulouse, and DECRG, World Bank, Washington, DC.

Munshi, K. 2003. "Networks in the Modern Economy: Mexican Migrants in the US Labor Market." *Quarterly Journal of Economics* 118 (2): 549–99.

Munshi, K., and M. Rosenzweig. 2005. "Why Is Mobility in India So Low? Social Insurance, Inequality and Growth." Economic Growth Center, Yale University, New Haven, CT.

Woodruff, C. 2001. "Remittances and Microenterprises in Mexico." Graduate School of International Relations and Pacific Studies, University of California, San Diego, La Jolla.

World Bank. 2006. "Nepal—Resilience amidst Conflict: An Assessment of Poverty in Nepal, 1995–96 and 2003–04." Report 34834-NP, World Bank, Washington, DC.

———. 2008. *World Development Report 2009: Reshaping Economic Geography.* Washington, DC: World Bank.

———. 2010. "Sri Lanka: Connecting People to Prosperity." Draft, South Asian Poverty Reduction and Economic Management Unit. Washington, DC.

CHAPTER 11

Summary and Conclusions

Today's transition from rural to urban economies is an immense development challenge. Urbanization may spur growth and reduce poverty, but it also goes hand in hand with inequalities. Developing country policy makers and the development community are thus looking for ways in which to manage the rural-urban transition that ensure inclusive growth.

Three Levels of Perspectives on Urbanization and Shared Growth: Sub-Saharan Africa

As noted at the outset of this report, rural-urban transformations have been the focus of two consecutive editions of the *World Development Report: WDR 2008, Agriculture for Development*, and *WDR 2009, Reshaping Economic Geography* (World Bank 2007, 2008). Part I of this report is an empirical exploration of some of the principal propositions of *WDR 2009*, using examples from three Sub-Saharan countries: Ghana, Mozambique, and Uganda.

Urbanization is inextricably linked to economic development. It accompanies, and in many ways drives, the structural transformation of economies that are largely agricultural to ones that are increasingly manufacturing and services-based. As part of this process, "leading" areas

191

emerge, characterized by average standards of living higher than those in "lagging" areas. The spatial inequalities that arise are often viewed as an inevitable part of the development process, rewarding higher productivity, economies of scale, and agglomeration effects in the more advanced sectors of the economy. Although leading and lagging areas often correspond to rural-urban divides, the same spatial disparities may be replicated on larger or smaller geographical scales—for example, in the form of North-South divides or intraurban inequalities.

Even if they are linked to the process of development, spatial inequalities can be far from benign. They may increase total inequality, which can diminish the impact of growth on poverty reduction. Spatial inequalities often correspond to ethnic, cultural, or religious divisions, leading to friction and unrest that may impede or even derail the development process. Although unequal outcomes are expected to some degree as a country develops, if left unchecked, spatial inequalities may become structural inequalities that translate into inequalities of opportunity. What, then, is the scope for public policy to manage the rural-urban transformation and urbanization in a way that promotes equitable development?

Our cross-country findings in chapter 2 suggest that few low- and middle-income countries fit neatly into the paradigm in *WDR 2009* that rural-urban welfare disparities first diverge and then converge once countries reach upper-middle-income status. Even in countries with the same levels of urbanization or GDP per capita, rural-urban differences may be enormous or relatively small. And, depending on the welfare measure used, almost as many cases of convergence of living standards can be found within countries over time as cases of divergence. The existence of so much diversity of experience at the country level implies that policies and institutions can play a crucial role in rural-urban transformations, a proposition that is explored in much greater depth in part II of this report, which describes and analyzes the rural-urban transformation in South Asia.

The decomposition analysis in chapter 3 provides some insights of the kinds of policies and institutions that could help to narrow rural-urban divides in Ghana, Mozambique, and Uganda—countries that qualify as "agriculture-based" and "incipient urbanizers," according to the categories put forth in *WDR 2008* and *WDR 2009*, respectively. The principal finding—that rural-urban inequalities in average household welfare stem primarily from differences in household endowments—suggests an important role for "spatially blind" policies and the kinds of institutions advocated in *WDR 2009*. These policies may include the universal provision of services such as education, health, water, and sanitation financed through taxes and transfers, as well as regulations affecting land, labor, and business development that do not discriminate on the basis of location. Because rural-urban welfare inequalities are strongly associated with differences in education attainment, policies must focus on the equal provision of education (both quantity and quality) to narrow productivity and income gaps between leading and lagging areas.

Nonmonetary welfare measures suggest that a significant rural-urban divide exists in more than just access to education. Stunting, an indicator of child health as well as the overall socioeconomic status of the household, is consistently found more in rural than in urban areas; adequate water and sanitation are consistently found less in rural areas than in urban areas, and in some cases are continuing to diverge. Thus the provision of spatially neutral institutions should also extend to increasing access to all basic services. Because rural areas are presently disadvantaged, the provision of "spatially blind" services might effectively entail a renewed emphasis on lagging parts of the country until these areas catch up.

Such investments in lagging areas are not intended to slow down the process of rural-urban transformation. Rather, because education and health are portable assets, expanded provision of them enables people to pursue a better quality of life in whatever geographical space they have chosen to make their home. However, improvements in basic services in rural areas may reduce excess migration to urban areas, because, as indicated in the case studies on South Asian countries in part II of this report, rural-urban migration choices are based not only on potential income but also on prospective access to services.

In contrast to the main policy thrust of *WDR 2009*, the findings in chapter 3 suggest that even in "incipient urbanizers" such as Ghana, Mozambique, and Uganda, policy makers must look beyond the provision of spatially blind institutions to the provision of connective infrastructure. As described in *WDR 2008*, such infrastructure is necessary both to support productivity gains among smallholder farmers and to promote the growth of the nonfarm sector and linkages between rural and urban economies. The effective delivery of services will depend in part on a higher level of infrastructure than currently exists in many rural areas of these countries. For example, a school is unlikely to be effective, or accessible, without a road to it. Likewise, the payoff to investments in portable assets depends in part on reducing the costs of trade for rural workers if they choose to remain in a rural area, or the costs of migration if they seek to move to an urban area.

The case studies of three African capitals in chapter 4 indicate that intraurban inequalities can be even starker than the rural-urban divide. Slums, in which hundreds of thousands of people lack access to even basic amenities, exist in close proximity to highly serviced luxury developments. Colonial legacies, weak land institutions, and poor governance all have a role to play in the kinds of spatial disparities on view in Accra (Ghana), Maputo (Mozambique), and Kampala (Uganda).

Local and national governments have recognized the urgent need to address the multiple issues—from inadequate legal frameworks and weak dispute settlement mechanisms to poor land management and corruption—that combine to create tight land and housing markets in each of these cities. As elaborated in greater detail in part II, land reforms are among the most challenging reforms to implement from a political economy perspective. However, intermediary measures such as efforts to improve land titling registration or codify existing laws are important steps forward. Evidence from other African cities suggests that tripartite agreements among governments, landlords, and tenants could help to improve tenure conditions. One example, from Nairobi's slums, required landlords to relinquish control of some housing units in exchange for formal title and assistance in improving retained units (Gulyani and Talukdar 2008). Such incremental but meaningful steps represent a promising approach in view of the entrenched vested interests in land and its ties to economic and political power.

The provision of adequate services for all urban residents remains a paramount challenge. Cohen (2007) recently remarked that "most urban analysts are still entering the city through the house and the bathroom, rather than through the workplace, the market, or as a site of creating long-term assets." Nevertheless, the challenge of urban governance—to provide adequate infrastructure and services—is vital to both human development and job creation. Indeed, as demonstrated in part II, diseconomies caused by overcrowded and underserviced urban living can outweigh agglomeration economies, deterring firms from locating in large cities. The dichotomy between the household and workplace is perhaps a false one: both rely on adequate public services and good governance to flourish.

Like the findings in chapter 3, those in chapter 4 indicate that policy makers in "incipient urbanizers" will need to look beyond the broad policy guidance in *WDR 2009*, which argues they should focus first and foremost on "spatially neutral" institutions. Within cities, targeted interventions such as slum clearance and housing construction may be an important policy step, even in countries that are only incipient urbanizers at the national level.[1] Indeed, as discussed in chapter 4, slum upgrading programs in Accra have already yielded important successes that could be replicated on a wider scale. But as indicated in *WDR 2009*, investments in connective infrastructure or slum upgrading will be effective only if the basic institutions are sound.

We hope that the findings of these chapters will spur deeper research and debate into the causes of spatial inequalities at the national and local levels. Land tenure in both rural and urban areas would certainly benefit from more in-depth analysis because of the evidence suggesting its profound impact on the rural-urban transformation (Shilpi 2010). Our research also demonstrates a need for more geographically sensitive poverty analysis of the kind generated by small area poverty maps, especially in urban areas.

Managing the Rural-Urban Transformation: Examples from South Asia

Now the focus shifts back to the national level. South Asian countries are at various stages of the rural-urban transformation. Indeed, these countries differ widely in their stages of agricultural development, urbanization, and living standards (chapter 5). Among the five major countries featured in part II of this report—Bangladesh, India, Nepal, Pakistan, and Sri Lanka—only Nepal can be classified as an agro-based country in which urbanization is at an incipient stage. The rest of the countries have experienced considerable declines in the importance of agriculture to economic growth and so are rapidly "transforming" (or urbanizing) countries. All countries have experienced substantial declines in the incidence of poverty, although the rapidly urbanizing countries have experienced higher economic growth.

Compared with cross-country differences, the pattern of rural-urban transformation within countries (chapter 6) suggests much greater variation in employment structure, urbanization levels, and economic well-being. Sri Lanka, the richest country in South Asia, has regions—such as Uva Province—in which the poverty incidence is comparable to that of poorer countries, and in which most people are still dependent on agriculture for their livelihoods. The Kathmandu Valley in Nepal, one of the least urbanized countries in South Asia, is nearly fully urbanized with a poverty incidence of only 3.4 percent. These striking intracountry differences in economic structure and well-being are also present in Bangladesh, India, and Pakistan.

A survey of the policy environment reveals that most of the South Asian countries implemented broad economic reforms over the last two decades (chapter 7). In Sri Lanka, an early mover, the first wave of trade and industrial deregulation began in 1977. By the early 1990s, the rest of the countries had implemented industrial and trade policy reforms. But in almost every country, agricultural reforms lagged significantly.

As for the factor markets, one of the most important conditions shaping the trajectory of economic development in rural areas is the land market (chapters 7 and 8). All South Asian countries have attempted to introduce some land and tenancy reform measures, but the actual implementation experience has been uneven at best. The land market in Sri Lanka is characterized by the predominance of public ownership of agricultural land. The distribution of landownership is unequal in most countries, particularly in Pakistan. In the labor market, restrictions on the hiring and firing of workers can create an environment prohibitive to business start-up and expansion. However, enforcement of these restrictions remains uneven, applying primarily to the formal urban labor markets.

In assessing the access to connective infrastructure, we find that although road densities are relatively high in South Asian countries (except Nepal), the intracountry differences in access to urban centers are striking (see chapters 7 and 9, which describe geographical linkages). Even in Sri Lanka, a country with the highest road density in South Asia, the relatively remoter regions are more than 15 hours away from the nearest city of 100,000 or more. These intracountry differences in access to urban centers correlate with geographical differences in economic structure and well-being.

By contrast, intracountry differences in the provision of health care and education tend to be small. Sri Lanka ranks highest in terms of the overall provision of health care and education and has also managed to provide them equitably across geographical space. Even though the overall levels of health care and education are lower in Nepal and Bangladesh, the intracountry differences are still small. By contrast, Pakistanis are subject to high inequality in health care and education along socioeconomic and gender lines.

Migration rates among adult male workers also vary considerably across countries (see chapter 10, which discusses labor mobility across areas). In the mountains and hills of Nepal where earning opportunities are limited, rural-to-urban migration is an important part of the livelihood strategy. By contrast, much of the work migration in India takes place within rural areas. However, the pace of migration, particularly rural-to-urban migration, has picked up in recent years in all of the South Asian countries.

The evidence on the patterns of rural-urban transformation thus demonstrates clearly that South Asian countries are not only experiencing different stages of structural transformation but also following different paths of transition. The uneven progress in the implementation of policy and institutional reforms also suggests that, despite their common colonial histories, these countries now face different constraints to rural-urban transformation.

The in-depth case studies reported in part II, while reinforcing some of the principal policy messages of *WDR 2008* and *WDR 2009*, yield additional policy insights for the rural-urban transformation. Here we summarize the major policy implications.

Land reforms that improve the access of the poor to agricultural land could ensure a more inclusive rural-urban transformation. As revealed by the case study, in Pakistan, inequality in the distribution of land has forced a large portion of the population to seek off-farm employment, thereby depressing wages, particularly in agriculture and manufacturing. The effect is not confined to rural areas. Self-employment in smaller cities and towns and manufacturing in metropolitan areas are also affected. These findings bolster the case for land reform that would increase the access of the poor to land. Even though drastic land reform remains politically infeasible in Pakistan as in most other countries, several policy measures can increase the access of the poor to land. These include increased access to credit to enable poor people to purchase land, land taxation to minimize the holding of land for speculative purposes, and measures to improve the efficiency of land sales and rental markets.

Flexibility in land market transactions is essential for ensuring a faster and more inclusive rural-urban transition. WDR 2008 emphasizes the need for land reform to both spur the growth of agricultural productivity and reduce rural poverty. *WDR 2009* highlights the need for flexibility in converting land from one use to another. According to the case study on Sri Lanka, restrictions on sales and subdivisions of agricultural land increase the cost of migration, resulting in slower urbanization and a higher incidence of poverty. Thus flexible land markets are needed not only at the urban fringe to allow physical expansion of urban areas, but also in rural areas beyond the urban fringe.

Investment in human capital remains a powerful instrument for undertaking a rural-urban transformation. The regression results confirm that educated people have better access to nonfarm jobs and can reap considerable positive returns in the labor market. The need to invest in human capital is much more urgent in countries such as Pakistan, where inequality in landownership may have led to underinvestment in human capital. When some of the institutional reforms (such as land reform) are politically difficult to implement, investment in human capital is an alternative strategy for promoting a smoother rural-urban transformation.

Investments in connective infrastructure are needed to strengthen farm-nonfarm and rural-urban linkages. WDR 2008 and *WDR 2009* give high priority to investments in connective infrastructure as a step toward agricultural transformation, urbanization, and regional convergence in living standards. The results from the case studies reinforce this policy recommendation. Improved connectivity can reduce migration costs substantially, facilitating better integration of labor markets across regions. In addition, the case studies indicate the benefits of targeting infrastructure investments to areas with high potential agricultural growth, where improved connectivity would have the greatest impact on productivity and farm-nonfarm linkages. Similarly, targeting investments in infrastructure and services in periurban and rural areas with existing concentrations of activities and access to markets could facilitate the further agglomeration of activities in these areas.

Combining institutional reforms and infrastructure investment would have a much stronger positive impact on rural-urban transformation than pursuing these goals separately. Sectoral employment and wage patterns over geographical space are shaped by complex interactions of access to markets and agrarian institutions. In Bangladesh, for example, the impact of access to large urban markets on farm-nonfarm linkages is particularly pronounced in areas with high agricultural potential. In Sri Lanka, the impact of land market restrictions is greater in villages closer to urban centers. The presence of interaction effects implies that countries may have to implement a package of complementary policies and investments to get a bigger bang out of their investments.

Investment in services combined with infrastructure investment can ensure better integration of labor and product markets in rural and urban areas, facilitating the clustering of activities and workers. Together, the Bangladesh and Nepal case studies demonstrate the importance of services in attracting firms and workers to a location. Firms in Bangladesh tend to move to periurban and rural areas that already offer agglomeration economies and better access to large markets. Meanwhile, migrants in Nepal value services (such as schools, health care centers, and access to urban areas) just as they value income prospects. These results indicate scope for investing further in infrastructure outside of metropolitan areas—whether rural, periurban, or small towns—subject to a location-specific cost-benefit analysis.

The relationship of the urbanization strategy to smaller towns and cities should be reconsidered. The empirical results suggest that smaller towns and cities in Bangladesh have not been able to attract manufacturing. The low clustering of manufacturing activities can be traced to these cities' and towns' dearth of infrastructure and services. Urban primacy, whereby Dhaka and Chittagong account for more than half of the urban population and receive the majority of public investments, is estimated to cost about 1 percent of economic growth (World Bank 2004). Connecting smaller towns and cities to national and international markets and providing better services could encourage firms and people to move to these locations, creating alternative engines of growth and sectoral transformation. The fact that migrants tend to relocate close to their regions of origin implies that investment in smaller towns will enable a faster convergence of living standards across areas.

Possible spillovers across sectors and areas in policy making merit attention. As revealed by the case studies, policies intended for one area may have substantial effects on others. For example, in Sri Lanka the productive inefficiency arising from the restrictions posed by the Land Development Ordinance in agriculture was to a large extent mitigated by the massive public investment in irrigation schemes. Such policies may have addressed the immediate concerns in agriculture, but they resulted in slower employment diversification, slower migration, and lower overall living standards. Similarly, the adverse effects of land inequality in Pakistan extend far beyond rural areas and into the smaller towns and cities.

In some cases, political economy considerations will be paramount. A political economy analysis was beyond the scope of our own research, but it is clear that the political environment can impose binding constraints on reform. This finding is particularly true of land reform because of the role of land in ensuring access to productive assets and political influence. With the exception of India, none of the South Asian countries has been able to implement marginal tenancy reforms, let alone broader land reforms, in recent decades. The country case studies demonstrate that the costs of inaction are likely to be high, whether for the rural-urban transformation, economic growth, or the convergence of living standards. These reforms will require a change in the mindset of policy makers and recognition of the importance of urbanization and rural-urban transformation in reducing rural and urban poverty.

Management of the rural-urban transition in a way that preserves growth and promotes equity is one of the major challenges facing policy makers in today's developing countries. The design and implementation of an effective policy mix rely in turn on having accurate information on the causes and manifestations of spatially based inequalities. We hope that the information conveyed in this report represents a modest step in the right direction.

Note

1. In "incipient urbanizers," the distribution of population is less than 25 percent urban and more than 75 percent rural. In "intermediate urbanizers," the distribution is between 25 and 75 percent urban (or 75 percent urban and 25 percent rural). In "advanced urbanizers," the population distribution is above 75 percent urban (below 25 percent rural).

References

Cohen, M. 2007. "Thinking Outside the Bubble: The Urban Crises of Land, Labor, and Capital." Paper prepared for Lincoln Institute for Land Policy Symposium, Rio de Janeiro, October 1–2, 2007. http://www.gpia.info/files/u1/wp/2007-05 .pdf.

Gulyani, S., and D. Talukdar. 2008. "Slum Real Estate: The Low-Quality High-Price Puzzle in Nairobi's Slum Rental Market and Its Implications for Theory and Practice." *World Development* 36 (10): 1916–37.

Shilpi, F. 2010. "The Effect of Land Market Restrictions on Employment Pattern and Wages: Evidence from Sri Lanka." World Bank, Washington, DC.

World Bank. 2004. *Bangladesh: Promoting the Non-Farm Sector in Bangladesh.* Report 29719-BD. World Bank, Washington, DC.

———. 2007. *World Development Report 2008: Agriculture for Development.* Washington, DC: World Bank.

———. 2008. *World Development Report 2009: Reshaping Economic Geography.* Washington, DC: World Bank.

Countries and Surveys Used for Consumption and Poverty Analysis

Table A.1 Countries and Surveys Used for Consumption and Poverty Analysis

Country (by World Bank Region)	Abbreviation	LSMS survey, year 1	LSMS survey, year 2	GDP per capita (2005 US$, PPP), year 1	GDP per capita (2005 US$, PPP), year 2	DHS survey, year 1	DHS survey, year 2
Africa							
Burkina Faso	BFA	1994	2003	729	982	1992–93	2003
Cameroon	CMR	1996	2001	1,678	1,870	1991	2004
Côte d'Ivoire	CIV	1998	2002	1,885	1,672	1994	1998–99
Ghana	GHA	1991–92	2005–06	886	1,209	1993	2003
Madagascar	MDG	1997	2001	823	884	1992	2003–04
Mali	MLI	1994	2001	737	933	1995–96	2006
Mozambique	MOZ	1996–97	2002–03	435	596	1997	2003
Nigeria	NGA	1996–97	2003	1,454	1,558	1990	2003
Senegal	SEN	1994–95	2001	1,293	1,429	1992–93	2005
South Africa	ZAF	1995	2000	7,319	7,466	—	—
Tanzania	TZA	1991–92	2000–01	837	880	1992	2004
Uganda	UGA	1992–93	2002–03	563	791	1995	2006
Zambia	ZMB	1996	2003	1,055	1,107	1992	2001–02
East Asia and Pacific							
Cambodia	KHM	1994	2004	769	1,291	2000	2005
Indonesia	IDN	1993	2002	2,487	2,873	—	—
Vietnam	VNM	1992	2002	997	1,780	—	—

Europe and Central Asia

Armenia	ARM	1998–99	2002	2,109	2,870	2000	2005
Kazakhstan	KAZ	1996	2002	4,591	6,748	1995	1999
Kyrgyz Republic	KGZ	1998	2002	1,408	1,556	—	—
Moldova	MDA	1997	2002	1,519	1,711	—	—
Uzbekistan	UZB	1998	2002	1,545	1,725	—	—

Latin America and the Caribbean

Bolivia[a]	BOL	1997	2002	3,508	3,565	1994	2003
Brazil[a]	BRA	1990	2002	7,235	8,017	—	—
Colombia[a]	COL	1996	2003	5,596	5,498	1995	2005
Dominican Rep.	DOM	1992	2003	3,493	5,014	1991	2002
Ecuador[a]	ECU	1994	1998	5,665	5,862	—	—
El Salvador[a]	SLV	1995	2002	4,707	5,018	—	—
Guatemala[a]	GTM	1998	2002	3,863	4,014	1995	1998–99
Honduras[a]	HND	1992	2003	2,744	3,044	—	—
Mexico	MEX	1992	2002	9,550	10,815	—	—
Nicaragua[a]	NIC	1993	2001	1,734	2,145	1997–98	2001
Paraguay[a]	PRY	1998	2003	4,069	3,706	—	—
Peru[a]	PER	1994	2003	4,978	5,894	1992	2000

Middle East and North Africa

Egypt, Arab Rep.	EGY	1995	2000	3,558	4,178	1992	2005
Morocco	MAR	1990–91	1998	2,825	2,977	1992	2003–04
Tunisia	TUN	1995	2000	4,422	5,444	—	—

(continued next page)

Table A.1 Countries and Surveys Used for Consumption and Poverty Analysis *(continued)*

Country (by World Bank Region)	Abbreviation	LSMS survey, year 1	LSMS survey, year 2	GDP per capita (2005 US$, PPP), year 1	GDP per capita (2005 US$, PPP), year 2	DHS survey, year 1	DHS survey, year 2
South Asia							
Bangladesh	BGD	1991–92	2000	712	901	1996–97	2004
India	IND	1993–94	2005	1,303	2,230	1998–99	1992–93
Nepal	NPL	1995–96	2003–04	818	938	1996	2006
Pakistan	PAK	1992–93	2002	1,799	1,937	1990–91	2006–07
Sri Lanka	LKA	1995–96	2002	2,520	3,092	—	—

Source: GDP per capita data from World Development Indicators, World Bank (2009).

Note: DHS = Demographic and Health Surveys; LSMS = Living Standards Measurement Study; PPP = purchase power parity.

a. Consumption and poverty measures are based on income instead of on expenditure or consumption.

Data, Methodology, and Results for Decomposition Analysis

To analyze the factors behind the rural-urban welfare inequalities, we used variations of the Oaxaca-Blinder decomposition to estimate the relative contributions of (1) the differences in household and community endowments or characteristics, and (2) the differences in the returns to these characteristics in accounting for differences in household welfare. These decompositions are simple descriptive tools that provide a useful way of summarizing the correlation among welfare differentials, endowments, and returns.

Data

The Ghana data are drawn from the 1991–92 and 2005–06 rounds of the Ghana Living Standards Surveys (GLSS3 and GLSS5, respectively). These nationally representative cross-sectional surveys are conducted by the government-run Ghana Statistical Service. The multipurpose household surveys provide detailed information on the household consumption of purchased and home-produced goods. The surveys are based on a two-stage (nonstratified) sample design. The Ghana Statistical Service used an amended sampling procedure to produce a self-weighting sample in GLSS3 and computed weights for GLSS5 (GLSS 2007). After the data were cleaned, the sample size was 4,498 households in GLSS3 and 8,652 households in GLSS5.

The Mozambique data are drawn from the 1996–97 and 2002–03 rounds of the national household living standards survey (Inquérito aos Agregados Familiares sobre as Condições de Vida, or IAF96 and IAF02). These nationally representative cross-sectional surveys are conducted by the National Statistics Institute. The multipurpose household and community surveys are similar to the World Bank's Living Standards Measurement Study (LSMS) surveys, including detailed information on household consumption of purchased and home-produced goods. A three-stage stratified cluster sample design was used for these surveys, with a sample of 8,250 households in IAF96 and 8,700 households in IAF02.

The Uganda data are drawn from the 1992–93 Uganda National Integrated Household Survey and the 2005–06 Uganda National Household Survey (UNHS) produced by the Uganda Bureau of Statistics. These standard LSMS-type surveys covered 9,923 households in 1992–93 and 7,421 households in 2005–06.

Model Specification

For intertemporal and spatial comparability of welfare, the log welfare ratio is the measure of welfare used as the dependent variable in the regression analysis. The welfare ratio is defined here as the nominal household consumption expenditure per adult equivalent divided by the applicable regional poverty line for the same survey year. Because of the spatial price variation across regions and rural and urban areas, the use of regional poverty lines in the welfare ratio improves comparability across these areas. The poverty lines are calculated to represent the same standard of living across different survey years, and thus dividing nominal consumption by the poverty line ensures comparability across years. Anyone interpreting the log welfare ratio should note that a value of zero implies that a household is living exactly at the poverty line.

The regression analysis was conducted at the household level. The right-hand variables in the regressions include: household size or adult equivalents, age and age squared of household head (as a proxy for experience), urban and regional dummy variables and their interactions, educational attainment of the household head or maximum educational attainment of the entire household, and the employment sector of the household head. In the Uganda regressions, we also used community-level variables indicating the presence of a secondary school, hospital, or tarmac trunk road. Community-level variables are not used in the Mozambique regressions because in Mozambique the community survey was conducted only in rural areas.

The regression results are shown in tables B.1, B.2, and B.3.

Oaxaca-Blinder Decomposition

Given any two subpopulations A and B (e.g., rural and urban areas of a given year or two different points in time), we assume that the logarithm of the welfare ratio for each group, denoted by $\ln C$, can be summarized by the linear regression $\ln C_j = \beta_j X_j + \varepsilon_j$, where j represents subpopulations A and B of the sample, and ε is a random disturbance term with a normal distribution and mean equal to zero. In this specification, the coefficients β_j summarize the influence of a variety of factors X_j on welfare. The difference in mean welfare ratios between subpopulations A and B can then be expressed as

$$\overline{\ln C_A} - \overline{\ln C_B} = \beta_A \overline{X_A} - \beta_B \overline{X_B},$$

where the bar over the relevant variables denotes the sample mean values of the respective variables.

As proposed by Oaxaca (1973) and Blinder (1973), we can add and subtract the term $\beta_B \overline{X_A}$ or the term $\beta_A \overline{X_B}$ and express the difference as either

$$\overline{\ln C_A} - \overline{\ln C_B} = \left(\overline{X_A} - \overline{X_B}\right)\beta_B + \left(\beta_A - \beta_B\right)\overline{X_A},$$

or

$$\overline{\ln C_A} - \overline{\ln C_B} = \left(\overline{X_A} - \overline{X_B}\right)\beta_A + \left(\beta_A - \beta_B\right)\overline{X_B}.$$

These decompositions produce two components: one that consists of the differences in average characteristics and another that consists of the differences in the coefficients. The only difference between these two expressions lies in how the differences in the characteristics $\left(\overline{X_A} - \overline{X_B}\right)$ and the differences in coefficients $\left(\beta_A - \beta_B\right)$ are weighted.

Since the original decomposition by Oaxaca and Blinder, numerous scholars (e.g., Reimers 1983; Cotton 1988; Neumark 1988) have extended the method by proposing alternative weights for the differences in the characteristics $\left(\overline{X_A} - \overline{X_B}\right)$ and the differences in returns $\left(\beta_A - \beta_B\right)$.[1] Because of the path dependence of the decompositions, a common practice is to average the results of the different "paths." We follow Reimers

(1983) and use as weights the average of the coefficients and the average of the characteristics so that

$$
\overline{\ln C_A} - \overline{\ln C_B} = \left(\overline{X_A} - \overline{X_B} \right) \left(\frac{(\beta_A + \beta_B)}{2} \right) + (\beta_A - \beta_B) \left(\frac{(\overline{X_A} + \overline{X_B})}{2} \right).
$$

Detailed decompositions can indicate which variable or set of variables is driving the endowment or coefficient effects.

Quantile Decomposition

By constructing counterfactual distributions using quantile regression estimates, we decompose differences in welfare distributions into a component based on differences in covariates and a component based on differences in coefficients. The counterfactual distributions are estimated by first obtaining quantile regression estimates at each percentile for two mutually exclusive subpopulations, A and B (e.g., rural and urban), and then predicting log welfare ratios using the covariates of the other subpopulation. These predicted values are then randomly sampled with replacement—with probability proportional to the survey weight of the observation—to obtain the desired self-weighting counterfactual distributions. Differences in log welfare ratios between the two subpopulations are then decomposed by comparing the predicted distributions with the constructed counterfactual distribution—see Machado and Mato (2005) for additional details.

Table B.1   Regression Results, Ghana

Dependent variable: log welfare ratio	1991–92	2005–06
Adult equivalents	−0.134***	−0.135***
	(0.008)	(0.007)
urban*adult equivalents	−0.022	−0.025**
	(0.014)	(0.011)
Age of head	−0.007*	0.006
	(0.004)	(0.004)
urban*age of head	0.012	0.003
	(0.009)	(0.006)
age of head squared (1/1,000)	0.076*	−0.049
	(0.040)	(0.036)
urban*age of head squared (1/1,000)	−0.075	−0.005
	(0.094)	(0.058)
Education of head		
primary	0.003	0.092***
	(0.036)	(0.032)
urban*primary	−0.015	0.043
	(0.065)	(0.051)
junior secondary	0.092***	0.153***
	(0.028)	(0.033)
urban*junior secondary	0.115**	0.097
	(0.047)	(0.049)
some senior secondary	0.186**	0.296***
	(0.081)	(0.060)
urban*some senior secondary	−0.031	0.136*
	(0.101)	(0.076)
completed SSS or higher	0.236***	0.498***
	(0.068)	(0.055)
urban * SSS+	0.270***	0.121*
	(0.093)	(0.072)
Employment sector of head		
secondary sector	0.153***	0.133***
	(0.047)	(0.043)
urban*secondary	−0.089	0.007
	(0.065)	(0.064)
tertiary sector	0.277***	0.209***
	(0.037)	(0.036)
urban*tertiary	−0.130**	−0.019
	(0.054)	(0.055)
other (unemployed)	0.148**	−0.056
	(0.062)	(0.047)
urban*other	−0.092	0.043
	(0.090)	(0.072)

(continued next page)

Table B.1   *(continued)*

Dependent variable: log welfare ratio	1991–92	2005–06
Region/ecological zone		
forest	−0.084*	−0.02
	(0.049)	(0.055)
urban*forest	0.163**	0.092
	(0.071)	(0.073)
savannah	−0.190***	−0.314***
	(0.058)	(0.069)
urban*savannah	0.263**	0.184*
	(0.106)	(0.108)
Urban	−0.020	0.090
	(0.198)	(0.160)
Constant	0.612***	·0.664***
	(0.111)	(0.100)
N	4,498	8,651
R²	0.399	0.413
F	54.975	71.663

Source: Authors' calculations from Ghana Living Standards Surveys.
*p < .10.
**p < .05.
*** p < .01.

Table B.2   Regression Results, Mozambique

Dependent variable: log welfare ratio	1996–97	2002–03
Adult equivalents	−0.178***	−0.131***
	(0.008)	(0.009)
urban*adult equivalents	0.052***	0.023
	(0.013)	(0.013)
Age of head	−0.007	−0.007**
	(0.005)	(0.004)
urban*age of head	0.025***	0.021**
	(0.009)	(0.009)
age of head squared (1/1,000)	0.074	0.099***
	(0.048)	(0.036)
urban*age of head squared (1/1,000)	−0.221**	−0.229**
	(0.100)	(0.099)
Education of head		
primary 1	0.143***	0.081**
	(0.025)	(0.037)
urban*primary 1	0.114***	0.104
	(0.043)	(0.066)
primary 2	0.281***	0.279***
	(0.067)	(0.071)

(continued next page)

Table B.2   *(continued)*

Dependent variable: log welfare ratio	1996–97	2002–03
urban*primary 2	0.278***	0.125
	(0.097)	(0.095)
secondary 1st cycle	0.504	0.596***
	(0.314)	(0.122)
urban*secondary 1st cycle	0.298	0.077
	(0.324)	(0.148)
secondary (2nd cycle) or higher	0.848	0.570***
	(0.550)	(0.204)
urban*secondary (2nd cycle) or higher	0.333	0.660
	(0.566)	(0.242)
Employment sector of head		
secondary sector	−0.019	0.173**
	(0.057)	(0.083)
urban*secondary	0.178**	−0.072
	(0.077)	(0.100)
tertiary sector	0.264***	0.314***
	(0.046)	(0.056)
urban*tertiary	−0.023	−0.045
	(0.076)	(0.072)
other (excludes primary)	0.020	0.019
	(0.042)	(0.076)
urban*other	0.051	0.239**
	(0.082)	(0.094)
Region		
northern (region1)	0.053	0.297***
	(0.049)	(0.049)
urban*northern	−0.515***	−0.139
	(0.118)	(0.097)
central (region2)	−0.069	0.518***
	(0.045)	(0.054)
urban*central	−0.159*	−0.345***
	(0.083)	(0.074)
Urban	−0.743***	−0.426**
	(0.199)	(0.197)
Constant	0.568***	0.162*
	(0.118)	(0.089)
N	8,241	8,700
R^2	0.266	0.244
F	45.747	30.393

Source: Authors' calculations from Mozambique Household Living Conditions Surveys.
*$p < .10$.
**$p < .05$.
*** $p < .01$.

Table B.3   Regression Results, Uganda

Dependent variable: log welfare ratio	1992–93	2005–06	1992–93	2005–06
Adult equivalents	−0.091***	−0.073***	−0.091***	−0.076***
	(0.007)	(0.004)	(0.006)	(0.004)
urban*adult equivalents	−0.001	−0.020*		
	(0.013)	(0.011)		
Age of head	0.001	0.006**	0.002	0.010***
	(0.003)	(0.003)	(0.003)	(0.003)
urban*age of head	0.008	0.023***		
	(0.008)	(0.007)		
age of head sq. (1/1,000)	−0.017	−0.021	−0.025	−0.055
	(0.032)	(0.031)	(0.030)	(0.029)
urban*age sq. (1/1,000)	−0.078	−0.200***		
	(0.090)	(0.066)		
Education of head				
some primary	0.105***	0.132***	0.106***	0.137***
	(0.019)	(0.024)	(0.019)	(0.024)
urban*some primary	0.094	0.021	0.085	−0.023
	(0.059)	(0.073)	(0.060)	(0.071)
completed primary	0.152***	0.268***	0.154***	0.276***
	(0.031)	(0.029)	(0.030)	(0.029)
urban*comp primary	0.083	0.018	0.073	−0.031
	(0.079)	(0.087)	(0.082)	(0.083)
some secondary	0.276***	0.429***	0.277***	0.436***
	(0.032)	(0.029)	(0.031)	(0.028)
urban*some secondary	0.119	0.080	0.113	0.027
	(0.072)	(0.077)	(0.073)	(0.073)
completed sec or higher	0.608***	0.789***	0.608***	0.793***
	(0.052)	(0.065)	(0.052)	(0.065)
urban*comp sec +	0.134	0.329***	0.134	0.295***
	(0.095)	(0.111)	(0.094)	(0.106)
Employment sector of head				
secondary sector	0.132***	0.054*	0.132***	0.057*
	(0.044)	(0.032)	(0.045)	(0.032)
urban*secondary	−0.152**	0.078	−0.154**	0.063
	(0.076)	(0.069)	(0.078)	(0.069)
tertiary sector	0.182***	0.277***	0.182***	0.279***
	(0.029)	(0.024)	(0.029)	(0.024)
urban*tertiary	0.057	−0.055	0.055	−0.070
	(0.055)	(0.056)	(0.055)	(0.055)
other (excludes primary)	−0.027	−0.008	−0.026	−0.007
	(0.039)	(0.037)	(0.039)	(0.037)
urban*other	0.325***	0.196**	0.311***	0.160*
	(0.107)	(0.095)	(0.097)	(0.091)

(continued next page)

Table B.3   *(continued)*

Dependent variable: log welfare ratio	1992–93	2005–06	1992–93	2005–06
Community				
secondary school	0.194***	0.126***	0.194***	0.124***
	(0.055)	(0.029)	(0.055)	(0.029)
tarmac trunk road	0.107**	0.123***	0.107**	0.122***
	(0.054)	(0.028)	(0.054)	(0.028)
Region				
eastern (region2)	−0.073**	−0.260***	−0.073**	−0.261***
	(0.035)	(0.028)	(0.035)	(0.029)
urban*eastern	−0.199***	−0.030	−0.197***	−0.029
	(0.064)	(0.070)	(0.065)	(0.070)
northern (region3)	−0.277***	−0.571***	−0.277***	−0.571***
	(0.042)	(0.032)	(0.042)	(0.032)
urban*northern	−0.056	0.037	−0.052	0.032
	(0.096)	(0.068)	(0.096)	(0.068)
western (region4)	0.026	−0.019	0.026	−0.018
	(0.037)	(0.029)	(0.037)	(0.029)
urban*western	−0.122	−0.073	−0.122	−0.071
	(0.082)	(0.062)	(0.082)	(0.062)
Urban	−0.073	−0.363**	0.102	0.160*
	(0.181)	(0.168)	(0.069)	(0.093)
Constant	0.171**	0.341***	0.149**	0.258***
	(0.069)	(0.076)	(0.065)	(0.071)
N	9,115	7,291	9,115	7,291
R^2	0.263	0.422	0.263	0.421
F	34.688	94.690	37.122	103.335

Source: Authors' calculations from Uganda National Household Surveys.
*$p < .10$.
**$p < .05$.
*** $p < .01$.

Table B.4 Average Household Characteristics: Ghana, Mozambique, and Uganda, Selected Years

	Ghana				Mozambique				Uganda			
	1991		2005		1996		2002		1992		2005	
	rural	urban	rural	urban	rural	urban	rural	urban	rural	urban	rural	urban
welfare ratio	1.70	2.22	1.98	3.46	1.08	1.39	1.29	1.77	1.19	2.07	1.84	3.79
equivalent	3.38	3.20	3.30	2.72	3.31	3.91	3.27	3.75	3.64	3.14	4.01	3.59
age of head	45.19	42.54	46.30	43.27	42.37	41.58	42.89	42.32	42.24	35.33	43.02	38.04
hd educ: primary	0.49	0.27	0.42	0.17	0.79	0.42	0.83	0.47	0.35	0.12	0.19	0.08
hd educ: jr. secondary	0.12	0.08	0.15	0.10	0.18	0.36	0.12	0.25	0.43	0.32	0.45	0.26
hd educ: some sr. sec. comp. sr.	0.34	0.46	0.35	0.43	0.02	0.15	0.03	0.15	0.09	0.13	0.14	0.14
sec. +	0.02	0.04	0.02	0.09	0.00	0.05	0.01	0.07	0.11	0.30	0.17	0.35
hd_edlev4a	0.03	0.14	0.05	0.21	0.00	0.02	0.00	0.06	0.02	0.14	0.04	0.17
hd: primary sector	0.74	0.20	0.72	0.17	0.87	0.29	0.88	0.39	0.77	0.13	0.71	0.15
hd: secondary sector	0.07	0.17	0.07	0.18	0.03	0.15	0.02	0.09	0.04	0.19	0.06	0.17
hd: tertiary sector	0.16	0.53	0.15	0.50	0.05	0.39	0.08	0.45	0.12	0.61	0.16	0.59
hd: other	0.04	0.10	0.06	0.15	0.05	0.17	0.02	0.08	0.06	0.08	0.07	0.09
coastal region	0.24	0.57	0.22	0.49								
forest region	0.47	0.31	0.48	0.39								
savannah region	0.29	0.12	0.30	0.12								
Northern (region1)					0.37	0.32	0.36	0.37				
Central (region2)					0.46	0.25	0.46	0.27				
Southern (region3)					0.17	0.44	0.19	0.36				
Central (region1)									0.28	0.62	0.26	0.59
Eastern (region2)									0.28	0.21	0.26	0.13
Northern (region3)									0.16	0.06	0.20	0.15
Western (region4)									0.28	0.11	0.28	0.13
comm: sec. school									0.05	0.05	0.14	0.40
comm: tarmac road									0.05	0.63	0.09	0.46

Source: Authors' calculations based on household survey data.

Table B.5 Decompositions of Rural-Urban Welfare Differences: Ghana, Mozambique, and Uganda, Selected Years

	Ghana							
	1991–92				2005–06			
Variable	Endowment	SE	Coefficient	SE	Endowment	SE	Coefficient	SE
equivalents	0.027	0.016*	−0.073	0.045	0.086	0.011***	−0.076	0.033***
agehd	0.004	0.012	0.510	0.391	−0.021	0.009**	0.132	0.262
agehd^2 (1/1,000)	−0.011	0.014	−0.161	0.202	0.015	0.009*	−0.010	0.130
hd educ: primary (P1-5)	0.000	0.001	−0.002	0.007	−0.006	0.002***	0.006	0.007
hd educ: jr. secondary	0.018	0.005***	0.046	0.019**	0.016	0.004***	0.038	0.019**
hd educ: some sr. secondary	0.003	0.001**	−0.001	0.003	0.023	0.003***	0.008	0.004
hd educ: comp. sr. secondary +	0.042	0.008***	0.022	0.008***	0.086	0.009***	0.016	0.009*
hd: secondary sector	0.011	0.004***	−0.010	0.008	0.015	0.004***	0.001	0.008
hd: tertiary sector	0.079	0.011***	−0.045	0.019**	0.070	0.010***	−0.006	0.018
hd: other	0.006	0.003**	−0.006	0.006	−0.003	0.003	0.004	0.007
forest zone	0.000	0.006	0.063	0.028**	−0.002	0.004	0.040	0.032
savannah zone	0.010	0.009	0.054	0.023**	0.041	0.012***	0.039	0.023
constant			−0.020	0.198			0.090	0.160
Total	*0.190*	*0.029***	*0.378*	*0.038***	*0.321*	*0.028*** ·	*0.281*	*0.036***
	33%		67%		53%		47%	

(continued next page)

Table B.5 *(continued)*

	Mozambique							
	1996–97				*2002–03*			
Variable	*Endowment*	*SE*	*Coefficient*	*SE*	*Endowment*	*SE*	*Coefficient*	*SE*
equivalents	-0.091	0.016***	0.188	0.046***	-0.057	0.019***	0.080	0.046*
agehd	-0.004	0.005	1.050	0.374***	-0.002	0.003	0.909	0.379**
agehd^2 (1/1,000)	0.004	0.006	-0.434	0.196**	0.001	0.004	-0.468	0.202**
hd educ: primary (1GR)	0.036	0.006***	0.031	0.012***	0.017	0.005***	0.019	0.012
hd educ: primary (2GR)	0.051	0.009***	0.024	0.009***	0.040	0.008***	0.011	0.008
hd educ: secondary (1CIC)	0.028	0.009***	0.007	0.008	0.038	0.007***	0.003	0.006
hd educ: secondary (2CIC) +	0.020	0.007***	0.003	0.006	0.054	0.012***	0.021	0.009**
hd: secondary sector	0.008	0.005*	0.016	0.007**	0.009	0.004***	-0.004	0.005
hd: tertiary sector	0.086	0.015***	-0.005	0.017	0.107	0.019***	-0.012	0.019
hd: other	0.005	0.005	0.006	0.009	0.007	0.003***	0.012	0.005**
northern region	0.011	0.011	-0.177	0.043**	0.003	0.012	-0.050	0.035
central region	0.032	0.010***	-0.057	0.029*	-0.065	0.012***	-0.126	0.028***
constant			-0.743	0.199			-0.426	0.197
Total	*0.186*	*0.030***	*-0.090*	*0.052*	*0.151*	*0.025***	*-0.029*	*0.037*
	194%		*-94%*		*124%*		*-24%*	

Uganda

Variable	1992–93				2005–06			
	Endowment	SE	Coefficient	SE	Endowment	SE	Coefficient	SE
equivalents	0.046	0.007***	-0.003	0.045	0.035	0.007***	-0.077	0.043*
agehd	-0.038	0.029	0.317	0.325	-0.088	0.020***	0.928	0.277***
agehd^2 (1/1,000)	0.037	0.029	-0.139	0.156	0.059	0.017***	-0.383	0.124***
hd educ: some primary	-0.018	0.004***	0.037	0.022*	-0.026	0.007***	0.006	0.026
hd educ: comp. primary	0.008	0.003***	0.009	0.008	-0.002	0.004	0.001	0.012
hd educ: some secondary	0.063	0.008***	0.026	0.015*	0.083	0.012***	0.020	0.020
hd educ: comp. secondary +	0.082	0.011***	0.012	0.008	0.119	0.016***	0.034	0.012***
hd: secondary sector	0.008	0.005	-0.017	0.009*	0.010	0.004**	0.009	0.008
hd: tertiary sector	0.102	0.014***	0.023	0.020	0.105	0.013***	-0.021	0.022
hd: other	0.002	0.002	0.023	0.007***	0.002	0.001	0.016	0.008**
com: sec. school	0.000	0.002	-0.007	0.005	0.029	0.010***	-0.020	0.016
com: trunk tarmac	0.060	0.029**	-0.010	0.033	0.046	0.013***	0.006	0.017
eastern region	0.013	0.006**	-0.047	0.016***	0.035	0.005***	-0.008	0.013
northern region	0.032	0.006***	-0.006	0.010	0.030	0.007***	0.004	0.012
western region	0.006	0.007	-0.024	0.016	0.007	0.005	-0.014	0.013
constant			-0.070	0.180			-0.335	0.171*
Total	0.401	0.036***	0.123	0.037***	0.443	0.030***	0.165	0.031***
	77%		23%		73%		27%	

Source: Authors' calculations based on household survey data.

Note: SE = standard error.

*p < .10.
**p < .05.
***p < .01.

Table B.6 Decompositions of Welfare Differences over Time for Rural and Urban Areas: Ghana, Mozambique, and Uganda, Selected Years

	Ghana							
	Rural (1991–92 to 2005–06)				Urban (1991–92 to 2005–06)			
Variable	*Endowment*	*SE*	*Coefficient*	*SE*	*Endowment*	*SE*	*Coefficient*	*SE*
equivalents	0.011	0.011	−0.002	0.035	0.076	0.017***	−0.010	0.041
agehd	−0.001	0.003	0.589	0.254**	0.005	0.005	0.180	0.390
agehd^2 (1/1,000)	0.001	0.003	−0.292	0.127**	−0.003	0.005	−0.111	0.198
hd educ: primary (P1–5)	0.002	0.001	0.012	0.007	0.001	0.001	0.014	0.006**
hd educ: jr. secondary	0.001	0.002	0.021	0.015	−0.007	0.005	0.019	0.023
hd educ: some sr. secondary	0.000	0.001	0.003	0.002	0.013	0.003***	0.018	0.005***
hd educ: comp. sr. secondary +	0.010	0.002***	0.010	0.003***	0.038	0.012***	0.020	0.014
hd: secondary sector	0.001	0.001	−0.001	0.004	0.001	0.002	0.014	0.011
hd: tertiary sector	−0.003	0.003	−0.011	0.008	−0.006	0.004	0.022	0.029
hd: other	0.001	0.001	−0.010	0.004**	0.001	0.002	−0.009	0.011
forest zone	−0.001	0.002	0.030	0.035	0.006	0.005	−0.003	0.025
savannah zone	−0.003	0.010	−0.037	0.027	0.000	0.001	−0.024	0.015
constant			0.052	0.149			0.163	0.206
Total	*0.019*	*0.021*	*0.365*	*0.031***	*0.127*	*0.024***	*0.293*	*0.034***
	5%		95%		30%		70%	

Mozambique

Variable	Rural (1996–97 to 2002–03)				Urban (1996–97 to 2002–03)			
	Endowment	SE	Coefficient	SE	Endowment	SE	Coefficient	SE
equivalents	0.006	0.008	0.156	0.040***	0.018	0.021	0.070	0.052
agehd	-0.004	0.004	0.002	0.259	0.012	0.012	-0.151	0.463
agehd^2 (1/1,000)	0.006	0.005	0.051	0.124	-0.013	0.012	0.034	0.248
hd educ: primary (1GR)	-0.007	0.002***	-0.010	0.007	-0.025	0.007***	-0.022	0.020
hd educ: primary (2GR)	0.001	0.001	-0.000	0.003	-0.001	0.011	-0.023	0.014
hd educ: secondary (1CIC)	0.004	0.002**	0.001	0.002	0.018	0.009**	-0.007	0.007
hd educ: secondary (2CIC) +	0.001	0.001*	-0.000	0.001	0.050	0.014***	0.002	0.008
hd: secondary sector	-0.001	0.001	0.005	0.003*	-0.008	0.003**	-0.007	0.009
hd: tertiary sector	0.009	0.003***	0.003	0.005	0.015	0.014	0.012	0.032
hd: other	-0.001	0.001	-0.000	0.003	-0.015	0.005***	0.023	0.011
northern region	-0.002	0.004	0.088	0.025***	-0.008	0.011	0.212	0.051
central region	-0.001	0.006	0.270	0.033***	-0.001	0.001	0.104	0.024
constant			-0.406	0.148			-0.089	0.237
Total	0.013	0.009	0.161	0.028***	0.043	0.033	0.157	0.052
	7%		93%		21%		79%	

(continued next page)

Table B.6 *(continued)*

Uganda

Variable	Rural (1992–93 to 2005–06)				Urban (1992–93 to 2005–06)			
	Endowment	SE	Coefficient	SE	Endowment	SE	Coefficient	SE
equivalents	−0.030	0.004***	0.070	0.031**	−0.042	0.009	−0.003	0.053
agehd	0.003	0.002	0.204	0.187	0.053	0.019	0.716	0.365
agehd^2 (1/1,000)	−0.001	0.001	−0.011	0.093	−0.037	0.015	−0.197	0.157
hd educ: some primary	0.002	0.001	0.012	0.014	−0.010	0.005	−0.016	0.026
hd educ: comp. primary	0.012	0.002***	0.013	0.005***	0.002	0.004	0.005	0.014
hd educ: some secondary	0.020	0.003***	0.021	0.006***	0.022	0.011	0.034	0.031
hd educ: comp. secondary +	0.014	0.003***	0.005	0.003**	0.024	0.019	0.055	0.019
hd: secondary sector	0.001	0.001**	−0.004	0.003	−0.001	0.002	0.026	0.015
hd: tertiary sector	0.009	0.002***	0.014	0.005**	−0.004	0.007	−0.014	0.042
hd: other	0.000	0.000	0.001	0.003	0.003	0.003	−0.010	0.011
com: sec. school	0.016	0.005***	−0.006	0.007	0.026	0.016	0.000	0.020
com: trunk tarmac	0.005	0.003*	0.000	0.007	−0.018	0.010	0.024	0.040
eastern region	0.005	0.001***	−0.050	0.012***	0.023	0.009	−0.006	0.014
northern region	−0.018	0.003***	−0.053	0.010***	−0.041	0.008	−0.022	0.011
western region	0.000	0.000	−0.012	0.013	−0.002	0.002	0.001	0.011
constant			0.168	0.103			−0.097	0.228
Total	*0.038*	*0.011****	*0.372*	*0.017*	*−0.002*	*0.034*	*0.497*	*0.037*
	9%		*91%*		*0%*		*100%*	

Source: Authors' calculations based on household survey data.

Note: SE = standard error.

*p < .10.
**p < .05.
***p < .01.

Note

1. The twofold decompositions are carried out using the Stata command "oaxaca" written by Ben Jann (2008) using the "weight (0.5)" option.

References

Blinder, A. 1973. "Wage Discrimination: Reduced Form and Structural Estimates." *Journal of Human Resources* 8: 436–55.

Cotton, J. 1988. "On the Decomposition of Wage Differentials." *Review of Economics and Statistics* 70: 236–43.

GLSS (Ghana Living Standards Surveys). 2007. "Pattern and Trends of Poverty in Ghana." Ghana Statistical Service, Accra.

Jann, Ben. 2008. "A Stata implementation of the Blinder-Oaxaca decomposition." ETH Zurich Sociology Working Papers No. 5. ETH Zurich, Zurich, Switzerland. http://repec.ethz.ch/ets/papers/jann_oaxaca.pdf.

Machado, J. A. F., and J. Mata. 2005. "Counterfactual Decomposition of Changes in Wage Distributions Using Quantile Regression." *Journal of Applied Econometrics* 20: 445–65.

Neumark, D. 1988. "Employers' Discriminatory Behavior and the Estimation of Wage Discrimination." *Journal of Human Resources* 23: 279–95.

Oaxaca, R. 1973. "Male-Female Wage Differentials in Urban Labor Markets." *International Economic Review* 14: 673–709.

Reimers, C. 1983. "Labor Market Discrimination against Hispanic and Black Men." *Review of Economics and Statistics* 65: 570–79.

United Nations. 2008. *World Urbanization Prospects: The 2007 Revision.* Department of Economic and Social Affairs, Population Division. New York: United Nations.

Index

source of rural-urban inequality in,
66–68, 74
Hungary, 27*b*

I

improvement index, 30, 32*b*, 40–44,
41–43*t*
income
contribution of nonfarm activities in
South Asia, 120, 121*f*
global trends, 36
land market restrictions and, 153–154,
153*t*
land ownership inequality and, 142
rural-urban convergence-divergence
patterns and, 4*f*, 9, 19, 44–47,
46*t*, 48
in South Asia, 114, 122*n*1
in Sub-Saharan countries, 52
upper-middle-income level as development threshold, 3, 18, 25–26, 27*b*
urbanization outcomes, 16, 16*f*
see also consumption
India
access to electricity, 136–137
agricultural subsidies, 127–128
agricultural tariffs, 126, 126*f*, 127*f*
agriculture's share of economic growth,
116–117, 117*f*
communications infrastructure, 137
contribution of nonfarm activities to
income and employment, 121, 121*f*
economic growth, 114
economic policy reforms and
outcomes, 126
educational access and utilization,
131, 133
Gini coefficient, 114
health care delivery in, 133
internal migration in, 176*b*, 177,
178, 197
labor market regulation, 130
land ownership distribution, 129, 142
land policies and institutions, 128, 129
per capita income, 114, 122*n*1
poverty patterns, 117, 120
poverty patterns across rural-urban
continuum, 160–161
poverty rate, 122*n*2
poverty reducing effects of agricultural
growth, 115–116

rural-urban inequalities, 117, 120, 133
stage of developmental transformation,
2, 3, 110
transport infrastructure, 134–135, 135*f*
urbanization effects on rural
poverty, 120
urbanization patterns, 118, 118*t*,
119, 172*n*3
See also South Asia
Indonesia, 2
inequalities, rural-urban
access to electricity, 137, 161,
161*fr*, 162*f*
access to water, 61
analytical methodology, 30–32, 48*n*1,
65–66
consumption patterns, 33, 34*f*
consumption ratio, 26, 26*f*
continuum conceptualization of, 10–11,
16*b*, 159–163. *see also* periurban areas
and smaller towns/cities
convergence effects of rural-to-urban
migration, 175
data sources, 28–30, 48*n*2
development patterns in South Asia, 113
in development process, 1, 191–192
divergence–convergence patterns, 3, 4*f*,
9, 17–18, 21, 26, 27*b*, 28, 36–44,
37–39*t*, 41–43*t*, 47–48, 69–70, 192
global patterns, 33–36, 34*f*
health and nutritional status, 35, 61, 87,
87*f*, 193
household endowments as factor in,
65–66, 70–72
intracountry differences in South Asia,
115, 115*f*, 122, 196
in living standards, 25, 115
national income per capita correlated
with, 44–47, 46*t*, 48
patterns across rural-urban continuum,
159–163
poverty rates, 27*b*, 28–29, 33–35, 34*f*,
57–63, 109, 117, 120, 159–160
research needs, 195
returns to endowments as factor in,
65–66, 69
school enrollment and attendance
patterns, 35, 61
scope of analysis, 26–28
sectoral employment of household head
as factor in, 66–68
social tensions and, 18, 113, 192

location decisions of firms in, 167–170,
    198–199
number of firms in, 165–166
policy recommendations to improve,
    3, 100–102, 194–195
proximity effects on wages and
    employment, 163–164
rationale for regional integration, 101*b*
slum upgrading efforts, 98, 99*b*
sources of growth, 15
sources of welfare increases in, 70
in Sub-Saharan Africa, 19, 21
taxation in, 98
undernutrition in, 35
WDR classification of country
    economies, 5*b*, 54*f*
welfare distribution patterns in, 82–87,
    88–90, 100, 194
see also Accra; inequalities in
    urbanization; Kampala; Maputo; peri-
    urban areas and smaller towns/cities;
    rural-urban transition
urbanization. *see* rural-urban transition

W

wages
    educational attainment and, 146–147,
        154
    effects of land regulation on, 153–155
    individual-level variables in Pakistan, 147*t*

land ownership inequality and,
    146–147
migration incentives, 65, 68, 81, 184,
    188*b*
proximity to large metropolitan areas
    and, 163–164
returns to age, 68
sources of inequalities in rural-urban
    transition, 3
waste management, 86
water supply and access
    in cities of Sub-Saharan Africa, 84, 88
    rural-urban differences in Sub-Saharan
        Africa, 61, 63*f*, 82
WDR 2008, Agriculture for Development,
    1–3, 7, 52, 109, 113, 191,
    192–193
*WDR 2009, Reshaping Economic
    Geography*, 1, 2, 3–6, 7, 18, 21, 25,
    79, 109, 113, 191
World Development Reports, 7, 18, 21, 25,
    52, 79, 109, 113, 191. *see WDR 2008,
    Agriculture for Development; WDR
    2009, Reshaping Economic Geography*
World Institute for Development
    Economics Research of the United
    Nations University, 27*b*

Z

Zamindari system, 142